Rabbit George and Me

A story based on the life of
Mary Stennett Smith
(January 2, 1846-May 15, 1932)

Rabbit George and Me

Veronica Hague

Matador
9 Priory Business Park,
Wistow Road, Kibworth Beauchamp,
Leicestershire. LE8 0RX
Tel: 0116 279 2299
Email: books@troubador.co.uk
Web: www.troubador.co.uk/matador
Twitter: @matadorbooks

ISBN 978 1788032 841

British Library Cataloguing in Publication Data.
A catalogue record for this book is available from the British Library.

Printed and bound in the UK by 4edge limited
Typeset in 12pt Adobe Garamond Pro by Troubador Publishing Ltd, Leicester, UK

Matador is an imprint of Troubador Publishing Ltd

This book is dedicated to the descendants of
"Rabbit George"
George Smith
(February 4, 1827-July 9, 1907)

CONTENTS

FROM THE AUTHOR

If you are to write a family history, or a story based on the life of one of your ancestors, you will need to know the facts. Census data is the crucial element underpinning your work. Your book will be read not because of your literary talent, but because of the factual information contained within its pages. If you are fortunate, members of your family will have undertaken much of this arduous work and, like me, you will be free to engage in the more interesting task of imagining the lives of the men and women whose existence led to your own.

It is, therefore, with much gratitude that I acknowledge the long and painstaking research conducted by George Schonhut and Charles Robin Hartley, son and grandson, respectively, of Elizabeth Smith Schonhut, the eldest daughter of George and Mary Smith. Their keen interest in their forebears made it possible for me to write *Rabbit George and Me* and to weave a story which I hope is of interest not only to present and future members of the family, but to those who wish to produce their own narrative history.

When you work on your family history, you will experience a newfound impetus to reach out to relatives, both near and distant, in order to uncover the memories and news from the multiple branches of the family. You will not only enjoy these communications, but will learn a great deal. With much pleasure I thank George and Mary Smith's many descendants, and the members of their families, who provided vital and interesting information: Robin Hartley, Nigel Hague, Gay Wadsworth, April Stern, Pauline Tear, Sally Foster, Louise Sampson, Jane MacCaw, Dorothy Goodswen, James Goodswen, Charles Hague, Cordelia

Sampson, William Hague, Elizabeth Sayers, Angela Hague, Charlotte Schoch, Adrian Sayers and Beryl Brown.

In addition, I am grateful to Pamela Thickett for serving as an invaluable connection to the descendants of George Smith and his second wife, Mary Crawshaw, and for generously sharing information about her great-grandmother, Margaret Laver. I am also thankful for the information provided by Sandra Pounder and Susan Lane, descendants of James Larrett Smith, brother of George Smith.

As you embark upon writing your family tale you will discover how much you don't know regarding your origins, whether it concerns the village in which you grew up or your family's business. I am grateful to Graham Hobson and the Greasbrough Community History Society for providing information on the village of Greasbrough during the time of George and Mary Smith. I also thank Kathleen Dickinson and Ann Brown, my friends from Greasbrough Primary School, for their interest and insights. In addition, I am grateful to Jean Bailey and Stephen and Amanda Pilgrim for their assistance in exploring the naming of Rossiter Road.

I am indebted to Dr. Charles Collinson for providing the document which marked the founding of Hague's of Parkgate in 1870, and to Roy Young, retired headmaster of Wentworth Primary School and expert on the history of Wentworth, for sharing his knowledge of that village during the time of my great-great-grandparents, William and Elizabeth Smith.

I thank Lincolnshire historians, Christine and Lou Hird, and Bernie Ayton of the Shireoaks and District Local History Society.

Sincere thanks to Robin Hartley and Ffion Hague who generously took the time to provide fact-checking and editorial review prior to publication. This book is a better work because of their involvement.

Writers need encouragement and with this book project, as with others, I have been blessed with the love and support of Steven McAuliff.

Finally, and most poignantly, I can attest to what you already know, or suspect, as you embark upon this story, or delve into your own family's tale. You will wish you had paid more attention to your history when you were younger. You will regret not asking questions of your parents, grandparents, aunts and uncles before it was too late. Those opportunities may be gone, but the chance to read this story, or to create your own, is now in your hands.

Veronica Hague
Lebanon Township, New Jersey, USA
December 2017

Email: rabbitgeorgeandme@gmail.com

"Rabbit George"
George Smith 1827-1907

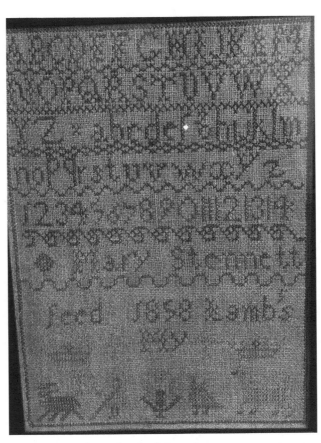

Sampler by Mary Stennett

Wedding of Elizabeth Smith and Albert Schonhut, August 1906,
Rossiter Villa, Greasbrough, South Yorkshire.

I

I am so happy the photograph of Lizzie's wedding has been passed down and that I can start my story with a picture. This book is my chance to tell you, my descendants, about your forebears and this photograph truly saves me a thousand words! Looking at our stern faces you must think we're at a funeral rather than a wedding, but sitting for a photograph was a slow job back in 1906. It took ages for everyone to sit still and you wanted to make sure you wore a serious expression and wouldn't go down in history looking like a grinning idiot.

In the photograph I'm sitting on the right with my husband, George, next to me. I'm wearing my best frock, swathed in black from neck-to-toe which a bride's mother wouldn't wear now, but was considered refined back then. The pitch black color set off my pale skin and light grey hair but, as usual, I was covered in too much material and I'd been hot and bothered all day. I envy you now when I see you jump into a pair of stretch trousers and pull a sleeveless top over your loose hair!

As you can see from the photograph, the stiff collar of my dress went all the way up to my chin and the sleeves ballooned out below my elbows and got in my way when I was working. All that day, I'd itched to unbutton the wristbands and roll up the sleeves, but Lizzie told me I would spoil the style. If only I had a style to spoil, I'd replied, a little too tartly considering it was her wedding day.

The truth is that Lizzie didn't want me to look as if I'd been working in the kitchen, even though that's exactly where I'd been most of the day. We'd brought in some women from the village to help but I'd had to make sure the beef and ham were cooked properly and the trifle wasn't brought out of the pantry until we were ready for it to be served. Each time I'd gone into the kitchen I'd had to close the pantry door to keep the cold in and the flies out. You didn't get a day off just because your eldest daughter was getting married. Not in the Smith family. Not in Yorkshire over a hundred years ago.

George's life ended the year after Lizzie's wedding, but mine lasted another twenty-six years on earth and many, many more watching from Far Yonder. Not everyone gets the opportunity to see what happens after they're gone. Far Yonder is a gift which is given to a precious few, usually to those who didn't have much of a voice during their lifetime. So the gift was given to me, but not to my husband. George had a say in every aspect of his life, as well as those of his children and the men who worked for him, not to mention many more people in Greasbrough and beyond who knew him or did business with him.

George Smith was a stonemason, farmer and builder who had three wives and twelve children. I was his third wife and the mother of his four youngest children. It is because of me and my children that this respected, intelligent and, fortunately, good-humored man became known to all as "Rabbit George".

Lizzie, the bride on that glorious summer afternoon, was our oldest daughter but Clement, standing to the right of her, looking down and off to the side as if he was meant to be somewhere else, was our oldest child. You can see from the photograph that my husband was tired. George was seventy nine years old and though he was pleased Lizzie was marrying Albert Schonhut, a fine young man from a family of pork butchers, he still had three more children at home and didn't know if he wanted to live to see them married or hoped he wouldn't have to suffer through any more weddings.

As it turned out, all our children were married within a few years but by that time, sadly, George was gone. I always wished we could have had a few more years together, but we were married for twenty-eight years which still seems like a miracle to me. So, instead of being sorry for the time we didn't have, I've always chosen to be thankful for the many years we were able to share. It's a hard fact of our existence, and one that is better accepted than fought, that everything must come to an end.

George might have been able to live on for a few more years, but by Lizzie's wedding he'd known he'd had enough. And he certainly wouldn't have wanted to be given time in Far Yonder. He'd thought enough and said enough – always in that order – in his eighty years on earth. I was happy to be given the gift, but I'm glad it's ending. This book gives me the chance to talk to you all and will bring my time in Far Yonder to a close.

On the day of Lizzie's wedding, I was sixty years old, nineteen years younger than my husband. You can see from the expression on my face that I was thinking of everything that still had to be done and was wishing the photographer would get on with it. It must be nice when a picture is taken in a split second, although I don't envy you the amount of photographs that are taken now. I feel sorry for the youngsters whose every move is recorded.

Seated on the ground next to me is our youngest, Effie. She was my fourth child and her father's twelfth, and must have known from the moment she came into the world that she would have to work hard to get our attention. More so than my three earlier babies, Effie can be given credit for the name "Rabbit George" sticking, as her father was sixty-two years old when she was born. Needless to say, it didn't take long for such a pretty little girl to discover that by being the youngest, as well as naturally dainty and feminine, she could wind her father, her half-brothers, and even her half-sisters, around her little finger. That left me and her older brother and sisters to keep her in her place.

During the time the photograph was being taken, Effie had grumbled to me that the grass was wet from the morning's rain and

3

that the longer she sat on it the more it would stain her delicate frock. Bertha, one of the groom's sisters, was sitting next to her and wasn't complaining. Effie's mutterings were more irritating to me that day than her usual complaints (as if I should have checked that the grass was dry before telling her to sit on it!) as she'd known I'd worried for weeks that it would rain on the day of the wedding, and we would be stuck in the house with the Schonhut family and Lizzie's and Albert's friends.

My husband built us a big house on Rossiter Road, but there were always enough Smiths' to fill it up and you didn't want your guests to feel you hadn't tried your best. You can't take sunshine or a dry, mild day for granted in Yorkshire, not even in the summer. Effie was seventeen years old and although she'd been the first that morning to shout down the stairs that the rain had stopped and the sky had turned bright blue, her excitement had dampened as quickly as the moisture had seeped into the folds of her flimsy dress. Effie lived to be ninety years of age, and her fondness for fine clothing would last until her slender body was finally laid to rest.

I'd shut out Effie's complaining only to feel Florence fidgeting behind me. In the photograph there are two young ladies named Florence – the first is our daughter who is standing behind me, and the second is Albert's sister, standing next to her. I'd desperately wanted to turn around and tell our Florence to stand still, but I'd had enough charges, step-children and, eventually, children of my own to know that a girl of nineteen is old enough to control her own arms and legs.

Florrie's discomfort had not been because she'd had to stand still for the photographer, but because of the scene she'd caused in the kitchen that morning. She'd started pestering me in the midst of all the preparations – as if that would get the response she'd hoped for – that she wanted to marry Arthur Holroyd. Florrie and Arthur were courting and he's a nice young man, but I'd said she could tell me all about her betrothal after Arthur had spoken with her father.

Florrie had started to cry, turning on the taps so quickly the tears must have been welled up behind her eyes just waiting for a reason to fall down her rosy cheeks. She'd said Arthur is an assistant at the boot dealers and isn't like Albert Schonhut who has his family's butcher shops behind him. I'd asked her why she would compare Arthur to young Schonhut at the same time six dozen trays of sausage rolls and pork pies – which went lovely with picked onions and a bottle of stout – were arriving from those very same shops!

Being too busy to pay any more attention to Florrie, I'd turned to take a tray from the delivery boy only to hear her pound up the stairs and slam the bedroom door. The three girls shared the back bedroom so it was no surprise when Lizzie came running downstairs screaming that Florrie had thrown herself on the bed on which she'd spread out her veil and it was all screwed up in a heap. Lizzie was a dressmaker and could work wonders with all kinds of material, but she looked as if a crushed veil would bring a premature end to the long and happy life she and her groom were about to start together.

I'd ignored all the fuss about the veil and told Lizzie to send her sisters downstairs where they were meant to be in the kitchen, and reminded her that as it was her wedding day she didn't have to do her household jobs. Florrie and Effie soon appeared announcing that they wouldn't be doing any of their jobs on the day of their weddings either. In all our years together, they hadn't learned that I liked to hear what they were going to do and not what wouldn't be done.

Finally, the camera exploded, the photographer shouted that he was finished and I jumped up to go back to the kitchen. I reminded Clement to help his father out of the chair. My husband was stiff from decades of physical work and, though he didn't ask for help, he would accept it when offered. I thought how nice it would be to sit in the garden with a cup of tea, or perhaps a little cream sherry, but there was still too much work to do.

Effie was swatting at the back of her dress and I decided not to tell her that a green stain had spread across her bottom. Bert Hague would soon notice and jump at the chance to brush off the back of her dress. Bert was nineteen and loved an audience and before the night was out he'd be imitating the Schonhuts' German accents and pretending to chase a pig around the table. He was so hilarious that people liked him even when he made fun of them.

I'd been surprised when Bert took a fancy to Effie who I'd thought too serious for the two of them to go together. But you can't predict love. And you can't today, in spite of all your gadgets. Considering his father's mineral water manufacturing business over in Parkgate, there had never been any doubt what the answer would be if Hubert Henry Hague proposed marriage to Effie Smith. I'd known it would suit Effie to be the wife of young man with a going concern although, of course, during the time he came courting she didn't know how hard she would have to work to keep that business afloat.

I'd worried that Florrie might feel hard done by when both her sisters married boys from local businesses, but she'd set her eye on young Holroyd and there'd always been the possibility that he could do as well as the Hague and Schonhut boys. But, in fairness, we'd known that wasn't true. There was no point denying it would be harder for Arthur who'd had some troubles growing up.

Arthur's father had died in a mining accident when he was a boy, leaving his mother with three little ones. What happened to the young widow and her children would have depended upon which pit her husband was working in when he was killed. Some of the coal owners, like the Fitzwilliam family up at Wentworth, gave compensation as well as a pension and housing allowance, but others would turn the widow out of her house within a few weeks.

After Arthur's father died he'd been taken in by a relative and his mother later got married again to a butcher named Oldfield, but for some reason Arthur didn't mix with everyone in his family.

It was unlikely he would catch up to Albert Schonhut or Hubert Hague whose families helped get them off to a good start. But that was never a concern for my husband who'd started out as a stable boy for Earl Fitzwilliam and went on to have his own building company. So Florrie's distress had been all for nothing which, as with us all, usually turns out to be the case.

I'd noticed Albert and Lizzie giggling together and been happy that my daughter had a husband who was as thrilled with her as she was with him. I'd smiled to myself thinking of my own wedding at St. George's Church in Doncaster. No-one would have imagined that George and me were as pleased with each other as these two young ones.

When a widower marries his housekeeper everybody thinks it's a practical arrangement and an easy way for a man with too many motherless children to get them brought up without having to pay for it. As if payment isn't made on both sides when it comes to all marriages! We were still happy, though we didn't show it. It wouldn't have been seemly and never would have been considering seven of George's children were with us on the day of our wedding, with five of them still living at home and little Georgie only four years old.

I'd become a mother to Georgie more so than to the older children as he'd been barely two years old when his mother died and I came to work for the family. Georgie had been the second boy to be given his father's name. My husband's firstborn, George, died when he was only fifteen. When, after his death, another boy came along, he too had been named George. I doubt you would do this today but, at that time, it was fairly common to give the name of a deceased child to a new baby.

I've had a long time to consider my life and where it began and ended. I was born in Lincolnshire and died in Yorkshire and, other than a number of years spent in Nottinghamshire, I didn't go much of anywhere else. I went to London once, and to Southport in Lancashire. You can imagine my amazement as I've watched you move away, seeing you go as far off as Australia, America, Canada, South Africa, Hong Kong, Switzerland, Saudi Arabia, Guernsey, Scotland, China, Uganda, Wales and Northern Ireland.

I've also been so interested watching you living in London, Newcastle, Bristol, Leicester, Southampton and Liverpool. And many towns and villages in Devon, Oxfordshire, Surrey, Shropshire, Cleveland, Lancashire, Worcestershire, the Isle of Wight, Cheshire, Cumbria and the Isle of Man. But I'm happy to see that many of you still live in Yorkshire and Lincolnshire.

When I was a girl a number of families moved from Lincolnshire to America or Canada, and later many went to New Zealand. They went where they could farm their own land instead of working for the landowners like my family did for too many generations. Now you move far away but you go back home to visit, you fly around on holiday and for your jobs and businesses. I wonder how on earth you know where you are when you wake up.

Yet, as you are about to learn, though the distance from Billinghay to Greasbrough is but seventy-five miles, it was a long journey from the muddy fields of Lincolnshire to the pretty garden at Rossiter Villa where we gathered for Lizzie's wedding on that sunny day in August 1906.

George Smith (1827-1907) and Mary Stennett Smith (1846-1932)

CLEMENT (1880-1942)
m. Dora Woodward

Wilfred (1911-1941)
Clement (1916-1983)

see extended tree

ELIZABETH (1885-1956)
m. Albert Schonhut (1881-1945)

George (1911-1962)
Joan (1917-2007)

see extended tree

FLORENCE (1887-1974)
m. Arthur Holroyd (1888-1955)

Arthur (1908-?), Effie (1910-2003),
Neville (1914-2004), H. Peter
(1916-2000), Ruth (1928-   )

see extended tree

EFFIE (1889-1979)
m. Hubert H. Hague (1887-1958)

Charles (1911-1995) Pauline (1920-2011)
Anthony (1924-1929) T. Nigel (1928-   )

see extended tree

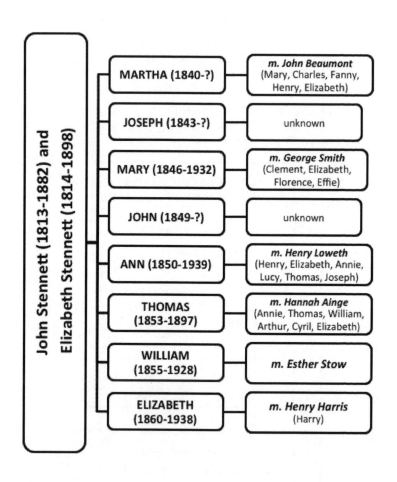

EARLY STENNETT ANCESTRY

JOSEPH STENNETT
(1780-1829)
m. Elizabeth _____
(1784-1854)

JOHN STENNETT
(1813-1882)
m. Elizabeth _____
(1814-1898)

Martha, Joseph, Mary, John, Ann, Thomas, William, Elizabeth
See extended tree

II

I know you like to be outside when the weather is fine and to potter around the garden, do a bit of weeding, cut the grass and clip the hedges. Even when it's dull and cold and you are cozy at home or in your office, you take a brisk walk, run a few miles or ride your bicycle to keep fit. You play golf in all weathers and enjoy football in the rain, and you feel healthy when you arrive home in wet clothes and dirty boots because you've been out in the elements keeping yourself strong. In the spring you sow seeds, happily kneeling down in the dirt so that later in the season you can pick your own tomatoes or lettuce, or a posy of flowers for the dining room table. The reason you like to touch the earth and feel the air is because you carry my family inside you.

It's a long time since the mid-1800's, and with every generation the physical and mental inheritances get less as the old gets mixed with the new. But when for hundreds of years your people labored on the land it takes a few hundred more for it to wend its way through the family tree. But, as you know, there is a big difference between getting tired and dirty for the pleasure of it, and being filthy and exhausted from six – or seven – long days, every week, every year, for subsistence wages.

I was born on January 2, 1846, coming after my sister, Martha, and my brother, Joseph. My parents, John and Elizabeth Stennett, christened me Mary and five more babies – John, Ann, Thomas, William and Elizabeth – followed. The youngest, Elizabeth, was named after my mother and my father's mother who was also named Elizabeth Stennett.

I christened my first daughter Elizabeth and she had a lovely granddaughter, Elizabeth Hartley, named after her. As it turned out, the two would become connected through more than their name as, sadly, my daughter's life ended while she was taking care of her little namesake.

In 1956 they were staying at the Hinton Wood Hotel in Bournemouth on the south coast of England. They'd gone for the sea air to help seven-year old Elizabeth during her convalescence from peritonitis. Lizzie and her granddaughter spent a lot of time walking up and down the chines which lead to the beach and, at the age of seventy one, Lizzie was stricken with congestive heart failure. Lizzie's son, George, and her daughter, Joan, rushed to Bournemouth along with Joan's husband, Arthur Hartley, and their son, Robin, arriving just in time to say goodbye to my daughter and to take care of the little one.

I am happy to know that the name, Elizabeth, continues in the family. My great-grandson, Robin Hartley, bestowed the name on his first child and she, in turn, named her first baby, Adele Elizabeth. Adele Elizabeth Sayers is a surgeon, and I enjoy picturing the confusion on my mother's and grandmother's faces if they could look down on Hull Royal Infirmary and see that the young woman who bears their name is not mopping the floor or cleaning up the patient, or even handing medical instruments to the doctor, but is the person performing the surgery.

My grandmother, Elizabeth Stennett, lived with us when I was girl. Her husband, Joseph, had died in 1829 at the age of forty nine, so she'd been a widow for many years. She lived with her sister, Mary Franklin, for a time and then came to stay with us. After a lifetime of labor in the Lincolnshire fields, my grandmother had not a penny to her name and depended upon my father to provide a roof over her head. A poor roof it was, filled with all of us.

My father didn't work in the fields but was a shepherd who tended the landowner's large flock. This meant he got a regular wage, if only a very small one. My grandmother was considered lucky that she had a son to take her in and didn't end up in the workhouse. In an official record of the people of Billinghay in 1851, Elizabeth Stennett is listed as sixty seven years of age, an agricultural laborer's widow, and a pauper. She died in 1854.

While no-one is described as a pauper today, I see that the lot of poor people hasn't changed and too many men and women still work their whole lives to be left with nothing except the charity of family or strangers. I know that national benefit programs are now available to help people, which is a good thing. However, if my husband had lived to witness them, he would say that being dependent on the government for the roof over your head and the food in your belly is a fate worse than death. He believed people should be paid fairly for their work, but be expected to take care of themselves.

This was one of the few topics me and George didn't agree on. I've always believed that you should help people who are worse off than you are because when I was a child I benefited from other people's generosity. The best thing to happen to me and my brothers and sisters is that we all went to school. At that time, many of the children of agricultural workers were barely taught to read and write, and education didn't become compulsory until after we were grown.

Fortunately, Billinghay had a school which we all went to on our fifth birthday and stayed until we were thirteen. We were only allowed to miss if we were really poorly, probably because it got us all out of the house for a few hours each day. I loved school and I learned to read and write, do multiplication tables and arithmetic, and I studied history and geography. We didn't do gym or sports because we had plenty of exercise working at home before and after school, but we played games in the breaks and I always joined in the skipping.

The school in Billinghay would not have been in existence when I was a child if it were not for good people who started charity schools before I was born, and later the church schools followed. It's easy to say that the people who paid for the charity schools were rich and had plenty of money and should, at the very least, spread it around. Personally, I'd like to see a situation where they don't get to hog so much of it in the first place, although I see that's not happened yet and I doubt it ever will. But not everyone who is rich is charitable, and not everyone who is generous is rich, so you can't dismiss the good things people do.

My great-granddaughter, Veronica Clinton (née Hague), works at a college in America bringing in donations for scholarships for students who can't afford to pay the tuition, and my great-great-granddaughter, Cordelia Sampson, travels to Ndali Lodge in Uganda every summer to help run a nursery school. Cordelia stays for months and has raised money to build a new facility there. This shows that for all the free education which exists in the world today, there are boys and girls who can't go to school unless someone is willing to help them.

I went to school until my thirteenth birthday, a date I hadn't looked forward to that year because I'd known it would bring my school days to an end. Just the week before my birthday, my sister, Martha, had come home on Boxing Day, struggling through the narrow doorway of our cottage with a heavy bag. My mother had quickly looked inside, glanced at Martha, cocked her head at me, and the bag had been dropped at my feet.

I'd been working on a sampler and had a long piece of wool threaded in my needle, so I'd ignored the bag and continued my stitching. I'd been anxious to finish my work as I'd already stitched the year, 1858, on the sampler and wanted to get it done before the year ended. My mother and my sister, Ann, kept telling me that it would be alright if it was a day or two into 1859 when I finished it, but that didn't seem right to me. I'd stitched 1858 on the sampler and had to finish it before December 31! We didn't talk about goals or deadlines back then but, as you know, setting a date to finish a job always gets it done.

Barely a second had passed from the time the bag hit the

ground before my mother gave me a sharp clip on the shoulder. I'd dropped my needle and stared as my sister turned her bounty upside down on the floor, emptying out skirts, pinafores, aprons, collars, and a sturdy pair of boots which, even from a distance, I could see had plenty of wear left in them.

Martha was six years older than me and for the past few years had been working for a family in Sleaford. The following year she would marry John Beaumont, an agricultural laborer from nearby Martin, and the year after that she would give birth to Mary Ann, the first of their five children. Martha would live into her seventies and outlive John by several years. During the early years she was in service, she would often come home with clothes and linens her employers no longer wanted. My mother must have told her to keep an eye out for some decent clothes for me so that I would be clean and neat when I started in service. I'd understood the message in this bag of clothes – it was time for me to leave home.

Elizabeth Smith Schonhut (1885-1956) and Albert Schonhut (1881-1945)

GEORGE (1911-1962) *m. Ethel Spittlehouse (1908-1995)*

PAULINE *m. Paul Tear*
Jacqueline *m. James Houghton* (Emily, Suzanna)
James *m. Johanna Rae* (Charles, Alex, Henry)

HILARY *m. Paul Hoskins*
Rupert

JOAN (1917-2007) m. Arthur Hartley (1914-1991)

CHARLES ROBIN *m. Judith Hewitt*
Elizabeth *m. Adrian Sayers* (Adele Elizabeth, Joe *m. Karen Buckley* (Logan), Joshua)
Clare *m. Steven Kitt* (Mia, Amber) *m. John Erskine* (Mabelle)
Fleur *m. Matthew Shaw* (Kara, Quillan)

ELIZABETH *m. James Ogley*
Richard *m. Karalyn Niven* (Isla)
Jonathan *m. Sarah Hellier* (Lucie, Charles)
m. Brian Brain

III

I'd imagined I would go out to service in Sleaford where Martha would be close by, but the first job I was offered was as a nursemaid with the Harrison family in Walcott, just two miles north of Billinghay. John Harrison farmed two hundred and fifty acres and the farmhouse was on High Street. I'd begged my mother to let me wait until I could find a position in Sleaford, but she'd known that it wasn't so much that I wanted to be near Martha, but that I was trying to delay leaving home. And though she would miss my help with John, Ann, Thomas, William and, especially, Elizabeth, who was just an infant, she'd made it clear it was time for me to earn my own keep.

I'd pointed out that Mrs. Harrison would be getting help with her children while she, my own mother, was losing my help with hers, but she'd reminded me that Ann was almost ten years old and was a good spare pair of hands. There was also the advantage of one less mouth to feed and one less girl – always wakeful, tossing and turning – in the bed. And, like Martha, I'd be coming home to visit and would find ways to help out. After all, I'd be only two miles away.

Young girls of thirteen are no longer made to leave home in order to earn their own keep and it would create a scandal to turn out a young teenager now, but it forced us to be independent and got us away from our families, whether bad or good. My parents were poor, but they gave me and my brothers and sisters whatever they could and the only thing they expected in return was something we could all do – work.

My brother, Joseph, had not waited until his thirteenth birthday and had been in a hurry to leave school as sitting in a schoolroom had been hard for him. By the time I left home, Joseph was already living at the farm of William Green where he worked as a carter. My oldest brother wanted nothing more than to be outside, no matter the weather, and was happy moving tools and produce around farmer Green's three-hundred acre farm with nothing but a mule and a two-wheeled cart to help him.

When you've moved a few times you learn to cope with the loneliness and strangeness of a new place. But I've never forgotten how homesick I was those first few weeks at the Harrison farm in Walcott. It didn't matter that it was only two miles away as it might as well have been the other side of the world. I could walk home on my day off but still felt as if I'd moved so far away.

I'd brought my sampler with me and each morning I made my narrow bed in the corner of the nursery and laid it on my pillow. One day, Mrs. Harrison noticed the sampler and compared it to a framed tapestry hanging in the upstairs hallway which her grandmother had made years earlier. A few days later, she'd told me that one of the farm workers spent his evenings doing carpentry work and she'd asked him to make a frame for my sampler. I'd gone down to the lower barn to go through the scraps of wood and he'd stretched out the cloth and framed it.

My sampler hangs today in the home of my granddaughter, Ruth Sampson (née Holroyd). I designed the sampler myself and put everything on it a person needs, knowing when I started it that it would go with me when I left home. At the top is the alphabet, which you need if you are going to read and write. Under that are the numbers, so you can count and add up. My name is on it, so everyone knows the sampler belongs to me. As mentioned, the year 1858 is stitched near the bottom, and is accurate because I finished it before December was done! I added "feed my lambs" from my favorite verse in the Bible where Jesus tells Simon Peter to "feed my lambs".

Like all children back then, we went to Sunday School. We read St. John and I told the teacher I liked this particular verse because it proved Jesus wanted his disciples to take care of the people. I knew it didn't literally mean to take care of the lambs, but my father had been happy when he'd looked over my shoulder when I'd been stitching one day and had seen these words and the drawings I'd added of a sheep and a shepherd holding a staff.

My father was always quick to show his feelings and he'd nodded his head up and down so fast I'd been afraid it might fall off. He'd then rubbed his hands over my hair and said he hoped I would always have my sampler because it would remind me where I came from no matter where I might end up. He'd said he hoped that was somewhere far away, quickly adding that he didn't want to get rid of me, but wanted all his children to have a better life than he'd had. John Stennett would be so proud to know that the sampler, along with its sheep and its shepherd, is still in the family.

I too am proud that my granddaughter has kept the tapestry and will pass it on to her daughter, April Stern (née Sampson), or to her daughter-in-law, Louise Sampson (née England), and they will keep it for their children. Although it reminds me of feeling so homesick in Walcott, it is proof that Mrs. Harrison was a kind woman who wanted me to feel at home. She let me hang it above my bed and told the children it belonged to me and to make sure it didn't get damaged.

Considering the racket the Harrison children made jumping up and down on the bed and the number of times it got knocked of its hook, it's a miracle it survived. But there it is hanging on the wall in Snape, near Bedale in North Yorkshire, and is a tiny bit of proof that I existed. And, imagine if I'd known when I was busy stitching that, thanks to April and Louise, a picture of my sampler would be sent to America almost a hundred and sixty years later, and that it would be sent without using paper, envelope or postage!

We should all strive to leave something of ourselves behind. Effie's youngest son, Nigel Hague, married Stella Jefferson, the daughter of a Greasbrough farmer. Stella loved to stitch tapestries and made dozens of cushions, rugs and pictures. She lives on through her tapestries, scattered as they are throughout the homes of her children and grandchildren. I didn't know when I was stitching that little sampler that it would be a comfort to me when I was homesick, but would also be a way for my family to remember me so far in the future.

The outcome of my life I most regret is that, other than this one small picture, there is nothing to show for all the work I did. From being a young girl in Billinghay to an old widow in Greasbrough, there was not a day that I didn't cook or clean or care for someone or something. But if all you do is housework, cooking and looking after children and the menfolk, you need to have faith that your work makes a difference because you will not be left with any evidence of your labors.

It's nice to have children, grandchildren, great-grandchildren and the succeeding generations to follow you, but children are only partly yours, even if you birth them, and with each generation the part of you they carry becomes smaller. Your great-grandchildren, or possibly an earlier generation, may not even know your name, which is why I treasure this chance to tell my story.

But, oh, how I envy my husband and the buildings he left behind! George built houses in Greasbrough which stand solid and strong to this day. It's marvelous to know that children run up and down the very same stairs he built and that when the owners come in and out of the front door, they are stepping on the stone he laid for the threshold well over a hundred years ago.

My husband also built two schools in Greasbrough which were attended by his children, grandchildren, and even six of his great-grandchildren: Robin and Elizabeth Hartley, and Jane, Veronica, Sally and William Hague. But while George Smith was laying brick, I was boiling potatoes and while he was mixing cement, I was adding the milk and butter, and when he put a rock-solid cornerstone in place, I was mashing the spuds in an enormous pot.

If all the mashed potatoes I made were baked into bricks, I could have built a cathedral.

Like my husband, some of you are leaving behind concrete proof of your labors. My great-grandson, William Hague, is the author of two books about famous men of the same name: William Pitt and William Wilberforce. And his wife, Ffion Hague, is the author of a book about the women in the life of her fellow Welshman, David Lloyd George, who I remember so well as a wonderful Chancellor of the Exchequer and Prime Minister.

Adrian Sayers, husband of Lizzie's great-granddaughter, Elizabeth Sayers (née Hartley), is the author of a novel about the miner's strike in Yorkshire in 1984. Adrian's pen name is Jack Marshall. Philip Goodswen, a great-grandson through Effie's daughter, Pauline, had a natural flair for drawing, and later in life painted beautiful seascapes for his family and friends.

The books and paintings will last forever, but I suppose someone has to peel the potatoes. And there is nothing more satisfying than a good helping of creamy mashed spuds.

Clement Smith (1880-1942) and Dora Woodward Smith

WILFRED (1911-1941)

CLEMENT (1916-1983) *m. Annie Hyde (1916-1996)*

ERIC *m. Jane Vessey*
Julie *m. Dean Ford* (Jack, Sam)
Wendy
Neil *m. Verity Morcom* (Isobel, Libby)

ANTHONY *m. Elizabeth Huttall*
Sarah *m. Philip Shaw* (Robert)
Joanne
Lesley *m. Nigel Bird* (Sophie)

IV

My mother taught me to peel potatoes and to scrape the skin really close to the surface because we couldn't afford to waste food. But she stressed that any green bits should be cut off because they could hurt an unborn baby. As a child I didn't believe that a baby in a woman's tummy could be damaged by a bit of green on a potato, but people believed this for many generations, both before and after my own. It has turned out to be true that the green on a potato is poisonous and shouldn't be eaten, particularly when expecting. It is fortunate that my mother knew this and that, in spite of never having enough food, she would not run the risk of serving bad potatoes.

Many years later, I would put what I'd learned about potatoes into regular practice at the vicarage of St. Luke's Church in Shireoaks. I was the cook in that Nottinghamshire vicarage, and it was where the foundation of my mashed potato cathedral was laid. Or, as you might say now, it was where my career in the mashed potato business really took off.

I stayed with the Harrisons in Walcott for a number of years, but the children grew older and I became restless and had known it was time to find something new. I answered an advertisement for the position with Reverend and Mrs. Brown in Shireoaks and, although I hadn't been employed as a cook before, they took one look at me and offered me the job. What they actually saw in me I never understood because, although I was now twenty years of age, I still looked like a scrap of a girl rather than a grown woman. The first words Mrs. Harrison had spoken to me when I'd arrived at the

Walcott farmhouse all those years earlier had been to question my age. She'd told me later she thought I was no older than ten and that my family had sent me out to service early.

I was always small and my arms and wrists were so thin it looked as if they might snap. And though a pretty face has got many a girl a good job – and still does no matter how many laws you might pass to stop so-called discrimination – Reverend and Mrs. Browne did not hire me for my looks. I was never pretty, either as a girl or as a young woman.

My eyes were pale and no bigger than slits – later my husband would tease me for being cautious and say that my narrow eyes were designed to take in the world slowly and carefully, which fit me to a tee. My lips were thin and my cheeks puffy which made me look like a squirrel storing up nuts, which I must admit also represented my character. I was blessed with a good head of hair, but it was a dull brown and always scraped back off my face so as not to get in the way of work.

You can imagine that I was a plain little thing. Not at all like many of the boys and girls who followed me. Some of you are so good looking now! I like to take credit where I can, but you didn't get your handsome or pretty faces from me. My girls were all bonnie and took after their father who, with his lively, twinkling eyes, was handsome at every age. Some of you resemble him today, particularly Charles Hague, my great-grandson through Effie, but it's fair to say that most of you got your looks from another side of your family.

However, in spite of my poor appearance, Reverend and Mrs. Browne seemed to agree that I was right for the job and took it on good faith that I could cook. Perhaps they thought that such a scrawny girl wouldn't eat as much as a big, round cook but, if so, they were mistaken. Like all my brothers and sisters, my appetite had never been satisfied at home, and Mrs. Harrison had soon become used to her little nursemaid always hoping for another helping.

I said goodbye to the Harrison family, to Walcott, and to Lincolnshire, and off I went to take up my new position in Shireoaks, just outside Worksop in Nottinghamshire. I'd felt adventurous leaving one county and moving to another, even though Nottinghamshire was just next door to Lincolnshire. In fact, Shireoaks put me on the border of Yorkshire and on the road towards Greasbrough, though it would be several years before I would answer the advertisement placed by Mr. George Smith, farmer, builder, father, widower.

During the years I was in Walcott and at St. Luke's vicarage, my future husband was busy farming and building, and making babies with his second wife, Mary Crawshaw. He had no reason to suppose that another Mary was heading in his direction. Thank goodness we don't know what the future is going to bring! George had already buried one wife and would not relish burying the second – the mother of his eight children – and taking on a third.

Shireoaks was a busy, bustling village with a colliery that had opened about twenty years earlier. I hadn't come across it by accident, but had heard about the village from my friend, Hattie, who had worked on another farm in Walcott. She'd moved to Shireoaks the previous year and had written many letters telling me that there was plenty of work and – of great importance to fun-loving, romantic Hattie – hundreds of strapping young men. It seemed that the place for me to look for work, and where I would start out with a friend, was Shireoaks.

The desire for adventure that got me on the road to Nottinghamshire didn't prevent me from feeling sad to be leaving Lincolnshire behind. But, just as George Smith didn't know another Mary was heading his way, I was not to know that I would have a son, Clement, who as a young man would move to Newark, a major town in Lincolnshire, and that his descendants would live in that area for decades to follow.

On the day of Lizzie's wedding when Florrie had been crying that her sweetheart was only a shop assistant, she must have momentarily forgotten that her brother, Clement, happily worked in a shop. She hadn't known, however, that far in the future she too would keep her own haberdashers shop, selling buttons, cotton and ribbons.

Clement always enjoyed working behind a shop counter, busily serving the customers and keeping the jars and drawers all stocked up. Later he became a grocery provisions dealer handling imported foods, which I'd advised him against – wrongly as it turned out.

When I was a young woman, wheat, meat and cheese started to be imported from America and Canada, as well as from Argentina and New Zealand. You will imagine that if I was apprehensive about importing food back then, it is beyond my belief what I've seen from Far Yonder with people eating not only meat and fish from far off, but vegetables that have come from the other side of the world. I shake my head when I see people in England eating food from as far away as China and Chile, and places that you have no idea where they are unless you open up the Atlas.

But what I've never understood is why the lesson wasn't learned from two terrible wars – the second of which was responsible for the death of one of my grandchildren – that a country as strong and independent as England must produce as much food as possible from its own soil. When the next war comes, as it surely will, how are people going to eat? I'm glad my time in Far Yonder is coming to a close because I've seen how quickly people seem to have no recollection of what they swore, not long before, they would never, ever forget.

Clement's oldest boy, Wilfred Smith, was a signal coder for the Royal Navy. On April 27, 1941 he was aboard the H.M.S. Patia heading up the Northumberland coast when the ship was attacked by German bombers. Wilfred was thirty years old and lost his life in the cold depths of the North Sea. He is buried in Tynemouth Cemetery, just south of Northumberland on the east coast of England. Did my grandson give up his life for his country so his country could give up on the necessity of being able to feed its own people?

My great-great-granddaughter, Rebecca Carruthers (née Foster), and her husband, Scott Carruthers, live in Tynemouth. They like to go down to the beach to look out at the sea and meet friends in the cafes and restaurants. I hope they both live to be old and to enjoy the beauty of their coastline for many long years. I ask only, as they look out at that dark, unforgiving water, that they pause for a moment to remember Wilfred. None of us must forget that when called, Wilfred Stennett Smith stood up and, without question or complaint, did what most of us are never asked to do.

V

It turned out that, contrary to my advice to Clement to stay working at a traditional grocers, he liked dealing with the imported provisions and did well enough that he was later able to move to Lincolnshire and open a shop of his own. From being young he was a big reader – like many of you now who like to have your nose in a book, or something that no longer looks like a book but apparently is one – and he opened an antique book shop in Newark. He realized that you put a book on the shelf and, other than a bit of dusting, it stays in place until it's sold, whereas food has to be continually stocked and rotated.

Grocery shops are different now, but the stock still has to be brought in and put on the shelves, although the likes of Clement are no longer standing behind the counter. I've seen you go into shops the size of a field of barley, marching in with your trolley to help yourself to the goods. I see the advantage of being able to serve yourself, but between the trolley, the till and the car, there's too much handling of your purchases.

I understand now you can avoid all that and you can sit at a machine, put in your order and drive to the shop to pick it up. This sounds easy enough, but it means you don't see the quality of the goods until you get home. I still think it was better in my day when all you had to do was walk to the shop, tell the shopkeeper what you wanted and be standing there looking at what you were buying before you paid for it. It was always a pleasure to walk back home with meat, bread and vegetables in your own basket. As soon as you got home, you put goods on the kitchen table or stored them away in the pantry and cupboards.

One of the big advantages to the village shops was that you could send youngsters on errands. For centuries, small children were given a note, a basket and a few coins, and off they would go to the butcher, the baker, the greengrocer and the newspaper shop, bringing back everything you wanted. You can't do this now because you have to drive to the shop, or you are afraid to send your children out alone. This is a shame and it seems my great-grandchildren were the last generation to be sent on errands and to know the satisfaction of bringing a basket full of goods home to their mothers.

It was, however, always possible that the child might come back empty handed. One day when she was very young, Veronica Hague was sent to Willey's in Greasbrough to pick up her mother's order. Unfortunately, Veronica was afraid to go in the butcher's shop, not only because of the glassy-eyed stare every customer got from "Sammy", the huge steer whose head took up much of the back wall, but because she believed that Jack Willey was going to lock her in the big fridge where he hung his carcasses. Jack had grown up with Veronica's father, Nigel, and enjoyed teasing his old pal's youngsters, particularly Vonz, as he affectionately called her.

That morning, Veronica set off on her errand, walking slowly up Campbell Street, but turning around as soon as she got to Main Street. She ran home and told her mother that Willey's shop was closed. Stella Hague knew Jack and Ann Willey wouldn't close their busy shop on a Friday morning, and took the basket and her daughter in hand and marched up the street. Finding the top half of the shop's stable door flung wide open, as she'd expected, Stella stepped into the shop, told Jack to stop teasing her children and, once again, tried to convince Veronica that he was only joking, Together, they walked back home with the weekend's joint of beef.

People will always have to eat and life is a never-ending cycle of cooking and eating, day-in-day-out, which makes selling food a good way to make a living. My great-great-grandson, James Goodswen, manages information and networks for a large chain of supermarkets. The work James does is completely different from that Clement did a hundred years ago, but the importance of the business hasn't changed.

Like me, Clement had been a late bloomer and almost thirty years old when he married Dora Woodward, one of our school teachers in Greasbrough. Today, several of my great-great-grandchildren are teachers and school staff. Robert Hague is assistant head at Hampstead School in London, Deborah Gill (née Stephenson) is a secretary at a school near Doncaster, and Charlotte Schoch (née Goodswen) is a teaching assistant for special needs children at the Phil and Jennie Gaglardi Academy in Comox on Vancouver Island in Canada. Clare Erskine (née Hartley) was a teaching assistant at Honiton Community College in Devon. She met her husband, John Erskine, a teacher of technology, while working there.

Edward Clinton, my great-great grandson in America is married to a teacher named Carla Castaneda. Carla's mother, Ruth Castaneda (née Girardi), is of Irish and Italian heritage, but her father, Roberto Castaneda, is from El Salvador which is where their wonderfully exotic name comes from.

You are proud when, like Clement, your son chooses a teacher for his bride! It shows he respects a woman's intelligence and won't manage his married life as if he is the only one who can make a decision or find the answer to a problem. I know sometimes it works best if you build a man up and let him think the good idea you just had was his, or pretend you don't know something when it was you who told him in the first place, but it is a better marriage if both husband and wife respect each other's abilities.

One of the main improvements I've seen from Far Yonder is women and men becoming more equal in education and work. It gives women independence and takes a big weight off a man's shoulders. I know that no matter how willing my husband was to provide for us all, he felt the burden that so much depended upon him.

I was sad when Clement and Dora moved away from Greasbrough, but pleased that they chose to put down roots in Lincolnshire, and proud and touched when they gave my family's name to both their sons: Wilfred Stennett Smith and Clement Stennett Smith. My son died at the age of only sixty two, the year following Wilfred's death, and the book shop passed to his second son, Clement, his only remaining child, who lived into his late sixties. I am proud to report that Eric and Anthony Smith, the sons of my grandson, Clement, live in Lincolnshire with their families to this day.

Many years later, my great-granddaughter, Gabrielle Wadsworth, would settle in Boston, barely twenty miles from Billinghay. Gay married Bruce Stephenson, the sales director at Elsoms Seeds in Spaulding – a much better prospect than shepherds and farm laborers! Gay and Bruce and their children, Mark and Deborah, have lived very different lives from those of my family.

Gay's mother, Effie Holroyd, is my granddaughter through Florrie. She and her husband, Reginald Wadsworth, lived in Lincolnshire during their later years so they could be near Gay and the grandchildren. A great-granddaughter of my Lizzie, Elizabeth Sayers, and her husband, Adrian, live in Epworth. It's nice to know that, thanks to Clement, Eric, Anthony, Effie, Gay and Elizabeth, I didn't leave Lincolnshire behind for good.

Nevertheless, not knowing that future generations would exist, let alone live in Lincolnshire, the day dawned when it was time for me to move to Shireoaks to start my job as the cook at St. Luke's vicarage. Reverend Browne and his wife were named George and Mary, which I later looked upon as a happy portent of my own marriage although, as you have already learned, it was not unusual to come across people with the same name as yourself or your family.

My husband, George, was the son of William Smith, but his grandfather and great-grandfather were both named George Smith. The name continued on, although has not been used as often. Our daughter, Elizabeth, named her son George, and Florrie's granddaughter, April Stern (née Sampson), named the eldest of her two boys, George, which would make my husband very happy.

George's father, William, married a girl named Elizabeth. William Smith, born in 1796, married Elizabeth Foulston, born in 1801. You will learn more about your Smith ancestors in this book. I know the repetition of names makes it difficult when you are researching or writing about your family because you have to keep explaining who you are talking about!

You don't limit yourselves to the same old choices of names any longer and have so many to choose from. The descendants of George and me include so many pretty names, both old and new, for the girls: Julie, Joanne, Sally, Joan, Florence, Pauline, Jane, April, Fleur, Suzanna, Lucie, Mia, Amber, Deborah, Kara, Jacqueline, Chloe, Clare, Isla, Lucie, Adele, Rebecca, Stephanie, Phyllis, Pamela, Gabrielle, Wendy, Lesley, Natalie, Nyah, Thea, Monica, Evi, Hilary, Diana, Margaret, Jessie, Frances, Hilda, Constance, Sarah, Ruth, Emily, Julia, Harriet, Veronica, Effie, Victoria, Rachel, Lucy, Charlotte, Cordelia, Hannah, Marina, Monica, Margaret, Gertrude, Isobel, Libby, Mabelle, Sophie and Mina. And Elizabeth!

The boys have good, strong names: Edward, Robert, Joseph, William, Wilfred, Clement, Philip, Peter, Hubert, Herbert, Neville, Nigel, Arthur, Charles, Rupert, Richard, Jonathan, Robin, Anthony, Eric, Neil, James, Frank, Harold, Walter, Alex, Cyril, Samuel, Jack, Mark, Leonard, Aaron, Joe, Oliver, Harry, Henry, Thomas, Alexander, Theo, Lucas, Joshua, Logan, Bailey, Quillan, Riley, Finley, Adam and Wesley. And George!

Over in Shireoaks, George and Mary Browne were never referred to by me or anyone else as anything other than Reverend and Mrs. Browne. Their three daughters, Ethel, Margaret and Eleanor, had been born one after the other and were still little when I arrived. The family had a young servant, Frederick Elliott, who, like me, lived in the vicarage.

You might think that I had an easy time of it cooking for only five members of the family, along with Fred and me. You might also imagine that the vicar and his wife were gentlefolk who went about their church duties and kept quiet evenings at home. This pleasant picture – and even a fuzzy image forming in my mind of me and a handsome collier living happily ever after in a little rose-covered cottage – had filled my thoughts when I'd stepped off the train in Shireoaks and made my way up to the vicarage. I'd been wrong in every respect.

Florence Smith Holroyd (1887-1974) and Arthur Holroyd (1888-1955)

ARTHUR (1908-?)
m. Edith Riley (1906-?)

EFFIE (1910-2003)
m. Reginald Wadsworth (1909-1992)
GABRIELLE *m. Bruce Stephenson*
Mark *m. Jacqueline Cowin* (Lucas, Chloe)
Deborah *m. Russell Gibb* (Adam, Alex)

NEVILLE (1914-2004)

H. PETER (1916-2000)
m. Alice Colclough (1922-2003)
PETER *m. Valerie Guy*

RUTH (1928-   )
m. Guy Sampson (1924-1992)
MARK *m. Louise England*
Harry, Cordelia
APRIL *m. Philip Stern*
George, Edward

VI

Amongst all the girls in the playground in Billinghay, I was the best skipper. When I was young, the older girls would turn the rope faster when they saw that I was the next one in, hoping to trip me up but instead giving me the chance to prove that I could clear the rope no matter how quickly it was turning. My brother, Joseph, had seen that I was faster than the other girls and made a skipping rope for me out of an old washing line. He told me that if I practiced by myself I would get even better.

Each day after school, as soon as I was done helping my mother, I would take my rope to the bare spot of dirt behind the house and my arms would fly, my feet barely touch the ground and my mind fill with nothing but keeping in rhythm with the rope. When it was tea time, John or Ann would be sent to fetch me and, though I would ignore their first call for me to come in, the spell would be broken and I would run inside. As much as I loved skipping, being last to the table usually meant getting less to eat, as I'd sit down to find my brother's and sister's hands already flying across the table.

As soon as tea was done, I would hurry back to my rope and skip until the last scrap of light left the sky. Having the ability to concentrate on a single task and shut out everything else is a wondrous gift. It's the gift given to inventors, athletes, musicians, artists, writers, scientists, singers, explorers and all creators. It's also given to those of us who like to work and who take pleasure in being productive, and mastering and completing a task. I was happy when I was skipping because I was getting faster and more confident, and at the end of the day I would climb into bed tired and contented. A blessed sleep would follow, and it was all thanks to skipping.

My first weeks at St. Luke's vicarage were such a whirl of activity, an endless race to meet the enormous demands of the household that I'd felt I'd been skipping from the minute I'd arrived. On that first day, I'd tapped nervously on the back door and immediately heard footsteps scurry across the slate flagstones of the kitchen. The heavy, weathered door had been flung open and a tall, lean woman with wavy black hair – which in all the years I would know her was never kept in place by her hairpins – had thrust her arms out to me. Mrs. Browne had grabbed me by the shoulders and literally pulled me into the kitchen. I'd been happy from that very first moment.

Many of you will have had the experience of taking a job which was described one way but turned out to be quite another. I'd realized immediately that although I would be the cook, as promised, I would also be in charge of the cleaning, washing and taking care of the children. I was a maid-of-all-work and, if anything explained why the vicar and his wife so quickly engaged me for the position it was because they knew I wouldn't have any silly ideas about only doing the work described in the advertisement. Not many people did back then, and certainly not someone whose only previous job had been nursemaid for a farmer's wife. You considered yourself fortunate to get work and did whatever your employer expected. If you were in service, you could only hope there were other servants to help with the work. St. Luke's vicarage had me and Fred.

The Brownes' had known they would not be met with resistance when they loaded me up with work, just as they'd known that the plain-faced daughter of a shepherd wouldn't have many marriage prospects and wouldn't soon be carried off by a husband, even in a village full of colliers. You must wonder why I was so contented at St. Luke's when people as decent as the vicar and his wife seemingly took advantage of me. It is because they didn't sit idly by while I ran between the range and the scullery, the nursery and the dining room, the bedrooms and the broom cupboard. Reverend and Mrs. Browne worked tirelessly, day in and day out, and it's natural to respect your employers when they work as hard as you do. When your boss knows how to work, you want to do an extra good job.

Many a vicar's wife would draw the line at holding Sunday School in her own home, but not Mrs. Browne. So many children attended Sunday School at St. Luke's that the church could not accommodate them all. Mrs. Browne solved the problem by holding one of the classes in the vicarage's parlor.

On my first Saturday evening in Shireoaks and, after skipping in perfect time for several days straight, Mrs. Browne announced that Sunday School would start at nine o'clock in the morning. She'd known I was too old to attend and I'd known I was not qualified to teach the youngsters, so I hadn't been sure why the announcement had been made. It became clear when she'd called Fred in from the coal shed where he'd been filling up the scuttles and, without saying a word, he'd clattered down the cellar steps in his worn out clodhoppers and come back up with four little chairs hanging on his back.

Fred was fourteen-years old and, like me, undersized for his age but, also like me, strong and fast. After several trips running up and down the cellar stairs, twenty five schoolroom chairs were scattered higgledy-piggledy across the parlor rug. Fred had gone back outside as quickly as he'd come in and Mrs. Browne had started to say something, but then shaken her head in resignation. She'd sighed and begun to arrange the chairs in some kind of order.

Immediately, I'd run out to the coal shed, grabbed Fred by the scruff of his neck and dragged him back inside. He'd been so shocked at being manhandled by me that he'd come without protest. I'd deposited him in the parlor and told him to put the chairs in a circle and to place a larger one amongst them. I'd been to Sunday School in Billinghay enough times to know that the teacher couldn't be expected to balance on a child's little chair.

Mrs. Browne was always so immersed in her duties and the hundreds of tasks she performed each week that she thought everyone knew as much as she did about the church and the vicarage. This meant she never explained what needed to be done. I'd known from my brothers and the farm hands in Walcott that you can't assume a boy will complete a job unless you tell him what to do every step of the way. If you want a young lad to clean the floor you must tell him to fill up the bucket with water, get the mop, wet it, wipe the floor, rinse the mop, and so on.

It was clear that Mrs. Browne had never told Fred how to arrange the chairs or, if she had, hadn't waited around long enough to make sure he followed her instructions. Instead she'd become used to doing the job herself. And it's hard to blame young Fred for not being able to read her mind or have enough experience to know what was required. My great-great grandchildren start jobs with companies which send them for training and orientation and something called onboarding, whatever that is. But, when you started work at St. Luke's vicarage, or most places back in the 1800's, you were thrown into the thick of things and had to muddle through as best as you could.

Beginning with that first Sunday morning when a whole gaggle of seven-year-old boys and girls had filed in through the kitchen and an hour later had filed out – each with a fresh-baked bun in their little hands – Mrs. Browne had turned to me to supervise Fred, and Fred had relied on me to explain what Reverend and Mrs. Browne wanted done. And I'd known I could work at St. Luke's for as long as I wanted. It turned out I would be thirty-one years old by the time I left.

One afternoon, a few weeks after I'd arrived, I'd been startled to see a face smiling at me through the kitchen window. It was Hattie, my friend from Walcott who'd encouraged me to look for a position in Shireoaks. I'd been so busy that I'd barely had time to think about her, but here she was rushing in the door, blurting out that she couldn't believe I hadn't come to visit her and how funny it was to see me in the vicarage instead of chasing the Harrison children around the farmhouse kitchen.

Hattie had babbled on in her thick Yorkshire accent – another portent of how my life would turn out – and then revealed what turned out to be the reason she'd chosen that particular day to visit her old friend: she'd heard the Shireoaks Colliery Band would be visiting the vicarage on Saturday afternoon. Could she come and help serve the tea?

Amidst the constant flow of visitors and the jumble of names and faces that had passed through the vicarage since my arrival, I recalled a foreman from the pit coming to the back door to see Mrs. Browne. It would only take a minute, he'd said, he just needed to make some arrangements. Now I realized that if I had cornered Mrs. Browne as soon as he'd left, I might have been informed of the Colliery Band's visit.

Instead, I'd assumed the foreman was a member of the church choir or one of the bell ringers making arrangements for next week's services. Or he could have been talking to Mrs. Browne about a miner's funeral, or a baby's christening, or a child's confirmation or, though it was unlikely a working man would take on jobs such as these, rushed arrangements for a daughter's wedding. But, instead, it seemed Hattie, who worked for a family on the other side of Shireoaks, was here to tell me that two dozen hungry men were coming for tea on Saturday.

Except for meal times with Fred – which lasted no longer than the three minutes it took us to shovel the food into our mouths and scoop a thick slice of bread around our plates – it was rare for me to sit at the kitchen table. But upon hearing the news of this additional task on a day which already included a hot dinner for the Bishop of Lincoln which I'd got myself in a real tizzy about, I'd sat down at the sturdy wooden table and rested my head on my arms. Hattie had quickly sat down on one of the children's stools, darting glances at the hall door to make sure Mrs. Browne wasn't about to appear.

One of the many things I loved about Hattie was that, unlike me, she was never a stranger. No sooner did she enter a house for the first time or meet a new person, she was as familiar with them as if she'd known them for years. I was to meet many such folk during my years in Yorkshire, and I was always happy to be reminded of the first friend I'd made when I left home.

My mind had quickly filled with egg sandwiches, jam tarts, apple pies, minced tarts, bread and butter, teapots, tea cups, plates, cloths and trays, and I'd started to do what I always did when I was feeling flustered. I'd picked up a pencil and paper and started to make a list. But Hattie had immediately snatched it out of my hand and urged me to listen to her. She'd begun to talk excitedly about a miner who played the trumpet and who she was sure would invite her to the Colliery dance next week if she could stick her nose in his face before he invited someone else.

I hadn't known anything about a dance and, if I had, I would not have expected to be invited. Nevertheless, I'd listened quietly and then, as soon as I could get a word in, asked her why she would want to go to a dance with a man she had to push into inviting her? If he liked her as much as she liked him, couldn't he find out where she worked and knock on the scullery door and invite her properly?

The expression on Hattie's face – which I would see on many faces in the years that followed – showed complete surprise that I might know the proper way to be invited to a dance, or anything else that involved a man and a woman. I'd known Hattie hadn't intended to be mean and I'd known that her honest reaction came from knowing me as well as she did. But I'd decided right there and then that I would never chase a man, no matter how much I might be tempted, and that I didn't want a husband or a rose-covered cottage if I had to throw myself at some unsuspecting fellow to get them. I didn't know how much this resolve would be tested when, years later, I would arrive in Greasbrough and begin my employment as housekeeper in the home of Mr. George Smith.

Effie Smith Hague (1889-1979) and Hubert H. Hague (1887-1958)

CHARLES (1911-1995)
m. Mabel Issott (1909-1995)
JULIA *m. Nicholas Ross*
James (Aaron)
CHARLES *m. Davina Smith*
Mark *m. Marietta Brown* (Harry, Evi)
m. Angela Turner - Robert, Lucy
m. Rachel McAteer - Emily

PAULINE (1920-2011)
m. Stanley Goodswen (1915-1981)
PHILIP *m. Dorothy Leigh*
Charlotte *m. Simon Schoch* (Alexander, Emily)
James *m. Kay Leonard* (Thomas, Hannah)
STEPHANIE

ANTHONY (1924-1929)

NIGEL (1928-   )
m. Stella Jefferson (1928-2008)
JANE *m. Robin MacCaw*
Marina *m. Ben Lewis* (Mina), Joseph
VERONICA *m. Rick Clinton*
Edward *m. Carla Castaneda* (Theo, Wesley)
SALLY *m. Robert Foster*
Rebecca *m. Scott Carruthers*, Harriet *m. Nicholas Heron*
WILLIAM *m. Ffion Jenkins*

VII

You're probably wondering if I had any fun when I was young, or if my youth was entirely taken up by work. Monday was my day off in Shireoaks and was a welcome break after cooking for the many guests who came for Sunday dinner at the vicarage. You will recall my saying that my career in mashed potatoes took off there, and it's no exaggeration to say that the cathedral's foundation and walls were built in that very kitchen.

But every Monday I would lie in bed for an extra hour or two and then go out with Hattie or one or two of the other servant girls from the village. We would wander arm-in-arm looking in the shop windows at all the hats, ornaments, frocks and pins we couldn't afford to buy.

In the afternoon when it was time for the miners to leave the pit, many of the girls would hurry to put themselves in their path, accidentally-on-purpose of course, but I would always try to steer us away from them. Many times I'd watched from the safety of the children's bedroom window as a long line of dirty men wove its way into town from the pit head. I'd seen enough to know that the weariness on the men's faces was no different from the grim expression I'd seen on the faces of the laborers when they came in from the Lincolnshire fields. If I'd dreamed that a collier would come courting and carry me over the threshold of a rose-covered cottage, I'd soon given up such a fancy. I'd known that my life wouldn't change with one of these exhausted young men.

As the years went by, a lot of the girls married local boys or one of the new pit workers and I can't deny that they were happy and excited to find a sweetheart and be wed. Hattie's pretty face and determination hadn't secured her the trumpet player, but she'd quickly dusted herself off and turned her attention to a joiner who'd moved to Shireoaks. The young man had found plenty of work doing carpentry on the new houses being built for miners and their families, and soon had my lovely friend to keep him warm at night.

Hattie would be interested to know – though it would be many years after her time – that my great-grandson, Robin Hartley, would successfully court the trumpet player in a colliery band. Judith Hewitt was an accomplished trumpet player, playing in several bands including that of the Silverwood Colliery in Thrybergh. Robin and Judy were married on March 6, 1965.

Time flew by in Shireoaks and ten years passed from the day my friend had first come to see me at the vicarage. On the morning of my thirtieth birthday, Hattie had, once again, flung open the back door and walked into the kitchen, bold as brass, as was her habit. She had come to tell me that she'd had enough of my excuses for hiding out in the vicarage and it was high time I found a husband and settled down. She'd said life was passing me by and I would end up a sour old spinster.

I'd replied that as I was now thirty years old I must already be an old maid. I'd added that she'd got a good husband, but some of the girls had wed ne'er do wells. And I'd reminded her that the collier's wives had a terrible time, not knowing from one day to the next if their husbands would get enough work, or even make it home alive at the end of the day. When I looked at those women, I'd told her, all I saw ahead of me was the same life of drudgery that I had as a servant, if not worse. Hattie had scoffed and said that was the way life was for a woman, and that I had another think coming if I thought being an old spinster would be any easier.

Hattie and I had argued for years about my refusal to act like all the other girls who preened and giggled with the village lads as if their struggles would magically be over if a miner or a blacksmith or a bricklayer would marry them. As far as I'd seen, that was when many a woman's troubles began. Hattie had told me, once again, that I was too stubborn to change no matter how old I got. With that, she'd hurried off to collect her little ones from her neighbor.

As always, Hattie had left me fretting over whether she was right and if it really was too late for me to be married. It's hard to get people to accept, especially those closest to you, that you don't want what everyone else seems to want. But it's hard to stop the doubts from entering your head when a contented friend pushes you to make the same choices she has made. And even harder still when you can't describe, even to yourself, what exactly it is you want.

Many of the other servant girls had made it plain to me that I should take more care with my appearance even when working, given the number of tradesmen and workers who came to the church and vicarage. The younger ones assumed that as the years drifted by I must be desperately hoping for a husband. They told me I should smile more and pretend to be interested when, as sometimes happened when I was out doing errands, one of the shop assistants talked to me or suggested going for a walk on a fine evening. I'd always ignored such chatter as I didn't want to start something I wouldn't know how to finish.

Along with everyone else, Mrs. Browne had urged me to learn to dance so that I could join in the fun with the many servants living in Shireoaks. But I'd steadfastly refused, insisting that I wouldn't be able to remember the steps, let alone manage the turns. In truth, I'd been too self-conscious to try and too pig-headed to let her change my mind. Hattie had been right when she said I was stubborn!

I did, however, start making more of an effort to wipe my face, brush my hair and change my greasy aprons. It wasn't considered respectable to use cosmetics when I was a young woman and by the time it was accepted I'd been too old to change my appearance.

But before my life ended, I did become the proud owner of a pale pink lipstick which I would carefully put on before a family do. I saw how much it brightened my white face and I often wished I'd been able to wear lipstick when I was younger.

As you know, many years later, cosmetics would be used by almost everyone. My granddaughter, Pauline Goodswen (née Hague), was always beautifully made-up and kept lipsticks all over the house. She was never more than a few steps away from livening up her face with crimson, red, mauve and even orange lipstick. This might seem like a frivolous habit, but I'm glad if it helped her as there were many times when my granddaughter needed to muster up strength to face the world. Pauline was dealt great sorrows in her life, first as a sister and, later, as a mother.

But, back in Shireoaks and at the urging of the other girls, I'd started taking a bit more care with my appearance. I'd also tried not to shy away from the villagers' friendly banter and would smile at the young men working in the shops and take a minute to talk to them as if it wasn't the waste of time I'd always made it out to be. Contrary to my fears, this did not result in the unwanted attentions of every ne'er do well in the village. In fact the only overture I received was an invitation to go to the fair with a young man from the baker's shop.

Traveling fairs often came to Shireoaks and I'd been to them any number of times with Hattie and the girls. This was the first time I'd gone to the fair with a young man and I didn't enjoy myself. He'd insisted that we spend most of our time on the roundabout, spinning faster and faster, which made me feel sick. He'd smirked at the poor people in the freak show and told me I was being silly when I'd said such things were cruel and shouldn't be allowed. And he'd laughed in a scornful way when I'd said that the figures in the wax works didn't resemble real people but looked like they were dead and should have been left in the ground.

The young man didn't invite me to go out with him again, which was a big relief because I'd spent much of the evening worrying what I would say if he asked me to go back to the fair the following night. Looking back, I remembered the occasion not because it was my first outing with a young man, but because when he'd rushed off at the end of the evening without asking me out again, I'd realized how anxious we become over something that isn't going to happen. The baker's boy didn't pester me further and I should have had fun with him at the fair even if he wasn't the perfect companion.

I told myself that paying attention to my appearance didn't mean I'd decided to follow everyone else's path, nor that being friendly meant I was looking to get wed. I found I felt better knowing I looked neater, and quickly discovered that everything goes better with a smile. Some of you will recall the style and elegance of your mothers, aunts and grandmothers, and the great care they took with their appearance even if they were only going out to the shops. I, too, would look on in awe and admiration at my daughters, Lizzie and Effie, and my granddaughters, Joan, Effie, Ruth and Pauline, all of whom looked as if they'd stepped out of the great fashion houses of London and Paris.

From them, I learned that elegance and fashion cannot be left to chance. In order to keep up-to-the-minute my granddaughter, Ruth, read "*Vogue*" magazine from cover to cover. She bought her bridal 'going away' outfit after seeing it on the magazine's cover. The outfit is in the Victoria and Albert Museum in London as a fine example of fashion in 1952. This tells you what good taste – and what instincts they had – for style!

I hadn't known anything about fashion back when I was in Shireoaks – nor at any time after that except what I learned from those glamorous ladies who by some miracle came after me – but it was fortunate I made some small changes and was a nicer looking and friendlier woman by the time I got to Yorkshire.

Looking back at my years in Shireoaks, I realize how dull I must have seemed to everyone I'd known there. I've been pleasantly surprised from Far Yonder seeing not only your fashionable looks but how welcoming and charming so many of you are, whether to friends or strangers. You're more like Hattie than me! It comes naturally to you but, like your good looks, I'm afraid you didn't get your outgoing nature from me, or even from my children.

My daughter, Effie, loved to get dressed up and meet friends at parties and teas, but the great humor and personable manner of so many of her line comes not from Effie, but from her husband, Bert. Bert Hague made friends with everyone he met and was so popular he barely had time to be at home, or at work. Effie and Bert's daughter, Pauline, could hold the attention of a room full of people by turning an ordinary, mundane story into such a hilarious tale that people would still be laughing the next day.

Pauline Hague married Stanley Goodswen, a butcher she met while cruising in the Mediterranean on the SS Montclair in September 1939. Pauline was traveling with her cousin, my granddaughter, Joan Schonhut, and the ship had already been in port in Tangiers and Gibraltar. But on September 3, Britain declared war on Germany and the ship was forced to return home to England.

The cruise had been brought to an early end, but a romance had just begun. Pauline and Stan soon married and settled in Stan's hometown of Redcar on the North Yorkshire coast. They made a beautiful home on the Coast Road, directly across from the beach and the North Sea. Their son, Philip, was born in 1942 after Stan had enlisted with the Royal Air Force. Stan was sent to India which meant he didn't meet his son until Philip was three years old.

Effie had Bert had eight grandchildren, but Philip was their first and their favorite. Though he was a very naughty boy, the grandparents loved having him to stay at "Fairleigh", their big house on Moorgate Lane in Rotherham. Philip in turn loved his grandparents, particularly Grandpa Hague, whom he adored.

Gay Wadsworth, Florrie's little granddaughter, would often visit Philip when he was staying at "Fairleigh". He would invariably get them into trouble as he would urge Gay, always dressed up in pretty skirts and dresses, to race him down the coal heap. Two blackened children would soon be discovered.

Philip knew many ways to get into trouble, but his most famous antic was flushing a pair of Effie's treasured diamond earrings down the toilet. Pauline loved to regale her family and friends with stories of her mischievous son, but was careful not to tell the tale of the flushed diamonds in her mother's presence. Fortunately, Effie loved Philip more than her jewelry and was able to forgive her grandson, even after learning that he'd sent her glittering diamond earrings down to the sewer.

Philip Goodswen inherited his mother's and grandfather's thirst for fun and their same gift for entertaining. Philip and his wife, Dorothy, were always popular in the Redcar and Saltburn area. He had such a marvelous sense of humor that as a grown man he would literally roll around on the floor laughing at a funny film or television show.

Sadly, Philip died at only sixty-six years of age, but his son, James, and daughter, Charlotte, are as friendly and fun-loving as their father. Happily, their own children are carrying the family's sense of humor into the next generation. Emily Schoch is dry and quick-witted, while her brother, Alexander Schoch, is practical and funny. Thomas Goodswen is easy-going and happy to be with friends or to simply amuse himself. And little Hannah Goodswen loves shoes and talking. Who could she possibly take after?

It must be said that in the case of Bert, Pauline and Philip, their thirst for fun was usually accompanied by an equally strong thirst for alcohol – beer, gin, sherry, wine, whisky or whatever was on offer – but they were known to be wonderful company at any time of day.

So to satisfy your curiosity about whether I had any fun as a young woman, I must confess that I didn't and certainly not when compared to the independence and adventures you enjoy today. Some of the girls in Shireoaks would go with their young men to one of the beerhouses, but a woman could soon get a bad reputation even if all she was doing was sipping a glass of ale and sitting with her sweetheart.

Fortunately, those narrow-minded attitudes changed over the century which followed, although sometimes I wonder if they've gone too far in the other direction and have reached the point where pleasure and self-indulgence come before work and family. But it's wonderful that you have choices and can decide amongst many different paths.

You might think that, along with my lack of fun and pleasure, I didn't have much ambition. But that wouldn't be true. Though I had few choices as I'd turned thirty years of age back in 1876, I'd known I didn't want to take the path that had been laid out for me on the day I was born. No matter how fond I was of Hattie, I couldn't simply follow her way. I decided it was time to leave Shireoaks and, once again, start afresh somewhere new. This time it would be in the Yorkshire village of Greasbrough.

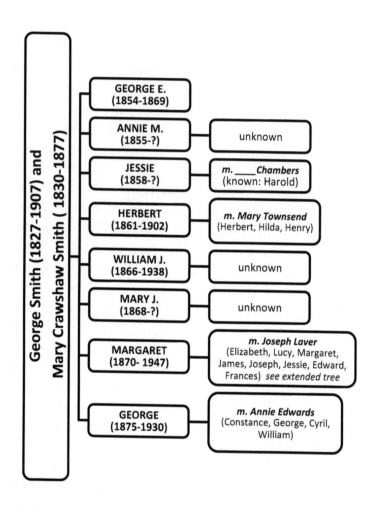

VIII

Films were invented during my lifetime, although they were short and silent and not nearly as entertaining as they are now. Later in life, I would go with my step-daughter, Margaret, to the Electra Cinema in Parkgate where her husband, Joseph Laver, played the organ. How lovely it was to go to the pictures and know that the sound accompanying the films came from Joe's long, clever fingers! We listened to every note and were quick to tell the audience to sit down and shut up if they got too rowdy.

If a film was made of my life – as if this book isn't excitement enough! – this is the part where the director would call for the children to be lined-up in an orderly row and be patiently standing, all neat and clean, ready to meet the new housekeeper. I would take my first steps into the Potter Hill farmhouse and Mr. Smith would introduce the children, starting with the oldest and quickly working his way down to the youngest. Everyone would nod politely and we would all smile at each other.

After the first greetings had been made, Mr. Smith would leave to take care of some important business and I would spend a few minutes talking quietly – in a friendly but firm tone – to the children. By the time the father came back, the housekeeper and the children would have burst into song!

The director is wrong. This is not how children who lost their mother just a few weeks earlier greet a strange woman who is moving into their home. And certainly not one whose father has told them they must obey.

It was a Monday morning in April when I took the train to

Rotherham. I'd promised Mrs. Browne – who'd been in a state of shock since I'd given notice – that my last day would be a Sunday and I would cook an extra big dinner and leave plenty of food in the pantry. She and her daughters had spent much of the previous week in the kitchen following my every move and taking notes for the young woman who would be starting a few days later.

Mrs. Browne said how much she would miss me, yet from the very first time she'd watched me peeling potatoes she'd known that one day I would say goodbye. Puzzled, the girls and I had turned to her for an explanation. Mrs. Browne had fixed her eyes on her daughters and said that a girl who works with her back so straight and her chin so high will know when it's time to leave. Her only surprise, she'd added, was how long it had taken me. But, as that had been clearly to her advantage rather than mine, she couldn't complain. You need to go faster, Mary, she'd added, if you're going to get what you want. I'd wondered if she'd been talking to Hattie.

Thus, with my back straight and my chin up, I'd stepped off the train at Rotherham Station with a small bag containing my clothes, my sampler and some little keepsakes the Browne girls had made for me. I'd asked the station master how I could get to Greasbrough and he'd arranged for me to get a lift with a tradesman who was on his way to make a delivery in the village. I'd been told it was just north of Rotherham and a distance of no more than two miles.

Within a short time we were passing Car House Colliery and cresting a hill. Greasbrough opened up in front of me with St. Mary's Church in the far distance and the mill standing tall in the center, surrounded by rows of terraced houses. I'd hoped we were going to the far side of the village so I could get a look around, but the driver had quickly come to a halt and pointed to Potter Hill Farm on the right.

Between the suddenness of the stop and my brief view of the village, I'd felt a keen disappointment. Mr. Smith had written with glowing descriptions of Greasbrough's many houses, shops and buildings, all surrounded by lush green fields. But, at least at first glance, I hadn't seen anything to equal his words. I'd reminded myself that, as a builder and farmer, he had contributed firsthand to creating what now lay before me and would, quite rightly, see only its beauty.

I'd soon learned, however, that this rose-colored view of his domain was shared by all Yorkshire folk who believe that their county, and each and every village within it, is superior to all others throughout the land. I was also to become familiar with the exaggerated expressions of sympathy for those who, like me, had the misfortune to be born elsewhere. This sentiment was always followed by a lot of "ayes" and numerous heads nodding in agreement that though I'd been dealt a serious blow by being born in Lincolnshire, I'd had the good sense to move to Yorkshire. Every man, woman and child born in Yorkshire believes that it is the only place not only to be born, but to live, and they pity those who must struggle through life outside its boundaries.

It's true, however, that Greasbrough residents have plenty to be proud of. Situated in the West Riding of Yorkshire, the village is recorded in the Domesday Book, the survey which was ordered by William the Conqueror, and completed in 1086, of most of England and parts of Wales. The village is listed as Geresbrook, and it is noted that a man named Godric has three carucates of land, and another man, Roger, has one plough and three villeins. This was hundreds of years before my time and I have no idea what is meant by carucates and villeins!

A few hundred years later, in the 16th century, the village was known as Gresbroke, or Gresebroke, and sometime after that, as Greys Brook. From these names, you will understand that Greasbrough stands between two brooks, which may also be where "brough" comes from. Greas does not, in fact, mean grease, but may refer to grass or gravel. Not only does Greasbrough date back to 1086, there is some evidence of a Roman settlement. All of this is valuable information, if only for us to be aware of how much happened on the earth on which we stand long before we ever came into being.

When I arrived in Greasbrough, the village was surrounded by farms and collieries, both of which provided plenty of work for the men. In the decades that followed, numerous generations of miners, chemical workers and steelworkers would be happy to live in Greasbrough where they could find a decent house, plenty of friendly faces, football and cricket teams, and a choice of pubs in which to down a pint or two at the end of the day.

Most importantly, the women of Greasbrough always knew that dinner, or tea, must be on the table the minute their husband came home from work. The wives kept their houses clean, got the children ready for school on time, hung out the washing on a Monday morning, and let their children roam for hours in the village streets and nearby fields, knowing they would return home, safe and sound, just as darkness fell.

In 1877, the farms in Greasbrough included Potter Hill Farm, the home of my new employer, Mr. George Smith. Thus, on a cloudy April day, having crossed the border from Nottinghamshire into Yorkshire, I'd arrived safely, ready to start my new position as housekeeper.

The eight children born to Mr. Smith and his wife, Mary, had been reduced to six living at home. The eldest, George, had died eight years previously, and Annie, the second born, was twenty two years of age and had left home a few years earlier. I'd been greeted, if you could call it that, by nineteen-year old Jessie who, holding a baby brother in her arms, had been staring anxiously out of the kitchen window.

Jessie had obviously been impatiently awaiting my arrival because as soon as I'd unlatched the gate and set foot upon the brick pathway leading to the house, she'd thrown open the back door and thrust the two-year-old child at me. I'd dropped my bag and taken the boy from her as she'd rushed past me muttering that she was Jessie and he was Georgie and she wouldn't be home for tea because she had so many fittings to do. She'd added that it would be a miracle if she had all the children's outfits ready for Whitsun. From this I'd gathered that Jessie was a dressmaker and that Greasbrough, like Shireoaks, set much stock in its Whit Sunday parade. I'd been right and during my first few weeks in Greasbrough, I'd barely seen Jessie without pins, material or buttons sticking out of her mouth or attached to her bodice.

I'd struggled through the open kitchen door with my bag in one hand and Georgie in the other. He'd screamed and tried to wriggle free, but I'd held on tight and he'd soon calmed down. He was obviously used to being passed around from pillar to post and had known there was no point in crying for his sister.

That day was the beginning of a lot of love between me and Georgie and he provided as much comfort to me as I did to him over the years, particularly at the beginning when I had to deal with the grieving older children. Georgie lived a good life but died two years before me in 1930, at only fifty five years of age, which was grievously upsetting especially coming only a year after the terrible loss of my little grandson, Tony.

What I hadn't known when I'd first held Georgie in my arms that day was just how much our lives would be woven together. When my husband passed away in 1907, his Will left first me, and then Georgie, a Life Estate in Rossiter Villa, our family home. My Life Estate lasted until my death in 1932, but as Georgie preceded me in death, his Life Estate ended before it could have begun. However, my husband's Will decreed that, after the two Life Estates were fulfilled, Rossiter Villa would go to a son of Georgie. This turned out to be George Albert Smith, the son of Georgie and his wife, Annie Edwards.

I'd understood that my husband wanted Rossiter Villa to go to a son, but I'd been disappointed when he decided to leave it to Georgie's line instead of to Clement, our own boy. Nor did my husband include his son, William, in his plans for the house, even though William was, by that time, his oldest surviving son.

But, as you know, Clement spent most of his life in Lincolnshire and would have had no need of a house in Greasbrough. As it turned out, our daughter, Effie, would be the eventual owner of the house, and Rossiter Villa would stay in the Hague family until 1971.

All that was far off in the future when I stepped through the back door of Potter Hill Farm in April 1877. My first impression had been one of pleasant surprise at the size of the kitchen. The range was as large as the one I'd left behind at the vicarage, and a large dresser held pretty blue crockery which must have belonged to Mrs. Smith.

Unfortunately, I'd soon noticed that there was no running water, but accepted that my time spent carrying wooden buckets, dripping and sloshing about in all weathers, was not about to come to an end. My arms were thin but strong from lifting iron pots and children, carrying buckets of water, scrubbing floors, beating rugs and washing clothes. I laugh when I see you driving out to the gym to lift weights and pump up your arms. If you want good arms, all you have to do is turn the clock back a hundred years or more and your biceps will get all the pumping you could ever need!

IX

Georgie had soon started to settle down and, happy at the prospect of being in charge of a roomy, bright kitchen, I'd begun to feel pleased that I'd accepted the position at the Smith home. But, instinctively, my hand patted the deep pocket of my skirt where I'd stashed the purse containing my savings. I'd decided in advance of accepting the job that the money I'd saved over my years in Walcott and Shireoaks would be my escape if I was unhappy with the widower or his children, or the conditions at Potter Hill Farm. I didn't have much, but it would be enough to get me back on a train and to a rooming house for a short time until I could find another position.

I'd learned a lot from my previous two jobs, not least of which was that I had a lot to offer an employer and they weren't merely doing me a favor by taking me on. As my first employer, Mrs. Harrison had been kind and caring and had made sure the children, as rowdy as they were, treated me with respect. When I looked back I could see I was lucky to work for such a nice woman and that neither she, nor Mrs. Browne, were ever mean or nasty to me no matter how busy or harried they might be. I hope you all work for decent men and women who help you learn, and that you get something out of every job that is more than just the wages.

Mrs. Browne made me take responsibility for my work and admit to a mistake when I made one because she saw it as a chance for me to learn. I remember some of those mistakes well, particularly the time I left a dozen cut-glass sherry glasses in the scullery sink and Fred came in and dumped a bushel of potatoes on top of them. I'd known the glasses were too good to be washed in the scullery, but I'd been rushed off my feet with the Women's Institute sherry evening and I'd put the glasses in the sink intending to move them later.

Before I'd had chance to get back to the scullery, Fred had rushed in and, without looking, had dumped the potatoes in the sink and every single one of the precious, shimmering glasses had shattered in pieces. My first reaction had been to blame Fred, but Mrs. Browne had taken me aside and reminded me that the glasses should not have been left in the scullery sink and that Fred wasn't to know they were there and, even if he had, he wouldn't understand the value of a cut-glass sherry glass if it rose up and bit him. By the time we get to Far Yonder, if not before, we've learned not to blame others.

Yet the most important thing I learned from Mrs. Browne was not to be intimidated by people with money and titles. Starting with those early days when I was a nervous wreck because the Bishop of Lincoln was coming for dinner, Mrs. Browne had reminded me that everyone has to eat and sleep (and something else which I won't mention, but she wasn't above pointing out) and there are few differences between us all. Much later I would learn that Mrs. Browne's attitude was shared by Mr. Smith, who had taken on Potter Hill Farm and started his own building company after he'd grown sick and tired of removing his cap and bowing to the Earl Fitzwilliam of the time.

Mrs. Browne had also always insisted that the many visitors who stayed at the vicarage left a tip for me and Fred. She said that guests make a lot of work for the household help and that the vails, as they were called, were the only way for a guest to compensate for the work and expenses they created. Those vails were stuffed safely in my pocket on the day I'd arrived in Greasbrough.

I'd walked around the kitchen opening the doors to the pantry and the scullery and could see they were in need of reorganizing.

Both rooms were a jumble of provisions and dishes and everything was in disarray. There was a pile of dirty washing in the scullery which meant tomorrow would be wash day. Jessie would later tell me that other than George's nappies, she hadn't had time to do any washing for over a week. At least I could be grateful that the poor little lad didn't have a sore bum.

The pantry included a set of glass cabinets and contained the family's best china. At the vicarage I'd grown used to the convenience of a butler's pantry which was invaluable for the storage of the good china and glasses – at least those that hadn't been broken. I'd liked the butler's pantry at the vicarage, even though I'd known from the start that it hadn't been laid out in the proper manner.

One day Mrs. Browne had laughed uproariously when I'd announced to her that the butler's pantry wasn't designed correctly. It should run between the kitchen and the dining room and not between the dining room and the scullery, I'd told her. I'd then added that the doorways shouldn't line up, but should instead be positioned to ensure guests can't see into the kitchen. I'd even admitted that one afternoon I'd sat at the dining room table to check the view and had been able to see straight into the scullery. Even if the butler's pantry had connected the dining room and kitchen as was proper, it should not be possible for a guest to see straight through to where the work was being done.

Mrs. Brown had been silent for a minute and then observed, rather quietly for her, that I was remarkably skilled in house design for someone who'd seen inside so few. It was one of the few times she'd said something which offended me but I'd pressed on, quickly sketching a diagram in the flour I'd spread out on the kitchen table for the mincemeat pies I was making. Mrs. Browne had put down her pen and dropped the never-ending to-do list which she carried clipped to a chain strapped around her waist. I'd remarked once that she was as chained to her list as a mule to its yoke and she'd shrieked with laughter and said if only she had a mule's strength she could perhaps get through her daily jobs.

But that day Mrs. Brown had stared with interest at the white powder scattered on the kitchen table and, as I'd guided her through the refashioned kitchen, scullery, larder, dining room and, finally, the butler's pantry, she'd immediately seen the superiority of my design. She'd particularly loved the bay window I'd added to the dining room, though I'd pointed out that was a pretty little extra and not essential to the design. I loved bay windows and liked to imagine sitting in a chair with a book, feeling the warmth of the sun shining in on me.

One day I would have not one, but four, bay windows of my own, though it would be years before I would have time to sit down with a book and feel the sun coming through the big, tall panes. Mrs. Browne had apologized for being so quick to dismiss my suggestions and said if only she had the money to make such masterful improvements she would take my design and follow it down to the last grain of flour.

I wouldn't have a say in the design of a house until my husband built Rossiter Villa for us twelve years after we were married. But that didn't mean I didn't have a natural eye for the best use of space. My great-granddaughter, Sally Foster (née Hague), shares my talent. She can walk into any house and re-design it in her head in a jiffy, needing neither paper nor flour. She's renovated houses in Ravenfield, Thrybergh, Helmsley and Tickhill, and in each has created a welcoming, organized, beautiful home.

Sally's husband, Robert Foster, has often wondered if he'll come home from work to find the kitchen and bedroom have swopped places. My daughter, Effie, also loved renovating, leading Bert to remark that his wife wouldn't be satisfied until the attic was in the cellar and the cellar in the attic. I know there were many times that Effie would have been happy to lock her husband in either one of them.

Before my first week was out at Potter Hill Farm, I would have set up the cupboards and shelves in a more efficient and logical manner. This would result in months of complaints from

Jessie that she could no longer find anything and that the kitchen should have remained exactly as her mother had left it. But on that first afternoon, I'd had to concentrate not on convenience and efficiency, but on food. I'd tried to judge from the collection of dishes jumbled together in the middle of the table what the family had had for their dinner and what, if anything, was left for tea.

Mr. Smith had written to me a few weeks earlier with the names and ages of the children. I'd known that William, Mary and Margaret would be coming home from school in a few hours and that I'd better have some tarts and buns ready if I wanted to get off on the right foot with them. Herbert was sixteen and worked as a stonemason for his father, from which I knew to expect him home at tea time, tired and hungry. Between the three in school, Herbert at work, Jessie out doing fittings and Georgie, still in my arms and already beginning to smile at me, I'd accounted for the six children.

But where was Mr. George Smith on the day his new housekeeper was to start work? It turned out later that he'd left Potter Hill Farm half an hour before I'd arrived because he'd eaten his dinner, read the newspaper and smoked his pipe and, even though Miss Mary Stennett was expected within the hour, he'd continued on with his day as was his habit. And, just as I'd discovered immediately upon stepping into the vicarage in Shireoaks, as I'd stood in the unfamiliar kitchen in a village I'd been in less than an hour, I'd known that in Greasbrough I would be doing a lot of skipping.

X

It takes your breath away when you look down from Far Yonder and look back at the meaning someone had in your life that you couldn't possibly have known when you first met them. Margaret Smith was but seven-years old when she leapt into the kitchen of Potter Hill Farm and into my life and the lives of my future children and grandchildren.

After jumping through the open back door and landing with both feet firmly on the mat, Margaret had stopped dead and stared at me with such a stern intensity that I'd felt sure I'd encountered my first foe in the Smith family. I'd calmly reminded myself that she was a young child who must have been anxious to finish the school day so she could get home to meet the new housekeeper. Now, I'd reasoned as she'd continued to stare at me, having found a stranger standing in the kitchen in place of her mother, she'd been stricken at the sight.

I'd worried about the Smith children since accepting the position and, while I would never let any child get the better of me, I'd felt apprehensive about meeting them to a degree I had not felt with the Harrison and Browne youngsters. Mary Smith, the mother of all the children, was gone and a new Mary had arrived to take her place. It was true that that place did not extend to the big bed in the main bedroom upstairs which I'd noted while chasing after Georgie in the otherwise empty house. Back in those days no child would expect to find a strange woman in their father's bed. But I knew that by taking charge of the kitchen and the running of the household I was, in the children's eyes at least, replacing their mother.

In the months ahead there would be struggles on both sides in the Smith house, some of which I would win and others I would lose. When I won, I would wrestle with myself not to let the satisfaction spread across my face, and I'd take great care to conceal my irritation during the times I lost. And though sometimes I would cry in frustration, I strived hard to make sure no-one saw my tears.

But one day, only a few weeks after my arrival, Mr. Smith had caught me crying in the pantry. Many, many times I'd asked William to leave his dirty boots in the scullery and not toss them in front of the kitchen door for everyone, including me, to trip over. A big lad of eleven was old enough to know better, but once again William had arrived home after dark, kicked off his boots and left them lying in the entrance. I'd reminded him to put them in the scullery and he'd turned on me, angrily shouting that I wasn't his mother and that I had no right to tell him what to do.

I'd been very upset because I'd spent a lot of effort making William his favorite forcemeat balls almost every day, as if I had nothing else to do but grind up stale bread, chop up parsley and thyme, mix it with suet and roll it into perfectly round balls, just to please one young member of the household. William didn't appreciate the amount of work involved in cooking three meals a day, seven days a week, for eight hungry people. This wasn't surprising considering the only time he spent in the kitchen was from the moment he dragged his chair out across the stone flags to plop down at the table, until the second he jumped up and scraped the chair back again.

During the time William sat at the table, he would answer his father's questions about school and his chores up at the fields with as few words as could be considered an answer. Whilst he hurriedly shoveled food into his mouth, he would snatch morsels from Mary's and Margaret's plates which, predictably, would set them screaming in protest. He would then lean across the table to tickle his little brother, and stare in mock surprise as Georgie shrieked with delight, spraying the contents of his mouth across the kitchen.

Mr. Smith would adopt a stern expression that I wasn't always sure was genuine, and would tell William to sit still, stop messing around and not to bolt his food. But the minute William asked to leave the table, his father would nod in assent and we would all breathe a sigh of relief as he disappeared through the door. In addition to putting up with his poor table manners – which Mr. Smith did not tolerate from Herbert or the girls – I was continually cleaning up after William, as well as making time to wash his muddy clothes when he came in from the farm fields or from playing with his army of village ruffians.

On the day William had shouted at me, Mr. Smith had watched me rush into the pantry and slam the door behind me. A few moments later he'd followed me into its cool, calm darkness. I'd been embarrassed that he'd seen me crying and had turned my face against a sack of flour wedged on one of the shelves. Mr. Smith had placed his hands firmly on my shoulders and told me to dry my tears, saying he would, again, warn William to mind both his boots and his manners. I'd realized later it was the first time he had touched me.

Embarrassed, I'd brushed away my tears and mumbled my thanks for his concern, and as I'd wiped my cheeks a white paste had come off in my hands. He'd smiled and said he didn't realize I'd come into the pantry to make pastry and that if I wanted to bake a pie and push it into anyone's face it should be William's and not my own.

I'd realized then that Mr. Smith did not blindly side with his children, but was willing to defend me. If I'd had any remaining doubts about staying in Greasbrough, those thoughts were gone at that moment. But as I'd stepped back into the kitchen, I'd known that the strong, supple hands that had pressed down on my shoulders had put an entirely new, terrifying, thought into my mind.

Yet on that very first April afternoon, it had been Margaret's fierce expression that had unnerved me. Fortunately, the staring contest which had taken place between us ended as soon as Margaret spied the tray of steaming jam tarts which I'd just taken out of the oven. She'd moved quickly towards them, while at the same time telling me they always ate rock buns after school. I'd replied that we didn't eat rocks in Lincolnshire or Nottinghamshire and she'd made a face at me like a good Yorkshire lass who, though but seven years of age, was aware of her superiority at being born in the best county in the world. In fact, I'd made rock buns at the vicarage on numerous occasions and, starting the very next day, rock buns were in the oven every afternoon at Potter Hill Farm for many years to come.

Margaret Smith Laver (1870-1947) and Joseph Laver (1869-1935)

ELIZABETH (1895-1934)
m. William Maxfield (1895-1952)
PHYLLIS (1918-2008) *m. Charles Thickett*
Pamela
Peter *m. Jane Wright*
Rachael *m. Edwin Holden* (Bailey, Nyah, Thea, Finley), Natalie (Riley)
MARGARET (1920-1993) *m. John Charlton*
Diana, Monica,
Clare *m. Richard Pattinson* (Victoria, Elizabeth, Robert)

SEVEN ADDITIONAL CHILDREN:
LUCY (1896-1950s) *m. Thomas Johnson*
MARGARET (1898-1968) (Mary Margaret)
m. Hayden Jones
JAMES (1899-1959) (known descendants include Frank Laver)
JOSEPH (1905-1957) *m. Mildred Hartley* (one daughter)
JESSIE (1906-1988) *m. Ellis Dowden* (Jessie)
EDWARD (1910-1981) *m. Effie Dickinson* (unknown)
FRANCES (1913-?) *m. Clifford Senior* (unknown)

XI

What neither Margaret nor I knew during that first hour we spent together was that our lives would be intertwined far beyond my employment as her father's housekeeper, and beyond the seventeen years we worked side-by-side in the family home prior to her marriage to Joseph Laver. On that April afternoon, we didn't know that I would marry her father two years later, nor that I would give her a half-brother and three half-sisters.

We also didn't know that in the year 2016 – an unimaginable date to those of us living in the 1800's – Margaret's great-granddaughter, Pamela Thickett, and my great-grandson, Robin Hartley, would each live in Devon in the south of England and would meet up occasionally. When Pamela and Robin get together they are not only extending relations between the two halves of George's family, but are continuing a friendship which began on an April afternoon in 1877. Pamela and Robin are both interested in ancestry, and have compiled much of the Smith family history you are discovering in this book.

I grew to love Margaret and we spent time together happily throughout the rest of our lives. Like most of us, there was much more to her than her serious face would ever reveal. Margaret's stern demeanor masked a highly-strung, superstitious personality. Starting as a young child, she believed lightening would crack all the mirrors in the house. Upon hearing thunder in the distance, she would anticipate its frequent companion, and rush around the house covering up the mirrors with sheets and heavy wool blankets. Neither the teasing she received from her brothers nor, later, her husband's patient, logical explanations could convince her otherwise.

Margaret and Joseph would have eight children – five girls and three boys – with, sadly, three of their daughters causing them much heartache. The first, Elizabeth, married William Maxfield, a man whom Margaret considered to be a poor provider and, therefore, unsuitable to be the husband of her pretty firstborn child. The marriage lasted, but Elizabeth died of tuberculosis at the age of thirty-nine leaving behind two girls, Phyllis and Margaret. Elizabeth had worked in a munitions factory during World War I which wouldn't have done her lungs any good, and spent a long time in a sanatorium in Keighley before her death.

Phyllis was fourteen and young Margaret only twelve years of age when their mother died. I am very proud of my daughter, Effie, who helped look after them. Later she arranged for Phyllis to get a job at Schonhut's butchers which led to her meeting a fine husband, Charles Thickett. My step-daughter, Margaret, was still living when her daughter, Elizabeth, died and was able to help her grandchildren, but she remained eternally grateful to her half-sisters, particularly Effie, who stepped in to make sure young Phyllis and Margaret got the care they needed.

You may need to stop for a minute and consider what relation the young girls, Phyllis and Margaret, were to Effie. Complicated families need a map if you are to find your way around without getting lost! Though with a difference in age of almost twenty years, Margaret and Effie were half-sisters, both being daughters of George Smith. Thus, when Effie helped Phyllis and Margaret, she was helping the granddaughters of her half-sister. This shows Effie had a powerful sense of the importance of extended family.

It's important to remember that "Rabbit George" had his first child at the age of twenty-seven and the last when he was sixty two, a span of thirty five years. Also worth noting is the difference in age between George, born in 1827, and his two youngest grandchildren, Nigel Hague and Ruth Sampson (née Holroyd), both born in 1928, just over a hundred years later. If you stop for a moment to work out the time span between you and your grandparents it will, in most cases, be a lot less than one hundred years!

George lived to know many of his grandchildren from his marriage to Mary Crawshaw, but died before any of ours were born. George and I had thirteen grandchildren, all born while I was alive which was wonderful. My son, Clement, had Wilfred and Clement; my daughter, Lizzie, had George and Joan; my daughter, Florrie, had Arthur, Effie, Neville, Peter and Ruth; and my daughter, Effie, had Charles, Pauline, Anthony and Nigel.

George and I also had eighteen great-grandchildren together, but I did not live to see them. Our first great-grandchild was Pauline Schonhut, daughter of Lizzie's son, George, and his wife, Ethel. Pauline was born in 1935 just three years after I died. That little baby is a grandmother herself now. Pauline married Paul Tear and they had a daughter, Jacqueline, and a son, James. Pauline's grandchildren are Emily and Suzanna Houghton, and Charles, Alex and Henry Tear.

Pauline was followed by a sister, Hilary, born in 1937. Hilary also married a man named Paul, in this case Paul Hoskins. They had a son, Rupert.

I would have loved to know my great-grandchildren, but I ran out of time. Hattie would be nodding her head saying she'd told me all along I was leaving marriage and family too late. Fortunately, she turned out to be wrong and I consider myself blessed indeed if the only price I paid for waiting was that I didn't live to be a great-grandmother. Becoming a great-grandparent is a rare privilege, however your life enfolds.

I never regretted waiting because it got me George. But it's easy to justify your choices when you get what you want. I'm not sure what I would be saying if Mr. Smith had fallen prey to one of the many ladies who called at Potter Hill Farm during my first year there. These ladies were always "just passing by" and "just happened to have baked a cake" which they must have been wandering aimlessly around Greasbrough with until it occurred to them that the new widower might be in need of something to satisfy his sweet tooth. Thanks to a lot of hard work, and some deviousness on my part of which I would not have previously thought I was capable, George didn't marry one of these ladies but, instead, chose me.

On that first afternoon in Greasbrough, Margaret's disappointment at not finding rock buns waiting for her after school had vanished at the same rate as half a dozen jam tarts had disappeared down her little throat. Yet even as she'd gobbled down the tarts, her solemn expression remained etched firmly on her handsome face. This tough exterior would be of great value when it came to her daughters, Ruda and Cissie.

Somewhat confusingly, all of Margaret's and Joseph's children were given, and used, two names. Joseph Laver was a music teacher and the second name of each of his children was in recognition of a composer or musician as a testament to Joe's passion. The only child to follow in his musical footsteps, however, was Edward Schubert Laver who played the drums but who, incidentally, hated his second name. It must have been hard to go to school in Rawmarsh bearing the name of a long-gone Austrian composer. But Edward played the drums which at least gave his father one child who'd learned at his knee.

Joseph would be proud to know that several generations later, through his daughter Elizabeth, he would have great-great-children who carry his musical gifts. Robert Pattinson is internationally famous as an actor, and is also a musician, and his sister Lizzy Pattinson is a singer and songwriter. This shows that genes never really go away, and certainly not to waste, because they will reappear a century later and everyone will exclaim that they have no idea where on earth he or she came from!

It's hard to know Margaret and Joseph and accept that their daughters, Ruda and Cissie, came from them. With a long marriage, eight children and Joseph's professional reputation, the Lavers' were a highly respectable family. They made their home at Spalton House in Rawmarsh, a large end-of-terrace house with two reception rooms – both furnished with a piano – and four bedrooms and an upstairs bathroom which was quite a luxury. Like the half-sisters who came after her, Margaret took care to be smartly dressed when she went out, always with an elegant veil covering her hat and tied firmly around her neck to prevent it from falling off. Her daughters' romantic antics would make more than her hat fall off.

Ruda had been christened Margaret Crawshaw Neruda (after a Czechoslovakian composer) and was always known as Ruda. She was a nurse who gave birth to a child without bothering to marry the father, or even reveal his name. Of course, plenty of folk were happy to speculate who the culprit might be and a fair scandal resulted. Ruda later moved to Cheltenham and eventually married but not until her daughter, Mary Margaret, was grown.

Cissie shared her sister's lack of concern for her family's position in the community. She was christened Lucy Armitage although I never understood who she'd been named after. There was a well-known Yorkshire pianist and composer named Reginald Armitage, but he wasn't born until two years after Lucy. However, Reginald Armitage had become famous while young so it's possible, although I don't recall, that Joseph gave the composer's name to his daughter some years after she'd been born.

But, whether or not Cissie had been named in an unusual manner, her life unfolded in the traditionally accepted way and she married at the age of twenty two. However, she soon left her new husband, though the couple did not get divorced probably because they couldn't afford to do so.

Cissie lived the rest of her life with another man who was completely devoted to her. She worked as a nurse and midwife in Kilnhurst and had no children. At her funeral in the 1950's her distraught lover threw himself into her grave! You can only imagine the scene that ensued as the grief-stricken man was wrenched off Cissie's coffin and dragged back up to ground level. Fortunately Joseph and Margaret were gone by that time and didn't have to bear witness to yet another event that they could not possibly understand.

All of this was very far off that April afternoon as Margaret wiped the jam off her lips and, in spite of her steadfast seriousness, a smile began to spread from the corners of her mouth. In my mind, I'd ticked off the children one by one. I'd met Jessie who would be busy making Whitsun clothes and so relieved to be free of too many household responsibilities she wouldn't pay much mind to the new housekeeper. Georgie and I were getting very well acquainted, and tomorrow afternoon's rock buns would make Margaret my firm ally. Mary and William would soon arrive home from school, and I would meet Herbert at tea time. That would account for all six children and before the afternoon was over I would have the full measure of what lay in store for me – good or bad – in the Smith home.

That would leave only one member of the family with whom to get acquainted. Mr. George Smith. The man I would make "Rabbit George".

XII

There were many ale houses in Billinghay when I was a child, although no-one from my family was ever to be found in one. One of my earliest memories was listening to my father ranting on about the fools who broke their backs to earn a penny and then willingly gave it back to the landowners at the end of the day. In my child's mind, I'd pictured dozens of grubby men standing in a queue waiting to hand over their pay, although even at that tender age I'd known there would be an equal number of women standing ready to grab the wages from the men before it could leave their hands.

I'd asked my father why the men gave their wages back when surely their wives would take it because it was needed to feed the children. He had sighed and, though he rarely took the time to sit with a child on his lap, my father had described the dilemma of a working man who deserves a reward for his daily work but, in giving himself that reward, will never be free of the work.

It wasn't, he'd explained, that he begrudged hardworking men the chance to soothe their aching backs with a good glass of stout, or the leisure time to talk to their fellow men while blessedly free of their bosses or wives. It was that the ale houses were usually owned by the families whose land the men worked, and spending money in their establishments was as good as tossing it back to them over their high stone walls.

That's what made him angry, my father said, adding that I was right that some of the men didn't get the chance to hand over their money because their wives stood, ready and waiting, to claim their wages from them the instant they left the fields on pay day. And that was a good thing because it saved the men from their own stupidity. With that, he'd stood up and I'd slithered off his knee onto the floor.

As a shepherd my father was often away from home and slept in a little traveling hut which he moved around with his flock. My father liked to talk and our home was much quieter when he was gone. As a child I would wonder how he tolerated the lonely days and nights with only his dog and his sheep for company. But as I grew up, I realized that he would have been happy to rant on about the landlords, the church, the monarchy and, always, the scarcity of money and food, with nothing but the wind to catch his words. The absence of an audience wouldn't bother him as he raged about the weather and the endless mud.

Unlike my brother, Joseph, who swore that he enjoyed feeling the rain falling upon him as much, if not more, than the warm rays of the sun, my father constantly railed against the wet, unpredictable Lincolnshire weather. It is fortunate Joseph enjoyed his time working outside as a carter for farmer Green as he didn't get to live beyond twenty years of age. Joseph was the second brother I would lose after leaving home.

While working in Walcott I'd been sent news of the death of my younger brother, John, who had been but twelve years of age when he passed. Years later my sister, Martha, had written to me in Shireoaks to let me know that Joseph was gone. I'd been so sad about them both, but doubly so with Joseph who had made me a rope so that I could be the best skipper at Billinghay school. Sometime later I'd visited his grave and thanked him for helping me and, without even worrying if someone would hear me, I'd talked to him a while about all the skipping I'd been doing, although of a different kind, since he'd made me that rope.

My father wasn't a man for conversation or a normal exchange of information or ideas. He didn't expect anyone to agree with him, nor did he seek to change the opinions of others. He just wanted to have his say and speak his mind and then go about his business. There have been good talkers in every succeeding generation and, whether or not they take after my father who cared not a jot if anyone was listening, many of his descendants have been blessed with the power of speech.

Effie's son, Charles Hague, could talk at length about anything and everything, and his son, also Charles Hague, has inherited the gift of the gab and never hesitates to speak up or tell a good story. Charles lives in South Yorkshire with his wife, Rachel, and their daughter, Emily. But, for those Hague men and my father, life wasn't just talk. There was always work to be done by Charles and his son at Hague's of Parkgate. And, as a shepherd, my father worked hard year-round, not only shearing and lambing when it was time, but mending fences and gates and taking responsibility for every single head.

When he was home, my father was a man in perpetual motion as he tended the vegetable garden, repaired endlessly broken doors, windows, latches and fences, and brewed his own ale. He drank this ale from his one and only prized possession – a pewter tankard which, he would remind us as he steered it to his mouth for that first satisfying swallow, belonged to his own father, Joseph Stennett, who he'd lost when he was sixteen years old. My father wasn't against a man drinking, he was merely against the wrong people profiting from his pleasure.

It is hard to get rid of the prejudices we develop when growing up, particularly if they've been ingrained in us by a loud, forceful parent. I'd carried my father's criticism of pub-dwellers through Walcott and Shireoaks, and it had colored my view of many of the young miners whose only opportunity to relax was to drink beer with their friends in the public houses. In Far Yonder you finally learn not to judge others. I regret thinking poorly of such hardworking men but I, too, saw the foolishness of handing over hard-earned pay to the coal owners and landowners who profited with every drink the miners purchased.

I had been, therefore, somewhat alarmed when I'd learned from Mary when she'd arrived home from school an hour after Margaret, that her father and her brother, Herbert, wouldn't be home for tea until six o'clock because they go to the pub on their way home. They go to The Prince of Wales on Sunday and Monday, said Mary, her wavy, chestnut hair bouncing on her shoulders in rhythm with her words, and The Yellow Lion on Tuesday. On Wednesdays, she said, they go to The Crown Inn.

Mary had continued with her litany of public houses, reporting that her father and brother go to the Bay Malton Inn every Thursday, and to the Ship Inn on Friday. Saturday is always different, she'd added after a quick intake of air, and they go wherever they feel like going. I'd wondered if each Saturday they rotated through the list of pubs in the same predictable order. It seemed that Greasbrough could put Billinghay to shame when it came to the sheer number of ale houses.

As today was a Monday, Mary had said, staring intently at me from the caverns of her deep round eyes, they would be going to The Prince of Wales which she described as being just down Potter Hill on the corner of Scrooby Street. They get there at five minutes past five, she'd added, her brown eyes twinkling, if I would like her to go to the Prince at that time and tell them to come home for their tea right away.

I'd laughed out loud at Mary's blatant attempt to ensure that her father would put me on the first train out of Rotherham the next morning, if not that night. I'd told her I had no intention of getting between hard working men and their ale, and that tea would be ready at six o'clock and not a minute before. Or after, I'd mumbled to myself wishing I could rant out loud with the same freedom my father had enjoyed in our humble little home. When you're a servant you can't speak your mind until you're in your own room and have only the walls to talk to which, of course, would not have bothered my father.

Tea at six o'clock was late in my experience, but I'd soon

78

learned that Mr. Smith wanted to make his day longer by downing his tools at five o'clock and having an hour to spare before tea. As he had his own business, and his son was his employee, they weren't handing over their money to their bosses, regardless of who might own the pubs in Greasbrough. And, if I'd been willing to have a more generous attitude about the young miners back in Shireoaks, I could see it was only fair that those lads should have some enjoyment with their friends at the end of the day. Maybe if I'd accepted this I would have had more fun myself.

Nevertheless, after hearing Mary's long litany of the Smith men's visits to the public houses, I'd checked that the money I'd saved was still tucked safely in my pocket, not knowing if I could live in a house with two drinking men. I'd also decided to ask my father for the measures of hops and water he used for his own brew, naively believing that if I made ale at Potter Hill Farm the Smith men might stay at home of an evening.

Later, I would laugh out loud at my ignorance! Mr. Smith and Herbert never drank at home, preferring the beer produced by the breweries, the company of their friends and neighbors and, just as importantly, the opportunity to do business with the other customers. How else could Mr. Smith ensure that if a stonemason was needed, or a builder was about to be chosen, it would be George Smith and his son?

I soon learned that not only did the men go to the pub on their way home each day, Mr. Smith returned later in the evening for an hour or two. He would come home a few minutes after ten o'clock and would quietly let himself in the house and lock up for the night. If Herbert went out after tea he was careful to be home before his father as there was always heavy work to be done the following day and Herbert was expected to be at the building site first.

Within days of my arrival, I developed the pleasant habit of sitting in the kitchen reading the newspaper or darning socks and stitching buttons on shirts when Mr. Smith came home. Not once in the thirty years I knew him did I ever see him drunk. He could hold his drink and knew exactly how much he could take. I came to accept the importance of Mr. Smith's pleasurable and practical daily visits to the village's public houses. Yet for many years I would still hear my father's voice ringing in my ears when I pictured those with the least to spare handing their money over the bar.

XIII

A few months after arriving in Greasbrough, I'd received my father's ale recipe. My brother, Thomas, had visited him and asked him to describe the ingredients and measurements. Our father's brews came from years of trial and error and there was no doubt as to the depth of his experience when it came to making ale.

Our father had learned to write as a child but, as I've already mentioned, his true talent was speaking. John Stennett liked nothing more than to stand and spout using his arms, and sometimes his legs, to add to the force of his speech. If he had been given the chance of the long years of education you enjoy today, he could have become a lawyer or professor.

And, given his gift of the gab, he would have made a fine politician. People would have voted for him not because he sought their approval or would have tried to convince them he was right, but because in his torrent of words they would recognize the passion of an intelligent man who cared about working men and women. Sadly, John Stennett would be long gone before his great-great-grandson, William Hague, became a famous politician.

Poor Thomas had struggled to keep up with our father's rambling instructions, as he'd described in exacting detail the delicate process of combining malt, hops, sugar and yeast. He'd also dictated pages and pages worth of commentary about wort and mash, the differences that might be expected when using hard or soft water and the unpredictable hazards that can come between a brewer and a perfect batch of ale.

A few years earlier, Thomas had worked at The Tally House

Inn in Blankney, a few miles outside Billinghay, as a servant to the landlord, John Greenham and his wife. Though a servant in a public house is a far cry from a master brewer, my brother's past proximity to a man and woman whose livelihood depended upon the delivery of consistently decent ale gave him standing in my father's eyes. This, in turn, gave Thomas the freedom to interrupt him or ask him to repeat a difficult step, and the result was an easy-to-follow timeless recipe for fine ale.

I'd been so grateful to Thomas for the time and trouble he'd taken to extract this information from our father. During that same year Thomas had wed his sweetheart, Hannah Ainge, and moved to Cheshire and had even less spare time than usual. Hannah came from Tysoe in Warwickshire and, when they got married, Thomas was a coachman for a wealthy family.

Thomas only lived to be forty-four years of age, sadly dying the same year as his son, and namesake, who had suffered from anemia since childhood and didn't live beyond his fifteenth birthday. My poor sister-in-law, Hannah, lost Thomas, her husband, and Thomas, her son, in the same year, both much too soon. She and Thomas had five other children, and Hannah later moved to Lancashire where most of my nephews and nieces became towel weavers. I hope you'll think of them when you wrap yourself in a big, plush cotton towel!

I've always thought it interesting how future generations can bring a family back to a place, yet with a much improved lot in life. My great-granddaughter, Gay Wadsworth, married Bruce Stephenson, a seed merchant. My great-granddaughter, April Sampson, married Philip Stern, a cotton merchant. Philip bought cotton from the countries where it was grown and sold it to textile mills around the world. Twice, he served as president of the Liverpool Cotton Association which controls the world's cotton trade.

The lives of Gay and Bruce, and their children, have been so different from those of so many of my family who didn't sell seeds, but toiled endlessly at planting them. And the lives of April and Philip, and their boys, are a far cry from those of my brother's children who didn't trade in cotton, but labored at the loom.

My husband knew instinctively what it would take me a lifetime to learn and most members of my family would never understand. When still young, George had given up working for wages as a stonemason for Earl Fitzwilliam and had turned to farming and building houses. George would tell all his children that it is essential in life to be positioned where the money is changing hands. He knew that to be successful you must have a share in the profits. Merchants and traders such as Bruce and Philip know this as, it turned out, did my children. Clement and Florrie opened their own shops, and Lizzie and Effie married young men with family businesses. Some things in life are not as accidental as they seem.

Many of the next generation also went into business. Clement's son, Clement, ran the book shop for many years after his father passed away. Lizzie and Albert's son, George Schonhut, continued to make a success of the pork butcher business in Rotherham. Lizzie and Albert's daughter, Joan Schonhut – who fondly remembered riding around in a pony and trap with her father visiting farms to buy pigs – married Arthur Hartley, a young man with a good head for business. Arthur established garage businesses in Parkgate and Rotherham in which Joan was also active. Years later Arthur and Joan's daughter, Elizabeth, and son, Robin, joined the family business. Robin and his wife, Judith, successfully ran the Wellgate branch in Rotherham during the 1970's and 1980's. Later, they too were aided by their daughter, Elizabeth, and her husband, Adrian Sayers.

George and Ethel Schonhut's daughter, Pauline, married Paul Tear whose family owns a company in Sheffield, founded in 1760, which produces precious metal alloys such as silver, copper and zinc. The company is now run by Paul and Pauline's children, Jacqueline Houghton and James Tear. Their products are used primarily in industry, although the company has also created such luxury items as a solid silver staircase for a privately owned boat. Can you imagine walking up and down a silver staircase?

Florrie's husband, Arthur, was in business for a time but his partners took it over during the First World War. Florrie's daughter, Ruth Holroyd, married Guy Sampson, whose family has been in the business of farming up in North Yorkshire for centuries. Ruth and Guy's son, Mark, and their grandson, Harry, continue to farm that same land.

Effie's daughter, Pauline, married Stan Goodswen, whose family owned butcher shops which were later run by their son, Philip. Effie's sons, Charles and Nigel, and her grandson, Charles, ran Hague's of Parkgate until the company was sold in 1989.

In more recent generations, family members and their husbands, wives and partners have owned a wide variety of businesses. Robert Foster and his family have owned Fosters of Thrybergh for four generations. The business started with a corner shop and has included a garden center, a gas station, a bonded warehouse, a supermarket, a bicycle shop and a laundry. For almost twenty years, Sally Foster (née Hague) ran her own business providing holiday rentals in Helmsley in North Yorkshire.

Steven McAuliff founded Animal Actors, providing animals for films, television shows, commercials and the theatre. His first job was to train a cougar for "The Magic Show", starring Doug Henning, on Broadway. Several years later, in 1976, he drove to Grand Prairie, Texas, to pick up Daisy, an elephant from South Africa. At that time, baby elephants were being culled and it was thought best to save their lives by selling them to zoos and trainers around the world. When Steven picked up Daisy in Texas to drive her back to his farm in New Jersey, she was six months old, stood five feet tall and weighed six hundred pounds. She performed "Summer in New York" at Radio City Music Hall in New York City, where she was extremely popular. Steven has also trained penguins, reindeer, lions, tigers, horses, an anteater, dogs, cats, numerous types of farm animals, and many more.

Ffion Hague runs her own consulting firm, providing board assessment services to companies in the United Kingdom and as far away as Australia. Mimi MacCaw is an independent jewelry consultant. Her husband, Ben Lewis, and his family own Young Voices International, producing concerts with school children in the United Kingdom, Germany, South Africa and the United States of America.

For many years, Clare and John Erskine ran an antique shop in Colyton, Devon. Clare is the daughter of Robin and Judith Hartley. John Erskine is from County Tyrone in Northern Ireland, and the couple now lives in Upperlands in County Londonderry where they are establishing a business. Upperlands is just a few miles from Cookstown which is famous for its linen mill. There is nothing more lovely than Irish linens! Also in the Hartley family, Joe Sayers, son of Elizabeth and Adrian Sayers, runs a successful men's hairdressing business.

My husband would be proud to know that so many members of the family have seen the wisdom of going into business for themselves. My husband was a wise man, and I often wish my father and brothers had shared his instinct for success and had been able to take the opportunity to change their lives.

In terms of opportunity – no matter how misguided – I'd seen a way for me to impress the Smith men and I'd soon begun brewing small quantities of ale at Potter Hill Farm, though with varying degrees of success. My father's warnings about water turned out to be crucial because Greasbrough is known for its soft water and, to this day, is nicknamed the 'saft watter town'. The village had numerous springs and you weren't considered to be truly born in Greasbrough unless, as a baby, you'd been sprinkled with water from one of the pumps.

As time went by I learned not to worry too much about achieving a perfect brew as my beer was drunk only by me in the form of a couple of glasses after the youngest children were asleep. Though I would be the only member of the household who would drink it, I was so glad we got the recipe from my father as he would live only a few more years, passing away in December 1882. John Stennett was sixty nine and, though his frenetic spirit would never be still, his body had been used up from years of hard physical labor. He was laid to rest in St. Michael's graveyard in Billinghay.

At the close of the day when Mr. Smith came home, he would find me reading the newspaper, darning socks, mending shirts, and sipping my beer. He would smile and nod his approval of his housekeeper enjoying her own ale at the end of a busy day. I would ask him if he'd like a drop and he would shake his head and say he'd had his fill, but he would sit by the range with me and tell me the news he'd learned that evening.

Mr. Smith always knew a great deal more about the village folk than I ever gleaned from my rushed trips to the shops or from snippets I heard from the children, though they always seemed to know a lot about the goings on in Greasbrough. After a few minutes of chatting, Mr. Smith would wish me goodnight and head up the front staircase, and I would put away my darning, wash my glass and hurry up the backstairs and into my little bed in the attic.

XIV

From my bedroom window I had a lovely view of Mr. Smith's fields, and could see all the way down Potter Hill to Main Street. As in Shireoaks, my room was in the attic tucked under the eaves, but there was just enough room for a small bed and a chest of drawers. Most importantly, the room and its little window were all mine. I would have welcomed another pair of hands in the house, but Mr. Smith did not keep any other servants and at least that meant I didn't have to share my private quarters. On that first April afternoon it had taken me only a few minutes to unpack my bag, place the ornaments the Browne children had made for me on the chest, and rest my sampler against the wall where it would stay until I found a good place to display it.

William had arrived home soon after Mary and had stuffed what was left of the jam tarts into his mouth. He had finally responded to Margaret's pantomime of pointing and nodding in the direction of the scullery door. Tall for his age and already a big strapping lad, he'd marched into the scullery to pick up my bag where I'd left it earlier in the afternoon. I'd placed it there after I'd noticed the back stairs leading off the scullery, knowing they would go to the first floor and then up to the attic. This was a house design which met with my approval as it would be easy for me to be up first in the morning without disturbing Mr. Smith and the children.

Margaret ran to lead the way, with William huffing and puffing as if my meagre possessions weighed a ton, which they did not. I'd followed the pair up the stairs while Mary stayed behind in the kitchen muttering that someone had to watch Georgie. I'd been grateful for her help, but suspected she did not wish to witness me moving into my room when perhaps her hope was for me to be returned to Rotherham Station before the day was done.

We'd stepped briefly onto the landing of the first floor and Margaret had pointed to the door of the bedroom she shared with Jessie and Mary. William forged on making it clear there wasn't time for chatter and that the purpose of his journey was to put Miss Mary's bag in the attic room and nothing more. He did it with a fair grace, however, laying my bag carefully on the floor and asking me if its placement was convenient for me. This was one of the few gentlemanly acts William would perform on my behalf, and I'd had no doubt that his father had left him strict instructions that, as he would be the first man to arrive home that day, he was to be responsible for making sure my luggage was taken upstairs.

William would grow into a fine young man but it would be a long time before we would become friendly. All those years later on the day of Lizzie's wedding, he'd walked around the kitchen, confidently familiar with his surroundings and sure of his welcome no matter how much time had passed since we'd last seen him. With a mischievous smile on his face, which he never lost despite his age, he'd enquired as to the whereabouts of his forcemeat balls. For a moment I'd thought he'd been serious and had flicked his wrist with a wet tea-towel. He'd laughed uproariously, knowing that after almost thirty years he could still get a rise out of me.

William and Margaret had left me alone in the attic room and I'd stolen a few minutes to myself. It was five o'clock and I had an hour before the two men would come home which was plenty of time to finish getting tea ready. Mary's information had been a great deal more useful to me than she might have intended, as there is nothing worse than not knowing when the master of the house might walk in the door expecting his food to be placed in front of him. Now I knew that the men always came home at six o'clock and – as I would soon learn--other than twice a year when Mr. Smith's sisters came for tea, we would set the clock by it during all the years ahead.

I'd had to get back down to the kitchen to take Georgie off Mary's hands, but I'd stolen a few minutes to peep out of my little window. I'd looked out at the farm as the rain poured steadily down the thick glass. The first thing that struck me was that although I could only see a portion of the thirty-six acres of Potter Hill Farm, it seemed some wheat and potatoes were started but much of the land was uncultivated. The past two or three years had been bad for farming and, although we didn't know it then, would only get worse. There was talk of an agricultural depression due to the disastrous combination of competition from imported food, high rents and poor summers.

Looking out of my attic window, it seemed there were more outbuildings on Potter Hill Farm's land than there were fertile fields. I soon learned that the barns and sheds were used to store building materials and equipment. As my husband dryly pointed out some years later, they turned out to be a better crop than wheat and potatoes.

By the time we were married, my husband had greatly reduced the time and money he spent on farming. This was fortunate as 1879 turned out to be one of the worst years ever for English farmers. There was little recovery to come afterwards mainly because of the increased importing, not only of grain but of cattle and sheep, and even cheese, butter and wool. Thousands of tenant farmers were ruined, and their laborers had neither work nor wages. I'd always worried about my family, but my father somehow managed to get by on his meager wages, helped by his vegetable garden and the numerous rabbits he trapped.

As I'd witnessed firsthand how imported foods destroyed the livelihood of our farmers in the 1870's and 1880's, you would think I would have been more enthusiastic when Clement got involved with imported products twenty-five years later. It was goods from countries like America and Canada where the weather, soil and wide open spaces made for bountiful harvests that did well in England. It would be natural, surely, that a young man should seek to make his living by selling them.

I know I've said this before, but I always believed that being dependent upon food from abroad is dangerous as it robs a country and its people of the skills and knowledge needed to feed itself. Anyone who has planted a vegetable garden knows how hard it is to get everything to grow and to get the produce in the quantities you want, if at all! The experience of doing it is the only way you can learn.

I hope the fears ingrained in me during my life turn out to be for naught, but I hope also that you grow some of your own food and can shoot well enough to bring home a pheasant, partridge or deer for your family's table. My time in Far Yonder is coming to a close and there are some things that can't be said enough. Knowing how to feed yourself is one of them.

Farming is a wonderful occupation if you own the land and keep it in the family generation after generation. My granddaughter, Ruth Holroyd, married a young farmer, Guy Sampson – after some skillful matchmaking by her older sister Effie Wadsworth! The Sampson family own Acclom House in Well, near Bedale in North Yorkshire. Acclom House was established in 1913 by Guy's father, Leonard Sampson, who came from a long line of farmers. Sampson's have farmed in Yorkshire since the twelfth century, which is a remarkable amount of time. During the fifteenth century, one of their ancestors was Lord Mayor of York which shows the family has been of prominence for hundreds of years.

Acclom House is now run by Ruth and Guy's son, Mark Sampson, his wife, Louise, and their son, Henry. The family farms about a thousand acres in the Vale of Mowbray, mainly wheat and seed barley, along with seventy acres of potatoes. Just think of all those lovely spuds waiting to be mashed!

After a few minutes in my room that first afternoon at Potter Hill Farm, it had been time to break away from my little view of the world and go back downstairs to the kitchen. I'd stopped to look in the tiny mirror which hung above the dresser and seen that the journey and my nervousness at being in a new place had taken its toll on my appearance. I'd licked my fingers and patted my hair down, straightened my apron and brushed bits of fluff off my dark blue skirt. Clumps of dirt were stuck to the hem so I'd rubbed the material together until it flaked off.

It was obvious that the attic room hadn't been used for a long time and before the evening was done I'd be bringing up a brush and dustpan to pick up the old dirt as well as sweep up the mess I'd just made. The room could wait until later, but I'd known my face and dress must look clean. The lessons from Hattie and the girls in Shireoaks had stuck. If a new housekeeper wanted to make a good first impression on the menfolk, not only must the kitchen be in shipshape order but she, too, must be neat and tidy.

I'd been used to working for the vicar and his wife, both of whom worked long, tiring days. But Reverend and Mrs. Browne were not engaged in hard, physical labor. I'd seen farm laborers worked to the bone, and miners drag themselves home in a state just short of total exhaustion. I, too, had always done a lot of physical work as there was no shortage of hard labor when carrying coal and water buckets, washing and ironing, lifting pots and pans and struggling with wriggling children. I'd worked hard at my heavy household tasks, but I knew that laborers and miners – and builders and stonemasons – worked harder.

Many times over the years I would remind Jessie, Margaret and Mary, as well as Lizzie, Florrie and Effie, that when a man deals with tons of stone and works it until it does what he wants, he isn't going to be persuaded that cooking, washing, ironing, mending, dusting, scrubbing and child rearing is so very hard to do. Not that any of those girls were shirkers or complainers, but I would sometimes suggest to them that, instead of trying to convince a man how hard you work, you might just as well get on with it and do a good job.

It may be that no-one knows how much we all do until we're gone, as I'm sure poor Mrs. Smith had known as she'd approached the end and worried how her family would manage without her. Those children and, in particular, her husband, had had no choice but to learn just how hard she had worked.

But marriage and family life isn't meant to be a competition and there aren't any winners unless everyone does their bit. If you want to be applauded, you should run a race or enter a competition because no-one claps when the fires are laid, breakfast, dinner and tea are on the table, and the washing is blowing high in the wind. At least no-one clapped in the Lincolnshire, Nottinghamshire or Yorkshire that I knew – and certainly no-one noticed that the walls of the mashed potato cathedral were climbing higher and higher.

But on that first afternoon, I'd known that the Smith men would notice a good tea when they got home from work – and from the public house. I'd found cold beef in the pantry which Jessie must have roasted the day before. Between making jam tarts and watching Georgie, I'd ground up the beef, boiled and diced half a dozen potatoes, rolled the meat and potatoes in pastry and sealed and crimped it at the top. I'd put the pie in the oven, ready to be brought out as soon as the men stepped in the door. It turned out nicely, accompanied with pickled onions and a loaf of bread. To finish, I'd made a tray of lemon curd tarts which I'd hidden from the children. They would get their share after Mr. Smith and Herbert had had theirs.

William, Margaret and Mary were sitting at the kitchen table and Georgie was in his high chair as the grandfather clock in the parlor clanged six long chimes. The kitchen door was closed against the rain which was still teeming down. Silence had fallen as we awaited the arrival of the men. Georgie was quietly smiling and waving his arms about in contented anticipation of his next meal, and William had somehow resisted the impulse to tickle him.

Suddenly, the door opened and a young man – a lad of sixteen to be exact – stepped into the kitchen. The heavy oak door slammed behind him. I'd realized later that from that moment on I'd known exactly what my future husband looked like.

Herbert was the spitting image of his father, with the same lean, strong body and handsome face marked by sallow cheeks and big, soulful eyes. Though I'd already registered some concerns about the Smith family's manners, I'd been certain Herbert wouldn't have let the door slam in his father's face. He must, therefore, have come home alone.

My mind had raced through the possibilities. Would Mr. Smith come through the scullery, perhaps being the only member of the family who knew to use the back entrance and go no further with his wet, muddy boots? Or – and I'd felt my hackles rising – had Mary purposely misled me when it came to relating the habits of her father and brother?

More worryingly, I'd wondered if Mr. Smith had been persuaded to take another drink instead of coming home in time for tea. Or could he be avoiding the awkwardness of meeting his new housekeeper? If he wasn't here in time for tea, I would face the difficult task of deciding how much of my lovely meat pie to set aside for my employer. Most alarming of all, how was I now to know when Mr. Smith would come home?

XV

An important event occurred when I was five years old that, even if I'd known about it, I would not have understood its significance or the effect it would have upon my future. I didn't know the people involved or the place in which it took place, yet it made it possible for my life to work out the way it did.

In 1851 a woman named Eliza Jackson was buried. The young widower who wiped his eyes and blew into a handkerchief as she was lowered into the earth was Mr. George Smith. He was aged twenty four, and his deceased wife had lived for thirty eight years.

I don't believe our lives are planned for us by a greater being as I've seen from Far Yonder how people make a mess out of what's laid out beautifully in front of them, and others work wonders with seemingly hopeless material. It is certain, however, that I wouldn't have become the third Mrs. George Smith if the first, and second, hadn't gone to their graves prematurely. Their absence – especially the gaping hole left by the second who had borne all eight children – made it necessary for the prospering widower to employ a woman to take care of his home and his children.

A housekeeper gets to know a lot about her employer and his tastes and habits. Though you are new to a man's home, you soon learn that his meal must be ready when he comes in the door. By the second day, you know to put the newspapers in the parlor and his pipe and tobacco on the mantel because as soon as he's finished his dinner – always served as the grandfather clock in the hallway strikes twelve – he'll go there to read the papers and smoke for quarter of an hour before going back to work.

You like this habit because you use the time to clear the table and start washing the pots. But often he'll call your name and you wipe the soap suds off your hands and hurry to the parlor door. He may say he fancies a bit of cow's tongue for tea and your mind will quickly run through the pantry shelves and you will add a trip to the butchers to your afternoon jobs. Or he may ask a question about one of the children and whether the girls could be doing more to help in the kitchen, or if the boys are keeping the coal scuttles filled.

Often you rush into the parlor when he calls and he will point out an article in *The Sheffield Daily Telegraph* or, his favorite paper, *The Sheffield and Rotherham Independent.* He knows you like to sit at the kitchen table and read the papers when he goes to the pub in the evening and he enjoys being able to tell you ahead of time what lies within their pages.

But sometimes he'll simply motion for you to sit down and you know he wants to tell you a bit about himself. A good housekeeper learns a lot this way and, though she wants to get on with her jobs, is well-advised to take the time to listen. And, anyway, why not take the rare chance to sit down?

During those first weeks in Greasbrough, I enjoyed hearing about Mr. Smith's youth and how at the age of fourteen he became a stable boy at Wentworth House. His father was the blacksmith on Earl Fitzwilliam's estate and helped his son get taken on, although he didn't follow his father's line of work but, after his time in the stables, became a stonemason. There was work for hundreds of men and women, not only at the big house, but also at the stables and at the hundreds of cottages and outbuildings which belonged to the estate.

Wentworth Woodhouse, always known locally as Wentworth House, is to this day the biggest private house in England. It has three hundred and sixty five rooms, one for every day of the year! If you walk down every passageway you will have walked five miles, so you can only imagine the number of servants needed to carry coal and water to all those rooms down all those corridors!

Mr. Smith worked for a number of years in Ecclesall Bierlow in Sheffield where the Earl also owned land and property. It was there that he met his first wife, Eliza Jackson. Just a few years later he would meet his second wife, Mary Crawshaw, in that same place. Mr. Smith described the beautiful countryside, the hills and parkland and, in particular, a marvelous bluebell wood.

I'd pictured him young and happy, holding Eliza's hand as they'd wandered through the blue-carpeted wood. I'd wondered if he'd also been young and happy holding Mary's hand as they'd strolled through that same wood. I'd decided that if it was pleasurable once there was no reason why it wouldn't be pleasurable twice, and I'd hoped he'd enjoyed his time courting these two girls as he'd had many sorrows since those carefree days.

I'd realized on the afternoons Mr. Smith asked me to sit with him, that for all the dozens of people he saw every day on the building sites and in the village and the public houses each evening, he didn't have anyone to talk to about himself. Though never alone, he was lonely. I'd understood that he must have enjoyed talking to his wives and that it might explain why he'd married Eliza when he was only twenty one and she was thirty five. He'd told me that she was fourteen years older than him and that the marriage had barely begun before she'd become sickly.

For years I'd watched Mrs. Browne stop what she was doing to sit down with the Reverend and listen intently as he talked about church meetings and problems concerning the dozens of committee members who were always knocking on the vicarage door. It appeared as if the vicar's wife was forever at the beck and call of her husband and that, no matter how pressed she was for time, she was expected to drop everything and give him her undivided attention. But as I'd watched them, I'd realized how much Reverend Browne depended upon his Mary, not only to listen, but to console and guide him.

From time-to-time Mrs. Browne would remind me that her husband had been Chaplin to Lord Lucan in the Crimea, and that because of what he saw there he had little patience for his troublesome parishioners. I imagine when you've stood witness to the hundreds of dead and wounded boys of the Light Brigade, you will be disgusted having to settle arguments over who is going to be in charge of the church fete.

I've always been glad that the vicar and his wife showed me this close, friendly side of a marriage. I couldn't recall ever seeing Mr. and Mrs. Harrison with their heads together. And, though children don't know everything that goes on between their parents, I don't imagine there was a single time when my mother and father sat down and talked like a couple.

But as I'd listened to Mr. Smith, I'd imagined that he'd always enjoyed talking to a woman and that the big age difference between the groom and his first bride hadn't been of importance to him. Eliza must have been a good listener and, being older, would have been able to understand and help him.

I hadn't been in Greasbrough more than a day or two before I'd been told, by both women and men alike, what a lovely woman Mrs. Smith had been and what a shame she had been taken too soon, only forty seven years old. Oh, those poor bairns and the widower whose heart must be broken!

Some of this was meant kindly, but I'd known it was also designed to make sure I didn't get any fancy ideas about my employer. As I would learn only too soon, there were more than a few ladies with an interest in Mr. Smith and who wanted to ensure that the new housekeeper was kept firmly in her place.

George and Eliza had lived in Ecclesall Bierlow during their marriage, and Mr. Smith had moved to Greasbrough only after he and Mary were married. Yet everyone seemed to know that Mary had been his second wife. I'd even heard one old fogey say, right in the middle of the butcher's shop, that Mr. Smith must have married his first wife for her money. As always with such tattlers, however, he didn't divulge how he would be privy to such information.

Before I'd gone into service I'd been warned by my sister, Martha, not to talk about the family you worked for, and I'd carefully followed this rule in Walcott and Shireoaks. I hadn't been about to stand outside Willey's shop in the middle of Main Street and gossip with an old nosy parker as to whether or not the first Mrs. Smith had money of her own.

Given that she had died in 1851, anything Eliza owned would belong to her husband and I suppose that's why people were curious. I've learned from Far Yonder that what people want to know about the most is somebody else's money. They'll ask a thousand questions about everything under the sun in an attempt to find out who has the money and, most importantly, how much.

In the same manner in which Mr. Smith would summon me to the parlor to listen to his stories, he would suddenly jump up, glance at the clock – though he always seemed to know what time it was – and hurry to the door. Sometimes he would be in the middle of a tale and it would be as if a gong had sounded which only he could hear. I would be left alone in my chair as though I was the lady of the house and my steward had come to report to me about the state of the grounds or the profits from the sale of the crops and livestock. I would have to shake myself out of my reverie and go back to the pile of pots that awaited me in the kitchen.

But as I would put the kettle on the hob to add hot water to the sink, I'd feel grateful that Mr. Smith talked to me. It was important to learn from him, instead of from gossiping neighbors, about his youth and, especially, about Eliza who was buried when I was but five years old and first dashing into the rope on the playground at Billinghay.

XVI

If you believe our hearts know what we need long before our minds catch up, then you will understand what I am about to say. If, instead, you think our hearts simply follow the path our minds set for us, you will read impatiently through my words. You will mutter that Mary is looking back and conveniently making sense of her life. Like all of us, Mary wants to find meaning and to justify her decisions and actions long after they took place.

But I hope you'll also consider that, though my approach to life was practical by sheer necessity, I traveled a path that led to me finding what I'd been in grave danger – as Hattie never failed to remind me – of missing.

I believe that before I accepted the position with Mr. Smith, my heart had known it needed a place to belong to and a man to call my own. And though I'd known my journey would be different from Hattie's straightforward path, my heart had understood what my friend urged me to do at the very same time I'd argued against it. Whilst I'd stood peeling potatoes, apparently ramrod straight, in the vicarage kitchen with my mind whirring as it wrestled whether or not to take the job in Greasbrough, my heart had already known what I must do.

We can think and analyze and churn something over in our minds until we believe we are sure, but when we make a change in our lives it is because our heart already has us on our way. When we say 'yes' to a new place or to a new job, or to a man or a woman, it is not because we are making a sound, rational choice but because we are following a yearning though it be deeply buried. The job or the new place gives us the ticket to finally take the trip that our heart began long before.

My heart must have been smiling on my first evening at Potter Hill Farm when Mr. George Smith arrived home. Stepping briskly into the kitchen, he'd found his new housekeeper on her hands and knees, her head in the oven and her bum stuck up in the air. That same bum was rocking side to side in rhythm with its owner's energetic scrubbing.

Dirt was our enemy back in the 1800's and it was an unending battle to get the better of it, particularly in coal mining villages like Shireoaks and Greasbrough. But living in coal country was no excuse for a dirty house. It just meant you had to work harder, scrubbing inside and out. Cleaning the range was a daily job and when I'd put the jam tarts in the oven that first afternoon I'd been alarmed to see that the Potter Hill range was in great need of sweeping out. It hadn't seen vinegar and water for quite some time.

If my heart had been smiling at the meeting that was about to take place, my mind had been given far too much time to think about it. As the evening had worn on and Mr. Smith still hadn't arrived home, I'd grown increasingly anxious about meeting him. After tea I'd put Georgie to bed and he'd settled easily as if he'd already known I'd be there in the morning and every morning to come. Herbert had gone out with his friends, Mary had retreated to her room, and I'd eventually convinced Margaret to join her and go to bed early. Jessie had returned home, rushing straight upstairs to the sewing table which was nestled under a window at the far end of the upstairs hallway, perfectly positioned to catch the last of the evening light.

I'd been exhausted from a long day which had begun in blessed, familiar Shireoaks and had ended in a strange new place. But I'd been grateful to get the kitchen to myself, and I'd dusted the plates and cups on the dresser and written a long list of jobs for the next day. I liked to know what I was doing from one day to the next and making a list sets you in good stead. It's also an absorbing task which forces you to rid your mind of worries, or at least add them to your list! I'd been too anxious to go up to my room and sleep, and I also believed I should be present and occupied when Mr. Smith finally came home. So, rather than sweep out the oven in the morning, I'd decided to get it done and cross it off my list.

When Herbert had marched into the kitchen at six o'clock and closed the door firmly behind him, we'd all stared at him. As we'd waited for an explanation as to the whereabouts of his father, he'd immediately provided the answer. He told us Mr. Smith had gone to a meeting of the School Board which he hadn't known about until a chap in the Prince of Wales mentioned that the Board was meeting at six o'clock up at St. Mary's.

Herbert had explained – very considerately I'd thought as it showed he'd understood that my knowledge of the village went no further than the kitchen in which I was standing – that there was talk of a new school being built on the corner of Harold Croft and Cinder Bridge. Upon hearing of the meeting, his father had quickly downed his ale and rushed off to Church Street.

From Herbert's information, I'd gathered that Mr. Smith wasn't a member of the School Board, but wanted to stay abreast of their plans. Months later, Mr. Smith told me that he attended every meeting of the Board, always sitting quietly in the back until such a time as he felt he needed to speak up. He said that was usually to remind the Board members that, as the ratepayers had elected them to their positions, they must address each and every one of the questions and concerns, including his own, of those members of the public in attendance.

Mr. Smith had added, with a twinkle in his eyes, that one of the Board members always responded to his comments by saying that an ambitious builder shouldn't be considered just a mere member of the public. Mr. Smith had laughed when relating this story and told me that you don't get the best contracts if you wait for permission to speak. You get work because you do a better job than anyone else, but also by standing up and pushing your nose into the discussions.

The only work I had my nose pushed into when Mr. Smith arrived home that first evening was a very dirty oven. Its condition was worse than I'd realized and it was lucky it hadn't caught on fire the past few days. But, though the oven hadn't yet gone up in flames, my heart surely did. Yet, just as the oven had proved slow to catch alight, my stubborn, practical mind would need a few weeks before it too caught on fire.

My new employer had entered the house through the scullery and suddenly appeared in the kitchen. Being startled and in a hurry to get off my knees, I'd jumped up so quickly I'd knocked my head on the range. With Mr. Smith standing in front of me I'd stood up, rubbed my forehead where I'd banged it and brushed my hands on my apron.

Mr. Smith had smiled at me and said in a loud, amused voice that he didn't know he'd employed a chimney sweep. When I'd gone to my room later that evening, I'd looked in the little mirror and seen a thick line of soot etched across my forehead. I'd thought of Hattie and the girls in Shireoaks and hadn't known whether to laugh or cry. But knowing they would all be doubled up laughing, I'd decided to join them and had lain down on the bed and laughed as my face was washed with tears.

Years earlier, Mrs. Browne had trained me and Fred to greet people properly and instructed us how to introduce ourselves to visitors. She'd said it wasn't only for the benefit of the vicarage guests, but would stand us in good stead in life if we could confidently state our name and speak to a stranger as if we weren't afraid they were going to bite us. I'd followed her training and had managed to look directly at Mr. Smith and smile, at the same time remembering not to look downward.

I'd said good evening, quickly adding that I was Mary Stennett which, in my discomfort, I'd been sure came out all in a jumble. How I'd wished Mrs. Browne was standing next to me at that moment! I would have been able to tell her that it was so much harder to be confident and mind your manners when you really were afraid. Not that I'd thought Mr. Smith might bite me as I'd seen right away, though it be a quick, momentary impression, that he was a gentleman.

But, oh, how I'd longed to be back in the familiar warmth of the vicarage kitchen. It was at that moment that I'd been most painfully aware that, if not for a decision entirely of my own choosing, I would be safely at home in that very same kitchen. Instead here I was in the house of a stranger.

Fortunately, my regrets had been fleeting, and I'd quickly realized that my fears were nothing more than nerves. The man who stood before me had such a kindly twinkle in his deep blue eyes that the only thing I'd been able to do was stare and smile. What a relief it had been to see that Mr. Smith was smiling back at me.

I'd been expecting to find a somber, sorrowful man at Potter Hill Farm. After all, a husband and father who'd lost his wife only a few short weeks ago, and had responsibility for several children as well as a farm and a business, must be weighed down with grief and worries. It was true that his eldest daughter, Annie, was already on her own, and Jessie was a big help in the house and Herbert in the business, but William, Mary and Margaret were still children and Georgie was little more than a baby. And they had all lost their mother.

I understand now you have counselors and psychologists who help people deal with grief and loss, but back in those days you muddled through. If you were a woman you might have a friend or relative you could talk to who understood that you were grieving and were feeling sad, or angry or lonely. Or, just plain exhausted.

Judith Hartley (née Hewitt) is the wife of my great-grandson, Robin, and is a gifted healer and counselor. She helps people work through their bereavements and deal with loss. She's also a medium and can make contact with people who are gone. I'm not going to say whether we've been in touch. You'll just have to wonder about that!

But even if my husband lived now, George would have been too proud to admit he needed help. A lot of men in England, and particularly in Yorkshire, make a point of appearing as if everything is alright even when it isn't. In fact, especially when it isn't. They may openly complain about the weather or their football team, and they may like to tell you that their rheumatism is bothering them. But if they are diagnosed with a fatal illness they won't tell you, and when their wife dies you will see them out the next day going about their business as if she'd meant nothing to them. Don't be fooled, they are dying inside but they are too manly, or too prideful, to let you see it.

My future husband was fifty years old when I first set eyes on him in the Potter Hill kitchen, but he was youthful and lively with sparkling blue eyes that seemed to be smiling even when he was serious. There was only a little grey in his brown hair and but a few specks in his bushy whiskers. I'd soon learned that he liked to call them his mutton-chops and he would rub them across Georgie's face and bare tummy until his little boy shrieked with laughter. Mr. Smith had few wrinkles on his face and his skin had a ruddy glow from being outside in all weathers. Except for the flat, almost sunken cheeks also borne by Herbert, he looked healthy and well-nourished.

If I'd been mistaken in expecting a mournful man, I'd been wrong again in imagining Mr. Smith – farmer, builder, father and widower – would be a big, tall fellow. He was no more than average height and lean and wiry but somehow, in all the years I knew him, I continued to think of him as a big man. Sometimes I would watch him from my window as he walked up Potter Hill with his hurried stride, and I'd always be surprised to discover anew that he was neither as tall, nor as big, as the picture of him I carried in my mind.

Whenever Mr. Smith arrived home, rushing through the scullery door as if he hadn't a minute to waste, we would all hurry and bustle around the kitchen like little marionettes. The children's friends would scarper off home as soon as they saw him, or heard his voice. It wasn't that we were afraid of him, or that his bearing was so great – and it certainly wasn't that we were idling until he came through the door – but it was as if we all got a bolt of energy from his presence and would suddenly spring into motion.

I'd been pleased with what I'd seen on that first evening and hoped fervently that Mr. Smith would find my work and demeanor – and my neat appearance – to his satisfaction. When I'd looked back I'd realized that everything I'd needed to know about my new employer and, of course, my future husband, had been made plain to me that night.

George Smith was a hardworking businessman who was willing to change his treasured habits in order not to miss an opportunity. He had a sense of humor and the confidence to use it when meeting a stranger. And he looked young and fit enough to live for many more years.

As I'd fallen into a sound sleep that first night I'd felt confident that Mr. Smith would be in need of, and be able to afford, a housekeeper for a long time. And, most importantly, I'd seen that he had the kindly, good-natured disposition which would make working for him a pleasure. If my mind was feeling calm and contented that night, my heart was already in flight. Though I knew nothing but its solid, predictable rhythm, my heart was quietly getting ready to take me on the journey of a lifetime.

XVII

I'd always enjoyed the story of Dick Whittington and his dream of going to London where the streets were paved with gold. Though I'd understood that Dick arrived in London to find more rats than gold, I'd kept the picture in my mind of a glittering city where poor young people went to seek their fortune. It's hard to replace an imaginary scene with the reality when you haven't had the opportunity to see a place with your own two eyes. That chance finally came when I was well into my seventies, and many years had passed since I'd first been drawn into the story of young Dick.

My step-daughter, Margaret, had always talked about us going on a trip to London and for more years than we could remember we'd tried, but failed, to find a time the pair of us could go. Finally, one dreary April afternoon in 1921 she'd called round and said it was a crying shame that at our ages – Margaret was now over fifty – neither of us had been to our nation's capital. She'd added that a train left Sheffield every day and it was high time we were on it.

We'd quickly gone through all the arrangements we would have to make if we were to go away for a few days and, even between us, couldn't come up with a single reason we couldn't make the journey. By that time I'd been a widow for well over ten years and, though I spent most of my days helping my children and grandchildren, I was no longer solely responsible for anyone, be it child or adult.

Effie had given birth to her second baby, Pauline, just the year before but could manage without my help for a few days. Lizzie's youngest, Joan, was four, and Florrie's fourth, Hubert Peter, was already five. Margaret's youngest, Nora, was only eight, but she would be well taken care of by her older sisters for a few days.

And so it was that a month later on a sunny May morning, Margaret and I arrived at Sheffield Victoria Station ready to board the Great Central Railway's fast train to London. We'd stood, excitedly and impatiently, on the platform with dozens of other passengers waiting for the train to come in. I'd looked down at the tracks and my mind had wandered to thoughts of my youngest brother, William, who had been born when I was eleven. William was the seventh child in our family, followed only by baby Elizabeth.

William had started out as a farm servant for John Bradshaw in Temple Bruer. Later, he and his wife, Esther, lived in Lincoln where William worked as a platelayer for the Great Northern and Great Eastern Joint Railway. The line had been built to move coal from Yorkshire to East Anglia. I'd known that he and his gang had worked on tracks in Lincoln and not on the line we would be traveling on but, as I'd studied the tracks, I'd imagined William walking up and down and getting on his knees to replace worn out rails and rotten sleepers.

I'd begun telling Margaret about William, pointing out that we didn't have to worry about the train being derailed because of men like him, though the railways worked them like dogs, six days a week from dawn to dusk, for very little pay. William lived to be seventy three, which was quite an achievement considering the type of work he did. But I'm certain his life as a platelayer robbed him of some of the extra years I enjoyed right up to aged eighty six.

As I'd started to speak, the train had thundered into the station and Margaret clapped both hands on her head and I'd thrust mine onto my legs in a vain attempt to stop my skirt from billowing up around me. I'd known Margaret didn't want to lose her hat, but I'm not sure why I'd been so worried about my legs being on display, given that I was well past the age of anyone wanting to look. They'd been hidden from view all my life and this wouldn't have been the time to start showing them off!

The train had screeched to a stop and the two of us had been pushed aboard by the force of the passengers behind us. Unlike most of you who have been all over the country and the continent, if not the entire world, I was not an experienced traveler. I regret I didn't have the chance to travel more than I did.

I'm not sorry, however, to have avoided being herded and pummeled and pushed by people who wouldn't dream of touching so much as your little finger until, all of a sudden, a train comes in and they feel free to thrust their bodies at you as if you were husband and wife. I can see from Far Yonder that it hasn't got any better. In fact, when I see people on aeroplanes practically sitting on your knee and pulling their luggage down on top of you, I am quite relieved to have missed it all.

The train ride to London, however, was one trip I wouldn't have missed for the world. The entire journey took only three hours, which is almost as fast as that same trip is now which you might find surprising. It seemed that in a flash we were disembarking at Marylebone Station. We jumped – literally in Margaret's case to avoid stepping into a puddle in her shiny new shoes – into a black taxi-cab. Before we'd had chance to sit ourselves down, the driver had spun the wheel and we'd sped through the busy streets to our hotel.

Between the train and the taxi-cab I'd already learned that, when it comes to travel, everything must be done at the fastest possible speed. I still don't see what difference it would make if a few extra minutes were added to each portion of a trip so that everyone could move around in a more dignified manner. I suppose if I was a more experienced traveler I would know that every journey is a race which must be completed as quickly as possible.

As this was the first time I'd been in a taxi-cab, I'd decided the best thing to do was to enjoy the ride before – as now I'd learned – it would suddenly come to an end. I'd sat back in a surprisingly comfortable seat and looked up in amazement at the city's tall buildings which were so many stories higher than those in Rotherham, or even Sheffield. While I'd been busy looking at the elegant buildings, Margaret's head had darted from one side of the taxi to the other as she'd anxiously scanned the crowds to see what the ladies of London were wearing.

As I might have expected, without warning, the driver had suddenly come to a stop and we'd practically gone face down out of our seats. The driver jumped out of the vehicle and grabbed our bags from where he'd secured them on the back, and opened the door. We'd practically slid out onto the pavement. I'd told Margaret to stop for a minute, and announced that I wasn't going to be rushed any further. We'd paused for a moment, patted down our skirts and straightened our hats. We'd then sauntered gracefully into the hotel, gliding up to the reception desk like two ladies of leisure who were down from the North for yet another seasonal visit to London.

Our room was on the third floor and we'd taken the lift which meant we'd had to rush to get in it before the boy closed the doors. I'd reminded Margaret of my vow not to be rushed anymore but she'd just smiled at me and said that before too long we'll be pushing up daisies so why slow down now? From that moment on, I'd stopped complaining. Not only might we be gone before we could visit London again, for much of my life such a trip simply hadn't been possible.

We found our room to be pleasingly spacious and comfortable. Margaret studied her elegant reflection in an ornate mirror and was able to assure herself that her outfit was as fashionable as any she'd seen on the streets of London thus far. We then set off to discover if those streets really were paved with gold. Unfortunately, it hadn't taken long for my long-held shining vision of London to turn into the same sad reality found by poor Dick Whittington. We barely ventured far from the hotel before seeing dozens of poor wretches who looked as if they hadn't had a good meal for a long time. We soon learned that they couldn't find work, let alone pieces of gold.

Both of us had been getting on in years, but we were still as fit as fleas and could easily walk the short distance from the hotel to Trafalgar Square to see Nelson's Column. From there, we went up the Haymarket to Piccadilly Circus. We soon became overwhelmed with the crush of people and decided to walk towards Hyde Park.

Though we'd barely been in London for more than three hours, with Margaret's constant unfolding, turning and folding of the map her husband had given her, we found our way around as if we'd never lived anywhere else. We ambled down Piccadilly, happy to leave some of the throng behind, when Margaret suddenly grabbed my arm and pulled me into an alley.

It turned out the alley was an elegant indoor street called the Burlington Arcade, lined with dozens of posh jewelers and antique dealers. With one glance I'd seen that though I was in a better position than many elderly folk in Greasbrough, there would be nothing on offer to make me hand over my money. It reminded me of walking round the shops with Hattie and the girls in Shireoaks, our noses pushed up against the glass, staring at what could never be ours.

Many years later my daughter, Effie, would visit the Burlington Arcade, a place more suited to her luxurious tastes. Effie was no stranger to jewels and owned some fine pieces herself. She would have loved to know her great-granddaughter, Mimi MacCaw, who worked for many years for Tiffany's on Bond Street and is a jewelry consultant in London. Mimi would have been a great help to my extravagant daughter who, for all her experience buying jewelry, never believed she got a fair price.

On the day Effie visited the Burlington Arcade, she'd stood outside a shop window staring at a display of necklaces and earrings studded with glistening precious stones. A jeweler had stepped out of the shop, greeted her politely and looked down at the magnificent diamond ring Effie wore on her left hand. The ring was composed of three diamonds, and had been Effie's reward to herself for helping to keep Hague's of Parkgate going during some difficult times.

Hague's of Parkgate had been founded in 1870 by Effie's father-in-law, Charles Hague. With his business partner, Ellis Law, Charles Hague had purchased a small soda water and ginger beer manufacturing business from William Collinson, a chemist in Masbrough. William Collinson hadn't wished to continue as a pop manufacturer, choosing to put into practice his skills and advanced education as a chemist and druggist. The descendants of William Collinson have included popular Rotherham doctors, Dr. Peter Collinson and Dr. Charles Collinson.

Hague's of Parkgate did well and, many years later, Charles Hague passed the company on to his son, Hubert Henry Hague – Effie's husband, Bert. But the thriving business soon encountered difficulties. As Bert was a primary reason for those difficulties, he hadn't been in a position to object when his wife purchased such an expensive ring. Bert's sole interest in the business was to serve as the company's sales representative, a job which allowed him to spend his days visiting the area's public houses where he would solicit orders for pop and soda water. With his love of talking and his friendly manner with all and sundry, Bert was not only an excellent sales representative, but a highly popular figure in the pubs of Greasbrough, Parkgate, Rawmarsh, Wentworth and Rotherham.

In spite of his lack of interest in the family business, Bert had a strong community spirit which he put to good use on Greasbrough Parish Council. He was always a favorite choice when he stood for election, and for many years served as a valuable and committed councilor.

Effie, meanwhile, had vowed to hold on to the business which supported her family. For many years, she and her eldest son, Charlie, aided by a number of loyal employees, managed the pop factory and kept it running. She also helped her husband settle a big problem he caused with the tax man which resulted in paying a substantial fine to the Inland Revenue.

Effie's desire to be compensated for the troubles her husband caused had begun many years earlier when she, Bert and their children were living in Greasbrough. Far too many times to count, Bert had arrived home as dawn was breaking over the village, having walked – always with his back firm and straight – several miles home through the park from the George & Dragon or Rockingham Arms in Wentworth. Knowing the landlords as well as he did, Bert was often invited for after-hours drinking. Reginald Cooper, a local builder, never forgot the day when he opened up his yard on Church Street at seven o'clock in the morning, only to see Bert Hague striding out of the park, wending his way home after a long night of drinking.

Bert spent a lot of time with his big pal, Tom Tullet, head gamekeeper for Wentworth Estate. Tom was an imposing man who carried a big stick which he used to clobber the many poachers he caught on the Estate, a practice which would get him into a lot of trouble today. One night after drinking into the wee hours at Woodnook, Tom's cottage in Wentworth Park, Bert downed his glass, said goodnight to his friend and headed out of the door. When Tom got up to go to work a few hours later, Bert was lying on the stone wall in front of the cottage covered in frost! Bert was a big man and it's lucky that this incident took place before he was afflicted with the diabetes that would later ail him. He was fortunate to make it home alive that day, although by the time Effie had finished with him I doubt he'd felt particularly blessed.

There was always plenty to drink at Tom Tullet's cottage. As head gamekeeper, he received gifts each year from the aristocrats and landed gentry who were invited to the shoots on Earl Fitzwilliam's estate. Tom would share these gifts with the other gamekeepers, but also got to keep many. One Christmas he received ninety nine bottles of whisky. It's lucky he had Bert to help him polish them off!

Bert and Tom spent a lot of time in each other's company and had many a good laugh. One evening they left the Prince of Wales in Greasbrough, marching briskly over to a pony and trap waiting for them on Potter Hill. A trap is a light, two wheeled open air carriage which seats two people. The men had left the pony facing uphill and as Bert, who weighed eighteen stone, and Tom, weighing more than twenty stone, jumped onto the trap at exactly the same time, the pony was lifted up in its shafts straight up off the ground. The pony would have weighed about five hundred pounds, but Bert and Tom between them matched, if not exceeded, the poor pony's weight.

It would be Effie who would diagnose the onset of Bert's diabetes. Her husband had a habit of relieving himself in the bushes in front of their house when he returned home late at night, and Effie wondered why a white crystalized powder kept forming on her prized shrubs. She finally deduced that her husband had become afflicted with diabetes. Bert would die in 1958 at the age of seventy one from a combination of diabetes and heart problems.

Back on the day Effie had visited the Burlington Arcade and the jeweler had stepped out of his shop, she'd looked on silently and intently as the dapper old man had gently taken her left hand and raised her fingers up to his face. After continuing for a moment to stare at her dazzling ring, he'd said, in a clipped and perfectly enunciated accent: "Madam, ladies have been murdered for less".

Effie had laughed with a mixture of surprise and pride, but had swiftly turned her diamonds into the palm of her hand and pulled on her gloves, never to remove them again when out in London. Personally, I wouldn't want to wear something if I had to worry about being robbed and murdered. But, for some men and women valuable possessions are worth even the serious trouble they can cause.

In Effie's case, the ring was worth far more than the sum of its precious stones. Firstly, it was her payment, though far from being the only one, for ensuring that her husband's business would not only continue to provide for them, but would survive to be passed on to their sons, Charlie and Nigel. Hague's of Parkgate remained in the family, managed by Charlie and Nigel, and, later, Charlie's own son, Charles, until it was sold in 1989. The family business had lasted almost one hundred and twenty years, and it was no small thanks to Effie.

But the extravagant purchases were not simply those made by a wife who wanted to show her husband that she knew her own worth. They were Effie's attempt to find solace for what she could never forget: that Hague's of Parkgate should have been passed on to three sons, not to two. But our little Tony didn't live to join the business, or grow to be a man, because he was gone before his sixth birthday.

Many years later Effie would suffer another grievous blow and would already know that if fine possessions hadn't take the place of her little boy, they would not help her face the loss of a young granddaughter. No matter how futile her purchases, my sorrowful daughter deserved to take some pleasure in her jewels, her antiques, her paintings and her fine house. And to be ever proud that a posh London jeweler stepped out of his shop to admire her ring.

XVIII

We'd stayed in London for three days and had the most wonderful time. Margaret and I had always been content in each other's company, which was just as well because we didn't know a soul in our great capital. I've often thought of the times in the future when if I'd visited London I would have been able to see so many of my relatives! Several of my great-granddaughters lived there at one time or another, including Jane, Veronica and Sally Hague, each of whom worked there for a few years.

April Stern (née Sampson), my great-granddaughter through Florrie, lived in London for ten years. She first attended the Cordon Bleu School and had a wonderful job preparing lunches for executives on Park Lane. She must know a lot about mashed potatoes, especially the fancy kind! Later, April worked as a secretary, first for a firm of solicitors and then for a property agent which means she knows about food, the law and houses which is really everything of importance.

Living in the capital was a lot of fun for a young woman in the 1970's, but it could also be dangerous. April was close to three bombs which were set off by the Irish Republican Army: the first near Selfridges, and the second close to her office in the City. A third incident took place in July 1982 when April and her mother, Ruth, were walking outside Harrods in Knightsbridge. A bomb was detonated in Hyde Park, tragically killing eleven soldiers and seven horses.

April, however, was destined to soon to leave the capital. She married Philip Stern in September 1982, and the couple made their home in the Wirral, Cheshire. They settled into the community and, over the years, would each serve as captain and co-captain of the Royal Liverpool Golf Club.

My great-great grandson, Rupert Hoskins, was also a long-time London resident. Rupert is the son of my great-granddaughter, Hilary Schonhut.

Many of the younger generation live in various parts of that sprawling city now: Mimi MacCaw and her husband, Ben Lewis, live in a beautiful flat in Harlesden, with their baby, Mina Stella Lewis. Mimi's brother, Joseph MacCaw, and his fiancé, Audrey Falkner, live in Deptford. Robert Hague teaches in Camden and lives in Wood Green.

Richard Ogley, a great-great-grandson through Lizzie, lives in London with his wife, Karalyn, who is from New Zealand, and their daughter, Isla. Richard is an executive with a well-known television station. And Emily Houghton, a great-great-great granddaughter, also through Lizzie, now lives in London.

It would have been marvelous if we'd been able to meet all these wonderful young people. We'd enjoyed ourselves, of course, but what a time Margaret and I would have had if we'd had all these young relations to keep us company!

Having seen the Burlington Arcade and, with neither of us inclined to purchase any of the merchandise, we'd continued with our sightseeing. We'd visited St. James Palace and then walked down to the Mall and headed toward Buckingham Palace. My mother had loved the monarchy and a portrait of Queen Victoria, dressed up in her jewels, velvet and furs, was one of the few pictures hanging on the wall of our home in Billinghay. My father would look at it and snort in disgust and sometimes point angrily at Her Majesty during one of his rants, but he accepted my mother's fondness for her and allowed the picture to grace our little home.

Like my father, I'd never understood why we were supposed to believe that the Royal family was better than the rest of us. After all, every man and woman in Great Britain knew that the monarchy was possessed of castles, palaces, lands, jewels and servants far in excess of what any family, large or small, could possibly use or need. But everyone seemed to accept that their place was high up above us all and no-one ever was ever able to explain, at least not in a sensible manner, why we should drop everything when royalty came to our village or town.

I know everyone enjoys a good show and there's nothing to match a royal pageant, but it seems quite wrong that we should stand in the street waving, bowing and curtseying to people who have power over us. Shouldn't we be the ones being driven by in a fancy coach while they stand and wave at us? But the only time that seems to happen is when our boys are sent marching off to war.

However, whether or not it was because of my mother's picture of the Queen on an otherwise bare wall, I'd been genuinely interested in Queen Victoria. Until she died in 1901, she had been our monarch since before I was born. I used to imagine her in Buckingham Palace with Prince Albert, and wonder what she did all day with so many servants to take care of her husband, her home and all her children. But I would remind myself that, as our Queen, she would have duties and responsibilities beyond the average wife and mother and that would account for most of her time.

Later, I'd wondered the same thing about Queen Mary who, as the wife of King George V, wasn't the reigning monarch but would no doubt be busy making sure His Majesty was taken care of and everything in the palace was ship-shape. And, of course, she'd have to be constantly dressing up for ceremonies and banquets which I would find tiresome, but Margaret and my daughters and granddaughters would have thoroughly enjoyed. Those girls would willingly change clothes ten times a day, and would have been happy to be born into the Royal family so they could wander around in finery, furs and diamonds, all perfectly suited to every occasion. Fortunately, they hadn't been born to spend their lives in a pantomime, but lived and breathed with the rest of us, so

I suppose there was nothing wrong with indulging their love of dressing up whenever they got the chance.

Whatever we thought of the monarchy, there we were in London and neither I nor Margaret wanted to miss the chance of going to Buckingham Palace. I must admit that as we walked up the Mall and the palace came into view, I'd felt a twinge of disappointment. Like everyone who sees Wentworth House on a regular basis, we forget that it's bigger than Buckingham Palace and that even though that palace is the home of our King and Queen, our big house is so much grander.

Though we'd been disappointed in the size of Buckingham Palace, we'd loved seeing the King's Guards dressed up in their brilliant red jackets and tall black busbies. Margaret had admired the tailoring of their uniforms and the straight backs of the young guardsmen who'd looked so strong and dignified. I'd admired their fortitude and the discipline that was required to guard the palace without showing any nervousness or fear. Margaret said that they are trained to be sentries and their job is to guard the palace gates and not be afraid.

I'd laughed thinking of my own time standing guard at Potter Hill Farm. My stepdaughter had quickly turned to me, her brow furrowed and a question spreading visibly across her serious face. I'd said that I wasn't laughing at Buckingham Palace or the Guards but was thinking of the times I'd been on sentry duty. She'd smiled and guessed, correctly, that I was referring to the times I'd had to shield her father from the invading ladies.

Margaret had quickly added that my objective had not been to protect her father, but to get him for myself. She'd then laughed so loudly I'd nudged her to be quiet in case someone in the crowd was listening. As Margaret had grown older, I'd related my guard duty stories to her. But she'd been such a sharp little girl that she'd known all along what was going on at the various entry points to Potter Hill Farm, whether it was the kitchen door, the front door or the garden gate.

I would enjoy sharing my guard duty stories with my great-grandson, William Hague, who, with his wife, Ffion, also lives in London. Their flat is close to the Houses of Parliament where William was Member of Parliament for Richmond, North Yorkshire, for twenty-five years. He also served for four years as Foreign Secretary, during which time he traveled the world many times over. William and Ffion are now The Lord and Lady Hague of Richmond. Having a cup of tea with them would be like meeting the King and Queen, only more exciting because we're related!

It's amazing to think that my grandmother was a pauper, my father a poor shepherd, and my great-grandson is a Lord. It shows you how people's circumstances can change in a few generations. It makes everyone more optimistic if you know you aren't stuck where you start in life. William was leader of the Conservative Party for a time, which means he and Ffion have a lot of experience dealing with visitors and reporters and with constant demands on their time.

When you have a prominent position you have lots of staff and assistants, known as gatekeepers, who manage your schedule and make appointments and turn people away when necessary. Funnily enough, the expression 'gatekeeper' came into being during my lifetime, just in time for me to use it. We'd always understood that gatekeepers serve as guards, like the wonderful sentries at Buckingham Palace. But later the word came to describe people who are guarding someone else's time and interests. I would enjoy speaking with today's gatekeepers because I would give them a very sound piece of advice: if you are the gatekeeper, you must stand at the gate.

You will think that sounds obvious, but it isn't because, unlike the King's Guards, you will have other duties. While you are supposed to be guarding the gate, you will be scrubbing pots in the scullery, stirring white sauce at the range, changing bed sheets, hanging out the washing, chasing Georgie around the back garden, or rushing down Potter Hill to the greengrocers. It won't be your fault, but you will be negligent in your gatekeeping duties. The gate will be, literally, unattended.

The King's Guards know they must never leave their posts and that it is their sworn, solemn duty to protect the King and Queen, even if it means sacrificing their own lives. I trust today's gatekeepers know not to leave their posts, no matter how many entry points there may be and however access may be achieved, which I understand is complicated nowadays. But back in 1877, my own gatekeeping duties required my constant vigilance if I was to protect not only Mr. Smith's time and interests but, what would become a matter of life or death importance to me, my own.

XIX

The invasion began with a rhubarb crumble, which was funny considering how much I'd always loved the sharp, tangy taste of spring rhubarb. When we were youngsters, we would climb over the wall of a neighbor's garden to snatch up some plump juicy stalks and scuttle back across the wall, carrying our bounty in our skirts and shirts, running home as fast as our legs would carry us. Once safely home, we would beg our mother for a cup of sugar so we could dip the pink and green stalks in it and enjoy the delicious mixture of sharp and sweet.

My mother used to mumble that we shouldn't steal the rhubarb, but she always said it in a half-hearted way as if she knew she was supposed to tell us off but didn't really believe her children were doing anything wrong. Most likely this was because the rhubarb patch in question was enormous and the house and garden of its owners so much bigger than our own. It was also a rare treat that kept us all quiet and, after some elbowing and jockeying to get the best position, we would be at peace with each other for a while.

Even our father wouldn't say much, telling us only not to get caught. But he would remind us not to take too much of any one plant and never to eat the poisonous leaves. My parents were scrupulously honest and so proud that only sheer necessity made them accept other people's cast-offs. But they seemed to believe that justice would look favorably upon a bunch of poor children helping themselves to someone else's plentiful rhubarb crop.

I hadn't immediately learned the name of the bearer of the

rhubarb which had unexpectedly arrived in a large, perfectly browned rhubarb crumble at Potter Hill Farm a few days after my arrival. However, I'd been sure that the person who delivered it hadn't climbed over any walls recently. The lady was short and exceptionally round, and looked as if her days were spent not only baking, but enjoying the fruits of her labors.

That this particular visitor got to the back door and stepped inside the kitchen before I was aware of her existence was my first warning that my gatekeeping skills had to improve. But I might as well admit that I'd found myself defenseless against a widespread local practice: that of walking straight into someone else's house without so much as a knock on the door.

Mr. Smith had made it clear to me that he had little use for visitors, other than his children's friends who were always welcome as long as they left when he arrived home for his meals. As you know, Potter Hill Farm emptied of all children, except its own, the moment Mr. Smith stepped across the threshold.

Though he was always hail-fellow-well-met when out, Mr. Smith considered his home to be a sanctuary where he could be assured of being free of the demands of others. He'd made it clear to me that he saw everyone he wanted to see during the course of his business day and his regular schedule in the village's public houses. If someone wanted to see him, they knew where to find him.

I'd agreed that visitors could be a nuisance and remarked that he should be happy he didn't live in a vicarage where the interruptions were constant. He'd laughed out loud and said that there was no possibility of him occupying a manse and that he hoped I'd had my fill of church people because I wouldn't find any at Potter Hill Farm no matter how thoroughly I might sweep its corners. In fact, he'd added, I would have to travel across the Atlantic Ocean and all the way to Utah Territory to find a member of the family who was a true believer. I'd been too busy to tell my employer that I had no idea where Utah was, although I was soon to learn.

Mr. Smith did insist, however, that William, Mary and Margaret should go to Sunday School each week as all the village children attended and the Smith children must, therefore, be present. Jessie and Herbert were now too old to go, although Jessie was frequently up at the church seeing her dressmaking customers. Georgie would be sent when he was a bit older. Needless to say, Sunday morning was always a rush to get the children ready to walk up to St. Mary's before the bells rang. Thankfully, by the time my four were old enough to go, they were able to attend Sunday School at the Methodist Chapel at the bottom of Potter Hill which was a lot closer.

The baker of the perfectly-formed rhubarb crumble which had arrived that morning turned out to be a Mrs. Jones. She'd stepped into the kitchen while I'd been in the scullery bringing in the washing in the nick of time before it got soaking wet. It was the second time that morning the rain had started teeming down and I'd been about to put the washing on the rack where it would dry.

I hadn't been expecting to find anyone in the kitchen. The children were at school and Georgie was having his rest and I'd jumped when I'd seen a dark, solid mass standing just inside the door. Seeing my discomfort, Mrs. Jones had let out a loud cackle and then slowly looked me up and down and remarked that I was a young little thing and would have my hands full with the Smith family. I'd decided not to acquaint her with that fact I could no longer be considered particularly young, but instead had started to introduce myself and to say that I was pleased to meet her.

Mrs. Jones had wobbled across the floor and placed her dish on the table saying she'd known Mr. Smith had a sweet tooth so she'd put extra sugar in the rhubarb and the crumble mix. This had puzzled me as, in the few days since I'd arrived, Mr. Smith had politely refused any of the cakes and buns I'd offered him. Perhaps Mrs. Jones knew him well or, more worryingly, maybe he didn't like my baking. I'd looked at the pie and thought about the extra sugar and how it would ruin the balance of the sweet and the sharp, and thought that even my brothers knew not to put too much sugar on their rhubarb stalks.

I'd thanked Mrs. Jones for baking such a lovely crumble and, using what I'd learned from witnessing Mrs. Browne's expert handling of unwanted visitors, had started to walk towards the door. This sets the expectation that the guest should leave, Mrs. Browne had instructed me years ago, adding that most people will follow you and, before they know it, they will find themselves outside saying goodbye. But, instead, Mrs. Jones had pulled a chair out from under the table, scraping it on the floor in the same rough manner as young William, and had sat down with a big heaving sigh.

Later that evening I'd written to Mrs. Browne asking why Mrs. Jones hadn't followed me to the door in the same way all the unwanted vicarage visitors had dutifully tripped after her. A few days later she'd replied saying that I hadn't been forceful enough. You must lead with a firm foot, she'd written, and never allow an uninvited visitor to sit down as you will have to work too hard to get them out of the chair to which they've helped themselves.

Your job, Mrs. Browne had reminded me, is to reduce the amount of work whenever possible and not to add time-wasting tasks. This saves not only your employer's time but also your own which, she'd added in her usual wry manner, is undoubtedly more valuable. She'd ended by saying she missed me greatly but was delighted to know that I was taking such masterful control of my new household.

Receiving Mrs. Browne's letter had made me realize how much I missed her and how little I shared her confidence that I was in control. With each passing day I'd felt the exact opposite was happening as, although I'd established numerous routines and set firm expectations with the children, I would easily become flustered when it came to their father. I'd even giggled and felt my face flush one day when Mr. Smith had complimented me on the tenderness of the meat in the stew, adding that there is no more valuable addition to a household than a good cook. I couldn't recall a single time when either Mr. Harrison or Reverend Browne had made me blush. It would take that tearful scene in the pantry before I would accept the true cause of my discombobulation.

Having failed to get Mrs. Jones back across the threshold, I'd spent the next few minutes learning more than I wanted to know about her circumstances. She'd been widowed the previous year, her children were all grown-up and the ones who'd given her grandchildren had moved far away which, she'd added wiping tears from her pudgy cheeks, shouldn't be allowed. She was lonelier than she could ever have imagined and her poor husband wouldn't recognize her sitting in the house all alone when for the past thirty years she hadn't had a minute to herself. She'd always had so much to do that even he'd sometimes told her to sit down and take the weight off her feet.

A substantial weight it was, I'd thought. But she'd added that she was so unhappy she wasn't eating right and had lost weight, and I could only imagine the size she must have been just one year earlier. It was on this particular day that I'd been forced to acknowledge, though only to myself, that I'd felt the first pangs of jealousy when faced with a woman who was interested in Mr. Smith. However, I'd quickly soothed such feelings by telling myself that he wouldn't be interested in such a big woman. I hadn't known for sure, but I suspected neither of Mr. Smith's wives had been large or fleshy. The children were all of regular height and lean like their father and, most likely, their mother, Mary Crawshaw.

At that particular time I didn't know about Eliza, the first Mrs. Smith, but imagined later that she'd been a dainty young woman. I'd stand at the sink scrubbing a mountain of dirty pots and picture Eliza, a pale but pretty invalid lying on a little settee as her young husband indulged her every fancy. Still later, I would struggle to force this image from my mind as it ignited in me flames of jealousy that my husband had not only loved Mary, the

125

mother of his children, but another wife before her. I'd had not one, but two, dead wives to contend with.

Years into our marriage I sometimes wrestled with jealous feelings brought on by the image of a much-loved Eliza. One day, in one of those self-pitying moods when we look for reassurance only to find the exact opposite, I'd asked my husband if Eliza had been like a delicate little flower he had loved and indulged. George had smiled and said he had been young and in love and very sad when she'd become so ill. But, he'd added, even when sickly, Eliza had been tough and had not allowed anyone to treat her like an invalid. He'd added that she was small and so slender she looked as if a gust of wind would blow her over, but people were much mistaken if they judged her by her slight appearance because she'd been strong until she was overtaken by the disease which killed her.

Unfortunately, this description of such a tough young woman had given me a new image to wrestle with, forcing me to waste valuable energy pushing away my jealous demons. I would calm myself down, however, by reminding myself that both Eliza and Mary were dead and I was very much alive. And it was comforting to know that my husband loved women whose small bodies housed genuine strength. It takes a strong man to love a strong woman.

Yet before learning of Eliza's daintiness, I'd known Mr. Smith would not be interested in a woman like Mrs. Jones. I'd known also that the rhubarb crumble was not a gift from a friendly villager who wanted to ensure a bereaved father and his children had a nice sweet, but was a ploy to get the widower's attention. As I'd struggled to listen politely to Mrs. Jones, I'd turned back to the pile of dripping washing.

Pulling the rack down from the ceiling, I'd started to fill it with the children's dresses, shirts and trousers. As I'd hung dozens of garments, Mrs. Jones had watched with such a look of sadness on her face that I'd felt guilty for having a house full of children, though none of them were mine. It wouldn't be long before any feelings of guilt or sympathy for Mrs. Jones, or the other callers I would meet, would be gone. It soon became clear that the friendliness they showed me, and the confidences they entrusted me with, were designed only to make me their ally. They showed an interest in me just to make sure I would be of use to them.

It would be another two years before I'd be able to sit back and chuckle not only at my own happy outcome, but at the gall and naivety of these ladies who hadn't seen me as a worthy competitor for Mr. Smith's heart. A few comments had been made that I had youth on my side, as if that was the only attribute I possessed. But the rest had dismissed me as merely the cook and the cleaner and, as any housekeeper worth her salt would know, her place is in the kitchen and with the children because a man such as Mr. Smith would have many marriage opportunities and would not have to resort to courting the paid help.

It was gall that made Mr. Smith's suitors dismiss me, but ignorance that didn't allow them to accept that many housekeepers did, in fact, marry their employers. Perhaps those ladies should have considered that it's hard to fight a competitor who has the full range of a man's home and who is growing daily in the hearts of his children. Or, at least, in some of them.

XX

I wish I could tell you that I grew to love all the Smith children and that when I married their father I'd been happy to have a ready-made family. I would be a better woman if I could say that the seven of them were as dear to me as if they were my own. The film version of my life would make it so and we would all skip off the screen hand-in-hand, stronger together, ready to face whatever the future might bring. Of course, we would all be singing – this time with the father joining in. But the only singing coming from the Smith children was when the young ones were at school or church.

I'd realized as that first summer in Potter Hill Farm began that the Smith boys and girls were mourning their mother. The weather didn't help as it rarely stopped raining and the entire summer was downright cold. William had continued in his rambunctious, insolent way to ignore my rules and requests, few as they were. The following year he would move out of the house, working and boarding a number of miles away.

I didn't miss William after he'd left and, although Mr. Smith's eyes were glistening and his voice scratchy on the morning his son departed, he'd known William needed to be tested. Working for his father and being waited on by the family's housekeeper would not bring out the good man William had inside of him, Mr. Smith remarked to me after his son had gone. He will always remember his mother, he'd added, but now he won't be reminded of her every time he comes home and finds she's not here. He'll remember her, but forget her as well.

Mr. Smith had paused for a moment that morning and I'd turned to face him afraid I would find tears running down his cheeks. But, instead, a wry smile had spread across his face. William won't find forcemeat balls waiting for him every day either, he'd added, and that will make him appreciate what his mother, and you, both did for him.

With Herbert's long, solemn face it was hard to know what he felt, though he was never any trouble to me and he was a great help to his father. But I'd seen his eyes light up when his sisters made a fuss of him and known that Herbert's loss of his mother had been softened by the older girls. Jessie constantly checked his shirts and trousers for holes, stitching them up often when he was still inside them. Herbert would act as if she was bothering him and tell her to leave him alone, but it was clear he enjoyed her attentions.

Annie often came around and, though she rarely stayed long, she'd pick Georgie up in her arms and hurry upstairs or dash outside to find William and Herbert. Years later, when in his thirties, Herbert made a very happy marriage to Mary Townsend and I believe he chose a bride well because he'd been close to his mother and sisters. Herbert was a good husband to Mary and a wonderful father to their three children, Henry, Hilda and Herbert.

One of the darkest times in my husband's life began in 1902 on the day Herbert died, suddenly and tragically, at the age of forty one. It had started as just another day at Smith's Builders with Herbert up on Church Street where they had almost finished the terraced houses opposite St. Mary's Church. Needless to say, those well-built houses stand to this day. One minute Herbert had been giving instructions to a young apprentice and the next he was on the ground. The terrified lad ran for help but by the time he'd returned with a doctor, Herbert was gone.

Not only had my husband lost another son, he'd lost his business partner and the future of the building company. Though my husband never fully retired, as the years had passed and he'd grown older it had been Herbert who'd built the houses and got the work done. My husband was seventy-five when Herbert died. He had no plans for Clement to join the business and, given that particular era and the fact that the owners of the company laid brick, mixed cement and moved stone, there had never been any discussion of one of the girls taking over the building firm.

Nor would my husband have considered bringing someone into the business from outside the family. The truest statement in the world is that blood is thicker than water. I am still surprised to see from Far Yonder that blood runs freely from our veins when we are cut. You would expect it to congeal in a thick mass the second it leaves our body.

Herbert's death had marked the beginning of my husband's decline and it had been clear that the business which he'd founded would go with it. He took care of Herbert's widow, Mary, and made sure she and the three little ones did not want for anything. But there would no longer be a business to pass on to the next generation.

George had started Smith Builders, Herbert had kept it going, and now it was to be over. It would be a long time before there were builders in the family again. But now our great-great-grandson, Mark Hague, is a builder in Huddersfield, where he lives with his wife, Marietta, and their children, Harry and Evi. Simon Schoch, husband of Charlotte (née Goodswen), is site manager for a company which builds timber frame homes in Canada. My husband would be proud of them both, and be truly interested to learn about how the life and work of a builder has changed in the century since his death.

Back at Potter Hill Farm that first summer it was clear that Annie and Jessie had no need of a new mother and believed my place was that of housekeeper and not a member of the family. I'd been certain that Annie had a high regard for all the work I did and was happy that her younger brothers and sisters were so well taken care of, but she had no interest in getting to know me.

Jessie continued to live at home for several years before she became Mrs. Chambers and, though she eventually warmed up to me, I spent a long time feeling a cold wind whenever Annie or Jessie blew through the house. There is no lonelier feeling in the world than being with people who are ignoring you. It's less upsetting to be in conflict with an angry boy, such as William, than to be disregarded.

Before I'd arrived in Greasbrough, Mr. Smith had written to say that he would instruct the children to call me Miss Mary. He'd thought Miss Stennett was too formal for someone who lived in the family home, and Mary would be too familiar. He was right and I'd been grateful that he'd set the right tone with the children.

The only one who had taken issue with this style of address was young Mary, who referred to me as Miss Stennett, unless she thought she could get away with 'her' or 'she'. Mary rarely could, as not only did her father and I correct her and remind her that it is rude to refer to another person that way, but Margaret, her younger sister by two years, was always quick to jump in and correct her sister.

"Miss Mary!" Margaret would exclaim in exasperation as Mary asked Miss Stennett for more bread or said 'she' had told her she had to wear an old dress for school because her favorite one was still damp on the rack. Or she had told 'her' she was going to her friend's house for tea after school and she didn't see why she had to ask 'her' for permission.

At nine years of age Mary had known perfectly well that refusing to say my name because it was not only the same as hers, but was the name of her deceased mother, would leave its mark. I'd tried to ignore her rudeness, knowing she was missing her mother deeply and she could not bear that, having been named after her mother, she now had to accept another Mary living in her home.

One morning Mary had become upset when I'd told her she couldn't leave the breakfast table until she'd cleaned her plate. She'd wailed that she wasn't hungry and why couldn't her mother come back? Why was there another Mary in the house when all she wanted was the real Mary, her mother, to come home to her own Mary? It had been a sorrowful scene and I hadn't taken offense as I'd seen how much little Mary yearned for her mother.

Mr. Smith had gently pulled her up from her stool and taken her to the big chair by the front window in the parlor. Usually he left the house immediately after breakfast, but that morning he'd put Mary on his knee and settled down in the chair with her. He'd spent a few minutes pointing out the birds flying outside the window. She'd nestled into the crook of his muscular arm, rested her head against his shoulder and soon joined in smiling and pointing to the starlings and swallows that swooped in the sky.

As I'd watched silently from the hallway, I'd heard her give a little squeal of delight when a baby blackbird landed on the windowsill. I'd been grateful to Mr. Smith for taking charge and I'd softened my heart towards Mary when I'd seen that all she wanted was comfort from her father.

You won't be surprised to learn that Georgie was my delight! Whenever I picked him up he would wrap his arms around my neck and his pudgy legs around my waist and hold on tight. I often wondered what thoughts ran through his little head and if he remembered his mother, but from the first day I'd known that however big the loss of losing her, I made him feel better. At the close of the days when William had challenged me and Annie and Jessie had ignored me, I would get Georgie ready for bed and I would lie down with him until he went to sleep. At those times I knew that in Greasbrough and Potter Hill Farm I had found the right place.

XXI

Just as I'd taken great comfort in Georgie, I'd known that Margaret found comfort in me. Though she was never short of friends, Margaret always came home straight from school and would sit at the kitchen table as the rock buns cooled on a wire tray right under her nose. Those big sweet buns stuffed with currants soon became a tradition which belonged to me as much as to her mother, and I'd known little Margaret was happy to have me waiting at home.

So much did Margaret come to value my presence that when I'd told her my sister, Ann, was getting married and I would be asking her father for two days off to go to the wedding, she'd become upset. That means you won't be here for me, Margaret had cried. I'd explained to her that even if her father approved of me taking the time off, I would be gone for just two nights and would be back, eager to see her and to get back to work.

Ann's wedding was taking place in Huntingdonshire where she'd worked for a number of years as a housemaid for Mr. and Mrs. Nathaniel Royds and their two children. Mr. Royds was the Rector in Little Barford just outside St. Neots and, judging from Ann's frequent letters, the rectory was a great deal quieter than the Shireoaks vicarage. The Royds' employed three other servants which seemed like a luxury to me who had only had Fred, good as he was after I'd taken him under my wing.

Mr. Smith had seemed taken aback that I was asking for a whole weekend off when I hadn't been with him but two months, but he'd quickly recovered from his surprise and said he would not stand in the way of a young woman being present at her sister's wedding. He'd asked if I had enough money for the train fare and had nodded approvingly when I'd assured him that I still had the vails I'd earned at the vicarage. I'd be able to buy my ticket and have plenty to spare. I'd already gleaned that my employer was careful with his money and I knew that his confidence in me increased every time he paid the bills at Willey's butchers and the Rhoadhouse shop, discovering they were less than he expected them to be.

I'd been excited to be going to Ann's wedding and had written to my family to say that I would take the train to St. Neots and fervently hoped some of them would be there. I'd been doubly happy to be going as I'd recently missed the wedding of my brother Thomas. Just a month after I'd arrived in Greasbrough, Thomas and Hannah had married in her home town of Warwick. It had been too far for me to go when I had just started a new position.

At least I'd be there to see Ann get married to Henry Loweth and to witness the start of their life together. Henry was a railway signalman from Yaxley in Huntingdonshire and they were to move to Lincolnshire after the wedding. Ann was twenty-seven when they married and they would have six children together. She was forty-eight years old when she had Joseph, her last. Sadly, though five of their children would be hale and hearty, their second youngest, Thomas, perished when he was but four-years old.

Just as on the day of my arrival, Mr. Smith had instructed William to come home at noon on the day of my departure, as was usual, but to stay to help with my bag when the delivery man – the same tradesman who had dropped me off at Potter Hill Farm a few weeks earlier – came to pick me up to take me to the railway station. I hadn't known until the day of my departure what Mary thought about my going away although I'd been sure she'd hoped I would be going for good. Like all the children, Mary had been told that I would be leaving immediately after dinner on Friday and would return on Sunday and that it was important they ate their dinner quickly – as if that was ever a problem – so that I could leave in time to go to my sister's wedding.

Earlier that morning I'd placed my little bag at the bottom of the back stairs, all ready to go. Mary had arrived home from school for dinner and had stopped dead in her tracks as she'd stared wide-eyed at the bag. In one of those instances where our faces reveal our feelings before we have opened our mouths to speak, her eyes had lit up and her pretty face broken into a broad grin. I'd caught her eye and she'd quickly dropped her smile and replaced it with a puzzled frown, but I'd seen her gleeful expression before she'd attempted to conceal it.

I'd realized that Mary had been hopeful that my claim to be going to a sister's wedding was a ruse for me to escape from Greasbrough for good. Or perhaps she hoped that her father had sacked me and was letting me leave under the pretense of a family wedding. But if my resignation or dismissal were too much for her to hope for, there was the chance I would be taken ill and unable to return or, if all else failed, train service to Rotherham might be cancelled forever and it would be impossible for me to get back to Greasbrough.

Without dropping my gaze from Mary's eyes, I'd smiled at her and said that I would be gone for two nights and would be back on Sunday afternoon. With that Mary had pulled her chair out from the kitchen table and sat down to eat her dinner. But after a few hurried mouthfuls she'd turned to her father and asked if she could please leave the table because Miss Green, her teacher, had asked her to be back at school before the other pupils. Her father had not noticed the exchange between me and his daughter and gave his permission for her to leave. Mary had gobbled what was left of her food, placed her plate in the sink and hurried out of the door.

Dinner had soon been done and as I'd cleared the table and hurriedly washed the pots I'd recalled Mary's ladylike teacher who, only the day before, had arrived at Potter Hill Farm hand-in-hand with her young pupil. Mary had bounded into the kitchen pulling

Miss Green behind her and the teacher, still holding Mary's hand, had asked to speak to Mr. Smith. I'd explained that Mr. Smith wouldn't be home until six o'clock when the family had their tea. Miss Green's fair face had furrowed in confusion and she'd stared down at Mary as if surprised to learn her father was at work and a housekeeper was in charge. Teachers are intelligent people and would know that this arrangement couldn't be considered surprising in the middle of an afternoon, so I'd guessed that Mary had purposely misled Miss Green into believing her father would be home.

Miss Green had soon recovered her composure and started to move further into the kitchen. I'd known I had to take control and so, with a vision of Mrs. Browne sitting on my shoulder and the aid of a broom I just happened to have in my hands, I'd begun to sweep the floor in front of our uninvited visitor. In order to stay out of range of my vigorous sweeping, Miss Green had quickly taken a step backwards and retreated to the doorway.

Realizing I'd successfully prevented her from stepping further into the kitchen and, most crucially, from taking a seat at the table, I'd rested my hands on my broom and taken the opportunity to study her. Mary's teacher was slender and nice looking but, given the fine lines on her pale delicate face and the crow's feet taking hold around her eyes, I'd guessed she was about the same age as me. That would make her over thirty and, for some reason, she wasn't married.

I would write to Hattie about Mary's teacher later that evening and, right on time, my friend's reply would arrive a few days later. Hattie's letter would include two full pages, in her heavy, round handwriting, about the likes of Miss Green who think they're too good for the village lads, but don't put themselves in a position to meet anyone else. Hattie said she knew this type only too well, which I didn't doubt as she always seemed to know a lot about different people.

In a postscript to her letter, underlined twice in thick

black ink, Hattie wrote that I needed to watch myself and not underestimate the lengths to which some young – and especially not so young – women will go to snare a husband. She'd added, underlined with an even thicker hand, that I still didn't understand this even though I was thirty one years old! I hadn't needed reminding about my age, but it was obvious that Hattie had gleaned the state of my fluttering heart, even though in my letters I'd written only about the day-to-day goings on in the Smith household.

Miss Green had begun to murmur that the Smith house was obviously a hive of activity and she would arrange to speak with Mr. Smith another time. In fact, she would send a note home with Mary the following day, and Mr. Smith could speak to her at the school at his convenience. She had turned and left and Mary had walked her to the gate and watched as her teacher sauntered elegantly back down Potter Hill.

On the day I was leaving for Ann's wedding I'd hurried to finish the pots so I could be ready for the driver and I'd remembered Miss Green's comment that she would send a note home with Mary. I'd imagined the legible, pretty handwriting the teacher would use when corresponding with her pupil's father. I'd pictured the visit Mr. Smith would make to her classroom the following week. An image had started to form in my mind which I didn't want to carry with me to St. Neot's.

I wanted my mind to be free to walk out of the kitchen, climb onto the delivery wagon, stand on the platform and board the train. I wanted to arrive in St. Neot's ready to enjoy my sister's happiness on marrying her Henry, and smile as my father proudly walked her down the aisle of the Little Barford church. I wanted to wake up on Sunday morning eager to catch the train back to Rotherham and hurry into the kitchen to do nothing more than clean and cook and look after the Smith family.

I didn't want to be at Ann's wedding burdened with a growing fear. I didn't want to worry that a chance I'd barely hoped for would slip away in the two days I'd be gone, or that I would awaken from a deep slumber before my prince came into view. As I'd stood at the sink, I'd been forced to accept that as eager as I was to go to Ann's wedding, a piece of me wouldn't be leaving Potter Hill Farm.

EARLY SMITH ANCESTRY
WILLIAM SMITH
(1709-?) *m. unknown*

GEORGE SMITH
(1727-?)
m. Hannah Parton
(1734-?)

GEORGE SMITH
(1756-?)
m. Charlotte Turner
(1769-1855)

WILLIAM SMITH
(1796-1864)
m. Elizabeth Foulston
(1801-1872)
daughter of Joseph Foulston
(1778-?) and Martha Batley
(1783-?)

Mary, George, Jane,
James, Eliza, Herbert
See extended tree

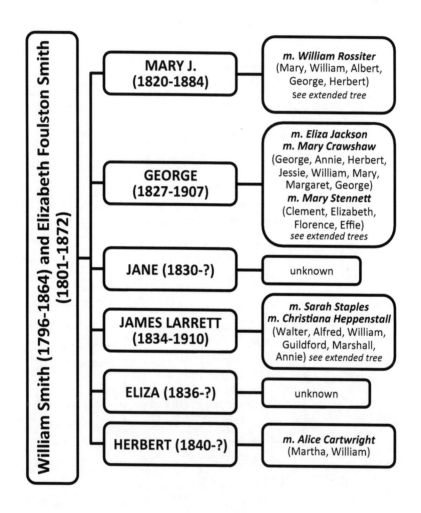

XXII

One afternoon in the early autumn of 1877, Mr. Smith called me into the parlor after dinner and asked me to sit down and make myself comfortable, saying he would be going back to work a bit later than usual. He said that since passing the age of fifty, he'd been giving a lot of thought to his life and to his origins, and found himself thinking often of his parents.

Mr. Smith had talked to me about his family during an earlier talk in the parlor and I was interested in learning more about them. His father, William Smith, had been born in Wentworth in 1796 and was the blacksmith at Wentworth Estate. William was the son of George Smith, born in 1756, and Charlotte Turner, born in 1769. Charlotte lived to the ripe old age of eighty six, dying in 1855. William's father, George, was the son of George Smith, born in 1727, and Hannah Parton, born in 1734. That's a lot of the same names to digest and mull over!

Mr. Smith's mother, Elizabeth Foulston Smith, was born in 1801 in Wombwell, Yorkshire, the daughter of Joseph Foulston, born in 1778, and Martha Batley Foulston, born in 1783. Joseph was from Darfield and Martha from Felkirk, two villages just a few miles from Wentworth.

The Smith family records go back to the generation before George and Hannah, having been traced back to a William Smith, born in 1709. Unfortunately, the name of his wife is not known. That particular William Smith was the great-great-grandfather of our own George Smith. Starting in 1709 and counting to the present day, the Smith family spans over three hundred years and includes eleven generations of descendants.

Mr. Smith kept a photograph of his mother in the parlor and, whenever I dusted it, I would stop for a minute to look at her. The photograph was taken in a studio like those taken of me, decades later, at the Gidden Studio in Southport which I'm pleased to know are still in the family's possession. In the photograph, Mrs. Smith is seated with a little book in her hands and I am always struck by her slender, delicate fingers. I don't know how she kept those fingers so fine considering how much work they must have done.

Mrs. Smith is a trim, elegant lady with a gracious smile and, with a white bonnet tied becomingly around her face, bears the mark of a fine lady, though she was neither born into privilege, nor lived a life of luxury. Elizabeth Foulston married William Smith on December 10, 1819 and the couple christened their first child, Mary, less than six months later on June 4, 1820. The weather must have been nice, and the evenings would have been long, that previous August! Mary had been followed by our George, and then Jane, James, Eliza and Herbert, born over a period of twenty years.

Mrs. Smith passed away on August 9, 1872 at the age of seventy one, following her husband, William, who had died eight years earlier on July 4, 1864, at the age of sixty seven. The couple share the same grave at Old Holy Trinity Church in Wentworth.

From looking at her photograph, I became fond of Mr. Smith's mother, particularly when I learned that as a widow she was lodge keeper at Thornwell Hill in Wentworth Park. Mrs. Smith was a gatekeeper! I'm sure she did a better job of it than I did, as by that time in her life she would have had fewer distractions and, unlike me, would always have had a welcoming smile for those passing through her gate.

The occupancy of Thornwell Hill Lodge would have been given to Mrs. Smith in lieu of a pension and was a testament to the importance of her late husband's position. The blacksmith was an important man in the big houses of the nineteenth century, producing everything to do with hot iron – horse shoes, hinges, equipment, tools, and much more. The blacksmith reported to the Master of the Horse, one of the Estate's senior professionals, usually a former military officer. At its peak, Wentworth House would have owned over one hundred horses, all crucial to every aspect of the Estate: farm work, transportation, riding, racing, hunting and social activity.

William Smith would have been taken on as an apprentice, most likely at the age of ten, starting during the time of William, the 4th Earl of Fitzwilliam, and lasting into that of Charles, the 5th Earl. Over the years, his role as the blacksmith would have included managing the blacksmith's forge in the stable block in the park, as well as the shop in the village. William would not live to witness the village blacksmith's shop being turned into a garage, as it was early in the twentieth century when Sibray Wheatsheaf returned from the First World War and opened up a garage to service the growing number of cars being driven around the village. Today, the property which housed the blacksmith's shop and, later, the garage, is a popular restaurant named 'Le Bistro', owned by Angela Hawkins.

William and Elizabeth Smith's children spent some of their childhood living in Lousy Bush, an idyllic enclave nestled at the bottom of a quarry where a gate provides access, one of several, into Wentworth Park. Lousy Bush consisted of two cottages and, traditionally, one was occupied by a keeper for the Estate, and the other by a woodsman. The census of 1851 records William and Elizabeth Smith residing in one of the cottages, though William was neither keeper nor woodsman, but the blacksmith. With the couple were Jane, James, Eliza and Herbert. The oldest two had left home by that time: Mary had gone to London where she had married, and George was with his first wife, Eliza.

Lousy Bush must have been a wonderful place to call home, but the cottage in which the Smith family lived would never belong to them, nor any keeper, woodsman or blacksmith. The Lousy Bush cottages were owned, like hundreds of others, by Earl Fitzwilliam. To the present day, the Fitzwilliam Wentworth Estate rents out numerous houses, farms and business premises on fifteen thousand acres in and around the village of Wentworth. The big house, Wentworth Woodhouse, is now owned by a private trust and is open to the public.

For many years in the mid-1900's the woodsman's cottage at Lousy Bush was home to Jack and Hilda Buttery. Jack was a woodsman for the Estate and spent decades clearing brush, felling trees and chopping wood, always setting aside the ash to be used up at Wentworth House. Ash lights easily and burns well and, on the Estate, was referred to as "gaffer's wood". Gaffer is Yorkshire for "boss"!

In addition to Jack's stewardship of the Earl's hundreds of wooded acres, he and his wife were in charge of opening up the gate at Lousy Bush for members of the Fitzwilliam family, as well as for the visiting aristocrats and gentry who wished to take that particular route into Wentworth Park. The gate also provided access to the 'iron stag' where guests were required to prove their marksmanship before being allowed on a shoot. Jack and Hilda Buttery were gatekeepers too!

Jack and Hilda's gatekeeping duties would most likely have ended with the 10th, and last, Earl Fitzwilliam, Thomas, who died in 1979. But they stayed on as tenants at Lousy Bush and never changed, no matter how many years passed, always preferring to live as if it was still the time period in which I lived. Just up the lane from Lousy Bush is Cortworth Cottage where my grandson, Nigel Hague, and his wife, Stella, lived for many years. Their children and grandchildren always enjoyed walking down to see Mr. and Mrs. Buttery when they were home for a visit.

Jack and Hilda Buttery were truly bewildered by the willingness of the Hague offspring to live so far away from Wentworth. But they would graciously open their garden gate to let in their visitors, and politely inquire about New York, London and Hong Kong as if they too were familiar with those far off cities. It was popularly understood that neither Jack nor Hilda had ever traveled as far as Sheffield, and that a trip to Rotherham or Barnsley was, to them, the equivalent of flying to the other side of the world.

On one particular visit, Jane's daughter, Mimi, was walking down to Lousy Bush with her mother and brother, Joe, when she heard the plaintiff mewing of a kitten. As a cat lover, Mimi could not ignore the sound of an abandoned kitten begging to be rescued. She'd taken the frail little creature to her grandparent's home and, after tearfully accepting that her new charge could not be taken back to Hong Kong, left the kitten with Nigel and Stella at Cortworth Cottage where, like its neighbors down in Lousy Bush, it enjoyed the rich, free life of a country cat.

But back in 1877, as I'd sat in the parlor of Potter Hill Farm, Mr. Smith had been keen to talk about his brother, James. When young, James had moved down south to work as a prison warder at Her Majesty's Convict Prison in Dartmoor, Devon. He'd married Sarah Staples in Smithfield in London in 1859, but two years later Sarah had died, at the age of twenty, and James had returned to Yorkshire.

In 1861, James married Christiana Heppenstall from Grimethorpe. At the beginning of that same year, James became head gamekeeper at Brodsworth Hall, an estate just a few miles north of Doncaster. Unfortunately, his tenure at Brodsworth Hall lasted less than two years as James had been dismissed in May 1862.

Mr. Smith had gone on to say, in a solemn voice, that as head gamekeeper, his brother had been entrusted with money far beyond his own wages. Just as his father, the blacksmith, had been in charge of paying his apprentices and workers, the head keeper would pay the wages to the other keepers out of money provided to him each week by the landowner or the Estate Office. The head keeper was also given funds to cover many kinds of expenditures, including food for the dogs, expenses related to prosecuting poachers, and money and ale for those who helped find nests. There were also expenses for night watchmen and the gun maker's bill. It's a big responsibility, Mr. Smith added, and it's essential that the head gamekeeper is a known and trusted man. That's why the job is often passed down within families.

James Smith had been made head keeper at Brodsworth Hall in spite of his family not being known there, and Mr. Smith had been certain that would have ruffled a lot of feathers. A year and a half later when the manager at Brodsworth dismissed him, James had taken off with much of the money that was meant for the keepers and for the payment of other expenses.

Within a couple of years, James had returned to Wentworth where the Smith family was well-known. In Wentworth, the Smith name had earned a great deal of trust and respect and, as William Smith had impressed on his errant son, was not to be treated lightly. James had later been given a job as a gamekeeper at Wentworth Estate, but left a few years later to move to Nottinghamshire.

Throughout that time, the first of James and Christiana's six children had been born: Walter and Alfred in Brodsworth, and William in Wentworth in 1866. By the time their fourth child, Guildford, was born in 1870, James and Christiana had moved to Sneinton near Nottingham. The last two children, Marshall and Annie, were born in Sneinton.

Mr. Smith added, with a puzzled expression on his face that, though his brother had been christened James Smith, he had added Larrett to his name. I'd commented that maybe he liked the sound of it, or he'd seen it as a way to set himself apart from others of the same name. A common problem, as you know! My employer had promptly replied that the way to distinguish yourself was by your behavior and your work, not by giving yourself a fancy name. I'd become silent at this terse, but nevertheless true, remark. But then Mr. Smith had laughed saying he, too, thought Larrett was a good name and perhaps he should have thought of it himself.

With that, the invisible gong had gone off in his head and he'd jumped up and rushed out of the Potter Hill parlor and gone back to work. I'd sat for a minute thinking about Mr. Smith's brother and his wife and children, and hoped they would turn out alright. I would learn more about them during my own lifetime and from Far Yonder.

James Smith died in 1910 at the age of seventy six while living at Thorneywood Rise in Nottingham, predeceasing his wife, Christiana. At that time, Nottingham was the heart of the world's lace industry and their children were employed as lace workers. Their eldest son, Walter Smith, was a lace dyer, and his wife, Mary Kine, a lace clipper. Walter and Mary had three children, George, Walter and Gertrude.

The second son of James and Christiana, Alfred, was a hosiery trimmer and, unfortunately, little else is known about him.

The third son of James and Christiana was William Smith. He started out as a lace winder and married Ada Elnor. William and Ada had seven children: Emma, Harold, William, Ernest, Annie, Ada and Albert. Emma, the oldest child, married Francis Graham and had a daughter, Shirley. Shirley married Gordon Atherton and stayed in the Steinton area.

William and Ada's third son, William, married Millicent Fisher and had two children: Irene and Constance, the latter sadly dying of meningitis at the age of two. Irene grew up to marry George Oakland and had four children: David, Allan, Sandra and Linda. Those children are the great-great-grandchildren of James Larrett Smith.

William and Ada's daughter, Annie, never married and was a member of the Salvation Army. She played the trumpet in the band. William and Ada's youngest son, Albert, married and had one son, John Smith.

Now we go back to James and Christiana and their fourth son, Guildford. Born in 1870, Guildford was employed as a cotton spinner. He married Annie Woods and had four children: Annie,

Sarah, Elsie and Guildford, a little boy who died during childhood. Annie became a cotton winder and married Fred Vertigan who was killed in the First World War. She then married Alfred Wall, a steeple jack, and had three children, Alfred, Edna and Cecil.

Guildford and Annie's second daughter, Sarah, was employed as an embroiderer. She married Tom Bowling, a soldier who fought at Ypres in the First World War. They had one son, Guildford Bowling. That boy married Joyce Daft and had two children, Susan and Jane.

Guildford and Annie's third daughter was Elsie, who married Albert Healey and had one son of the same name.

The fifth child of James and Christiana Smith was Marshall, a lace maker who married Mary Cook and lived in Nottingham. Marshall and Mary had six children: Harold, Ada, Ethel, George, Guildford and Lewis.

The last child of James and Christiana was Annie. Annie married William Stanley and had five children. The only two to survive infancy were Jane and James. James Larrett Stanley was born in 1898 during his grandfather's lifetime. James Larrett Smith must have been happy to know that the name he'd bestowed upon himself was to live on through his grandson.

James Larrett Smith (1834-1910) and Christiana Heppenstall (1839-?)

WALTER (1862-?) *m. Mary Kine*
George, Walter, Gertrude
ALFRED (1864-?) *unknown*

WILLIAM (1866-?) *m. Ada Elnor*
Emma *m. Francis Graham:* Shirley *m. Gordon Atherton*
Harold
William *m. Millicent Fisher:* Irene *m. George Oakland* (David, Allan, Sandra, Linda), Constance
Ernest, Annie, Ada, Albert

GUILDFORD (1870-?) *m. Annie Woods*
Annie *m. Fred Vertigan, m. Alfred Wall:* Alfred, Edna, Cecil

Sarah *m. Thomas Bowling:* Guildford *m. Joyce Daft* (Susan, Jane)
Elsie *m. Albert Healey:* Albert
Guildford

MARSHALL (1874-?) *m. Mary Cook*
Harold, Ada, Ethel, George, Guildford, Lewis
ANNIE (1876-?) *m. William Stanley*
Jane, James Larrett

XXIII

I've always fondly remembered a bright, sunny Monday morning walking up Potter Hill with my mind filled with thoughts of lovemaking. This will surprise you as you think sex and romance hasn't so far been a part of my life. You're right, but that doesn't mean I didn't think about it, often more than I would have liked. Once it enters your mind, it's hard to get it out, as I'm sure you all know.

This isn't such a problem for you now as it seems you can have sex with anyone of your choosing, and you don't have to be married or even spoken for. It wouldn't be seemly for me to comment from Far Yonder on the love lives of my descendants, except to say that you've been free to do what many of us could only dream of back in the 1800's!

Not that we were all pure and innocent. My youth could have been more fun if I'd been a girl who blushed and giggled and who, in spite of her protests, spread her thighs in the cornfield, and kissed and cuddled in the haystack. This sometimes worked out well, as it obviously had for Mr. Smith's parents. But a girl often got what I hadn't wanted – marriage to the first lad who got her with child. I hope you appreciate how fortunate you are to have control over the consequences of your fun!

I've noticed that nowadays people talk about lovemaking in a very free and open way. My husband wouldn't approve of it as, though he bore the name "Rabbit George", he wouldn't tolerate people talking about sex in public. If the men on the building site started to joke about their antics, or if he heard such talk in the public house, he would interrupt the teller of the tale and tell him to keep his stories to himself.

Those same men might have been surprised to learn that, after I became his wife, my husband often talked to me about sex. I was also certain that George had spoken in a similarly open manner to Eliza and Mary. Like I've said before, my husband enjoyed talking to his wives and had no reason to end his conversations at the bedroom door.

You might say it's easy for a man to disdain open discussion of sex when, firstly, he was living in the nineteenth century and it wasn't talked about like it is now, and, secondly, George Smith was a man with nothing left to prove. When you're "Rabbit George" and your brood serves as a constant reminder to all of your virility, you have no need to show-off.

But not all men have their reputation speak for itself in such an obvious way, and it isn't surprising if they sometimes feel the need to let people think they're a bit of a lad. There were plenty of other "rabbits" around even if they weren't given the recognition! There still are. Again, I don't want to comment on the love lives of our descendants but the "rabbiting" didn't end with my dear husband. It's just that now you can control the consequences.

"Rabbit George" would never admit that his nickname and his children gave him an advantage in proving his manhood. Not that he would have imagined it could ever be called into question. But if anyone approached him with a smile and a wink, a sure sign they were about to make a remark about his "rabbiting", he would stop them before they could get out the first word.

Staring at them dead-on in his usual confident manner, he would say that while he never forgot for a minute that he was blessed to have sired twelve children, he had also never been free for a minute from shouldering the responsibility of them. This remark would bring a swift end to the topic of sex, but would turn it to everyone's next favorite subject – money.

Much to the frustration of his companions, my husband also refused to discuss money in public. He believed it to be a similarly private matter and, like sex, not a subject to either brag about or to disclose intimate details. He believed that talk of money should be confined to business transactions only and he liked to remark that whenever two men talked about money, one of them, if not both, would be unhappy by the time the conversation ended. If more than two men talked about money, he would add, it was likely all of them would be unhappy at the end of the discussion.

I'm happy to say that he and I often talked about money and that, in spite of the times in which we lived, he considered me a worthy partner when it came to helping him manage his business and household accounts. I credit the school in Billinghay with providing me with a good grounding in arithmetic and making it possible for me to understand and manage finances. Education is so important and I wish I could have stayed in school for many more years. I hope you know how lucky you are – in so many ways!

But it was me who was feeling lucky that Monday morning as I'd walked up Potter Hill on my way back from Willey's, with my mind flooded with imaginings about lovemaking and romance. It might have been the warm autumn weather which had surprised us all by settling in a few days earlier and had been a rare treat after such an awful summer. Or it might have been that I was feeling more confident about my position in the Smith household and, especially, my employer's good opinion of me even if it was limited, as far as I knew or dared to believe, to my skills in the kitchen and my efficient, thrifty running of his home.

My good spirits that morning were also buoyed by the fact that Mr. Smith had finally grown tired of the procession of ladies and their offerings of baked goods. Just the day before, he'd forbidden any more food deliveries from one of our regular callers, Mrs. Bowman, a widow who'd been dropping off tasty meat pies each week for the past few months. Mr. Smith and the children were enjoying her pies to a degree which made me nervous, even though having a good pie to pop in the oven once a week saved me some work.

But when both Mr. Smith and William asked when Mrs. Bowman would be bringing round another pie, I'd known I had to step in and take the upper hand. Mr. Smith's interest in Mrs. Bowman might be limited to her pies, but it hadn't escaped my notice that the recent widow was a handsome woman who was always smartly turned out. To add to her attractions, she had her own cottage at Nether Haugh which I imagined was a very cozy place in which to receive gentleman callers. And I knew that Mr. Smith was often at Nether Haugh where his friend, David Yeardley, farmed. Mr. Smith and Mr. Yeardley were such good friends that my husband made David Yeardley co-executor, with our son Clement, of his Will.

A few days had passed and Mrs. Bowman had graciously dropped off another pie. She'd looked spry and not in the least bit fatigued from her walk down The Whins, up Cinder Bridge, down Main Street and up Potter Hill. She was always polite and friendly and not nearly as pushy as some of the other callers, so I'd felt guilty standing at the back door thanking her for the pie, knowing it must be the last. But I'd known that I must end her growing popularity in the Smith house and the only thing to do was to render her pie inedible.

Later that morning I'd slathered a mountain of salt and pepper across the crust, carefully injected more salt into the pie's center, heated it up in the oven and served it for dinner. It's a sin to waste food when so many go hungry and it had been with a heavy heart that I'd spoiled Mrs. Bowman's perfectly lovely pie. Right on schedule, Mr. Smith had come home at noon for his dinner and sat down at the table. He'd taken one mouthful and spat it out onto his plate. Mr. Smith has good table manners and the children were so surprised to see their father spitting out food that they'd laughed out loud. Furious that he'd been served bad food, he'd glared around the table – instantly quietening the children's laughter – and fixed his eyes on me.

I'd quickly ordered the children to put down their forks and not to take a bite. Even William had listened to me and let his fork crash down onto his plate, further annoying his father although thankfully shifting his focus from me to his son. I'd hurriedly cleared everyone's plates away and asked Margaret to set out clean ones.

With a flourish – which later I'd feared was a sure give-away – I'd brought a meat and potato pie out of the range, perfectly browned and ready to serve. Margaret had started to giggle, while Mary had looked at me with her eyes narrowed and a question spreading across her bonnie little face. These two clever little girls had known that if but one dish was made for dinner each day, how come a second pie was already baked and ready to be served?

I'd apologized to Mr. Smith for serving bad food, and mumbled that Mrs. Bowman must have made a mistake with her ingredients. He'd said that I was to get rid of the woman and her bloody pies, and everyone else's for that matter. Mr. Smith rarely swore, at least not at home, so I'd known he was upset. However, from the start he'd looked with suspicion at the offerings people dropped off, genuinely preferring his food to be prepared at home.

One thing Mr. Smith could not tolerate was inconsistency. He expected every dish to look and taste exactly the same every time you made it. He wasn't a cook and didn't know that each joint of beef is different from the last, that the range will be hotter one day than the next, or that eggs and butter and flour don't always mix exactly the same way each time. He didn't know and he didn't want to know. Remember, this is a man who got stone to do what he wanted it to do, and all he asked was that his food should look and taste as he expected.

I'd known this as clearly as I'd known that the extra salt would make Mrs. Bowman's perfectly delicious pie taste absolutely horrible. So I'd smiled and assured him there would be no more pies from Mrs. Bowman or anyone else. Then I'd served him an extra big helping of meat from my own perfect, steaming pie.

I'd known immediately upon arriving in Greasbrough that Mr. Smith was considered quite a catch. I'd learned also that Yorkshire women weren't inclined to sit back and wait for love and romance to smile upon them. They took it upon themselves, just as Hattie had in Shireoaks, to conjure up ways to bring a man to their door. It seemed the tried and true means of doing this was to get to his door first.

Just recently I'd prevented a Miss Johnson and a Mrs. Wright from becoming habitual visitors by telling them Mr. Smith insisted that his family's food be made at home. This statement hadn't been true when I'd said it but, fortunately, had become true soon enough.

After several unwanted visits from poor, lonely Mrs. Jones, I'd finally got rid of her by whispering – in a sisterly, confiding manner – that my employer insisted I work every minute of the day and not waste time gossiping with visitors. She'd looked at me with genuine sympathy, saying she didn't know Mr. Smith was such a taskmaster and, in that case, I was welcome to him.

Mrs. Jones's comment was evidence that she believed she had a chance of attracting such a man as Mr. Smith, and that it was she who was dismissing him as a suitor rather than the other way round. From Far Yonder, I've noticed that men often have a cockeyed view of their own attractiveness to the opposite sex. But Mrs. Jones was proof that women could be just as silly. One thing, however, had become abundantly clear to me during my first few months in Greasbrough – I was in coal country and there were too many women mining the Smith seam.

I'd come back from Ann's lovely wedding feeling stronger than when I'd left. I'd decided to do battle with my jealous feelings and force myself to believe that Miss Green's interest in the Smith family was no more than that of a teacher for a favorite pupil.

My reward for getting a grip on myself had been to learn that Miss Green had a real reason to speak to Mr. Smith. She needed his permission for Mary to play the lead role in the Nativity Play which the children performed at school every December.

I'd been relieved to hear that the pretty teacher's visit hadn't been a ruse to stick her nose in Mr. Smith's face though, to be fair, Miss Green wasn't the forward type. But my relief had soon been tempered by the news that young Mary was to play Mary. If the Smith house already had one Mary too many, I didn't know how we were going to make room for the Virgin Mary herself.

It could have been the fine autumn weather, or my growing comfort in the Smith home, that had put sex on my mind as I carried the pork sausages home from the butchers that morning. Or it could have been that I'd been pondering, as I often had, how the Virgin Mary could have given birth without having relations with Joseph nine months earlier. It might have been that I'd become keenly aware I'd be thirty two years old come January, and that the mother of the Messiah and me had one very significant thing in common. Not that I'd received a visit from an angel, or given birth to a baby boy. Not yet.

XXIV

I still get nervous when I watch you boarding aeroplanes and see how much you trust those big hulking machines to carry you safely across continents and oceans. Aeroplanes were invented during my lifetime, but I always believed my feet should stay on the ground. In the early 1900's I read about the brave Wright brothers over in America, and before I died in 1932 it had become possible to fly to many places in the world, including as far off as Australia.

Years after those original men and their flying machines took flight, my great-great-grandson, George Stern, studied Aerospace Engineering at university. He went on to get a job in traffic management in Leeds which just shows you how many vehicles are on the road, and the number of aeroplanes that are up in the air, if someone has to monitor who's going where and when they are going. I don't think anyone other than the station master and the kindly tradesman had known that I could get a lift from Rotherham Station to Greasbrough on that April morning back in 1877.

George Stern also worked as a ski instructor in Canada, so it's obvious he's happy when he's up high. His brother, Edward Stern, lives in China, where he works in hotels and studies at Wuhan University. Edward speaks Mandarin which is hard for me to even imagine! The boys' mother, my great-granddaughter, April Stern (née Sampson), and her husband, Philip, visit Eddie in China which is a very long way to fly. They also ski every year in Europe and America so it seems all the members of the Stern family like to be up in the air.

Here in Far Yonder, I calm myself about the dangers of you all flying around by imagining that the plane is the body of an angel and the wings are the angel's wings carrying you safely to your destination. I understand that you are willing to take the risk of flying so you can travel far and wide, and you accept that being packed in like sardines, strapped to your seat, staring in front of you for hours on end is what you have to endure to get to faraway lands.

I see that the airlines at least give you your dinner and a drink, and I'm sure it's nice and warm in the cabin and you can snuggle under a blanket and go to sleep. That is, unless you are a daredevil like my grandson, Nigel Hague, who seems to think that traveling on the wings of the aeroplane is a better way to see the world.

Nigel, the youngest of my daughter Effie's four children, was a little devil when he was a child. Fast and athletic, he was good at any sport he took up, whether it be football, cricket or, in his later years, squash. Nigel got his sportiness from his father, Bert, who in his youth played football for Rotherham Town. Bert also played for Yorkshire Amateurs and always remembered the summer of 1914 when the team was on tour in Germany. Just as years later in 1939, Bert's daughter, Pauline, would be on a Mediterranean cruise which was swiftly terminated when Britain declared war on Germany, Bert's football tour in Germany had been cut short. On August 4, 1914, Britain declared war on Germany and the players had to leave that country immediately to avoid internment.

Nigel was also a good shot and brought home many a dinner of pheasant, partridge and grouse, as well as venison from Scotland and ducks, quail, teal and widgeon from Ireland. Accompanying Nigel on the trips to Scotland and Ireland was Arthur Hartley, husband of Lizzie's granddaughter, Joan Schonhut. Arthur was a Greasbrough lad, the son of Walter Hartley and Amelia Dowling. The Hartley family lived in Greasbrough for many generations and the majority of the men were either miners or iron workers. The Hartley and Dowling girls all went into service until they were married. But Arthur, being in business, was in a better position than most and on their trips he and Nigel would go shooting and deerstalking during the day and eat a good dinner and drink Guinness and Scotch whisky in the evening.

Arthur's son, Robin, was fortunate enough to be invited to go wildfowling with them one year. At just sixteen, and with his own 12-bore shotgun, he joined the menfolk on their annual wildfowling trip. Also shooting with them that year was Eric Skin of The Black Lion in Firbeck, a popular public house near Worksop.

Nigel's shooting prowess had begun when he was seven years old and his father bought him an air rifle. At that time, they lived at Rossiter Villa which was number 9 Rossiter Road, and a Miss Grayson lived next door at number 11. On the day Nigel became the proud owner of a new air rifle, he'd naturally been eager to put it to use and had roamed around the back yard looking for targets. A group of blue tits were gathered in a tree close to the next door neighbor's wall. Seizing upon the tempting target of such sweet little blue and yellow birds, Nigel had picked up his new rifle and started firing. Within seconds, five dead blue tits landed in Miss Grayson's back yard.

Miss Grayson had a maid named Annie Lizzie, and a few hours later the young girl knocked on the back door of Rossiter Villa. Bert opened the door and greeted his neighbor's maid with his usual welcoming smile.

"What can I do for you, Annie Lizzie?" asked Bert.

"Miss Grayson says you have to come and look at her tits!" Annie Lizzie tremulously replied.

Needless to say, Bert never missed an opportunity to entertain his pub mates with this tale. But he would make it clear that, all humor aside, he'd gone back into the house that day and boxed Nigel's ears for shooting harmless little blue tits.

Always a lad, young Nigel's idea of courting was to throw stones late at night at his sweetheart's bedroom window at Manor

Farm on Church Street in Greasbrough. He always hoped that pretty Stella Jefferson would open her window before her two sisters, Marjorie and Mary, discovered him, and definitely before their father came bursting out of the back door. Jack Jefferson was a marvelous shot and Nigel knew that he would need all his athletic abilities to keep out of his way.

It turned out that World War II would get Nigel out of his future father-in-law's hair, as he was conscripted at the age of seventeen and sent to Germany as a member of the occupying forces. He returned and married Stella on May 16, 1949, beginning a wonderful marriage which lasted until Stella passed away on November 26, 2008, almost sixty years later.

Not too long before Stella died, her husband, a keen hillwalker, expressed his desire to climb Scafell Pike, the highest peak in England. Nigel had recently celebrated his eightieth birthday hiking up Helvellyn in the Lake District with his family, or at least those who were willing to join him on such a strenuous walk.

On the day of the Helvellyn hike in September 2008, some of the women in the family chose to read and relax at their lovely lakeside hotel or go shopping in nearby Grasmere, rather than risk life and limb on an unforgiving peak. Ffion and Veronica, however, chose not to read or shop but took off with Nigel and the menfolk. Also with them were some experienced climbing friends who'd joined them to hike three thousand feet up into the clouds. It wouldn't be everyone's idea of an eightieth birthday celebration, particularly as the walkers went across Striding Edge, a dangerous sharp ridge from which hikers fall to their deaths every year. Fortunately, they all made it back down again.

There are many good walkers in the family. April and Philip Stern have trekked in the Himalayas several times. Nothing seems to stop any of you from doing what you want to do!

Nigel had told Stella that in addition to climbing Scafell Pike, he wanted to jump out of an aeroplane as he'd been disappointed that during his time in the Army he hadn't qualified as a paratrooper.

Stella told Nigel that if at the age of eighty he was crazy enough to do stupid things, he should at least do them for charity. And so, for Nigel, a new passion was born and he soon completed a treacherous climb of over three thousand feet up Scafell Pike in the Lake District, raising tens of thousands of pounds for the National Society for the Prevention of Cruelty to Children (NSPCC).

Sometime later, Nigel abseiled down Hoober Stand in order to raise money for the Wentworth Cricket Club. Hoober Stand was built for Thomas Watson-Wentworth, the Earl of Malton, after he fought for the British government against the 1745 Jacobite rebellion. King George II elevated the Earl to the 1st Marquess of Rockingham. The views are beautiful from Hoober Stand, but it is a strange looking building and is one of a number of "follies" in and around Wentworth Park. The building has no practical purpose and, though its walls have a distinct slope, I doubt they were designed for people to walk up and down.

Like the Stern family, Nigel likes being up in the air. His next stunt was to parachute out of a plane at ten thousand feet, landing in Grindale, near Bridlington, again raising tens of thousands of pounds for the NSPCC. But the best was yet to come.

In May 2012, Nigel took his first trip on the wings of an aeroplane. On behalf of the NSPCC, he stood on the wings of a small plane and flew over parts of Yorkshire. He must have enjoyed it, because he was to do two more wing walks.

On June 6, 2014, then aged eighty-five, Nigel was strapped onto the wing of a bi-plane and flown across the English Channel from Calais, France to Lydd, Kent. The date was chosen to coincide with the 70th Anniversary of the World War II D-Day landings. The wing-walk was Nigel's personal tribute to the servicemen who lost their lives in the invasion of Normandy. His son, William, was Foreign Secretary at the time of the commemorations and had joined Queen Elizabeth II and many other heads of state in France.

At the same time William Hague stood solemnly with the

dignitaries in Normandy, Nigel was up in the air strapped to the wing of a plane flying for forty minutes in the open air across the English Channel. He had mentioned to his son that he ought to fly over the exact spot where the ceremony would take place, to which William had promptly informed him that if he so much as attempted to enter a designated "no-fly zone" he would get a missile up his backside!

I have no idea what a "no-fly zone" is except I wish I could have had one in the kitchens of Shireoaks and Potter Hill Farm. Keeping flies off the food was a constant battle and I spent many hours of my life swatting bluebottles with a rolled up newspaper. But I don't think it was the risk of flies bothering Her Majesty and all those presidents and prime ministers that forbade Nigel from flying over and waving down to his son that day.

That wing-walk raised a great deal of money for Lost Chord, a dementia charity based in Maltby in South Yorkshire. Nigel said that the only problem he had when he was up on the plane was that a fly got into his goggles! I suppose that's because he wasn't in the "no-fly zone"!

Nigel's last wing walk took place in December 2015 at an event for the Save the Children Fund where he joined numerous other – equally mad – people who jumped out of aircraft and traveled on the wings of planes. Between them, they raised over three million pounds. Nigel was eighty-seven by then and had to finally accept that his barnstorming days were over! He had thoroughly enjoyed doing his charity stunts, and was fortunate that Beryl Brown was on hand to provide much-needed companionship and moral support.

I'd like to think that my husband and I could take credit for our grandson's tough attitude, but it's more likely he got it from his father's side of the family. Bert Hague had fighters in his family, most famously his cousin, James William "Iron" Hague.

"Iron" Hague was a boxer and the British Heavyweight Champion from 1909 to 1911, winning many of his matches with knockouts. When he returned from winning the title in London in 1909 – a knockout in the first round – thousands of people lined the streets of Mexborough, Yorkshire, to welcome him home. "Iron" Hague also served in the military. He joined the Grenadier Guards in World War I and saw action in several battles, including the Somme in 1916. After a lifetime of boxing and fighting for his country, "Iron" Hague died at the age of sixty five at home in Mexborough, where he is buried in the local cemetery.

Many of the men from the Smith and Stennett families joined up when they were needed, serving in numerous branches of the military. We will always remember my grandson, Wilfred Stennett, who didn't come home, as well as all those who were lucky enough to survive. During World War II, Lizzie's son, George Schonhut, rose to the rank of captain in the Army and was responsible for supplying food to the British army in Italy and North Africa. Florrie's oldest boy, Arthur Holroyd, was a Major in the Army and his brother, Peter, was also in the service.

George Schonhut and Arthur Holroyd enjoyed some adventures together during their lives. In 1952, George entered his Rolls Royce in the Monte Carlo Rally in the south of France. At that time, you could enter the Rally with your own vehicle, although later it would be considered astounding that you would enter such a race with your own Rolls. Arthur had joined his cousin on the Rally, during which the pair encountered a number of mishaps. First they hit ice and spun off the road, losing too much time to keep up with the leaders. But they carried on to Monte Carlo, whereupon a lorry ran into the back of them which meant they could not qualify for a prize for the most prestigious car. I'm sure they enjoyed being in the Rally as much as they would have enjoyed winning.

My grandson, George, lived a good life and his time would come to a close, though much too soon, doing something he loved. George Schonhut died on the course at Thrybergh Golf Club in 1962 at the age of fifty one.

Because of the Second World War, many of that generation served in the forces. More recently, some of the young ones have shown an interest in the military. Lucy Hague, a great-great-granddaughter through Effie, enlisted in the Army and later trained for a computer job with the Ministry of Defense. There are a number of young men who lean towards a career in the military, including my great-great-great-grandchildren Charles Tear, Alexander Tear, Henry Tear and Joshua Sayers. Young Joshua is in the Royal Air Force Air Cadets and hopes to be a pilot in the Royal Air Force. I'm relieved to see that nowadays pilots sit inside the plane and don't have their heads sticking out of the top. Nor do they fly on the wings, like Nigel.

I'm glad the adventurous, patriotic, and volunteer spirit runs through the family. It's important to serve your country and community. Some of my great-great-grandchildren are doing more than their bit: Jonathan Ogley is a fireman in Worcester, a very dangerous job. Not everyone is capable of rescuing people from burning buildings, but it's wonderful when those who able are willing to do it.

Fleur Shaw and Kay Goodswen are health visitors with the National Health Service, visiting patients in their homes. Fleur's husband, Matthew, is a chemist and water pollution expert. Mark Stephenson is a director of a company which provides supplies to dentists. Everyone has a full set of teeth nowadays which is marvelous. There is nothing more important than your safety, your health and your teeth! I hope you appreciate them, most especially the privilege of having clean water running right out of the tap.

Sometimes the most important things we do are not for pay, but as a volunteer. I wasn't able to join civic clubs and organizations when I was working, and didn't have time when I was married and had step-children in addition to my own four. By the time my children were all grown, I was busy helping with the next generation of the Smith family. Charity begins at home!

But many of my great-grandchildren go far beyond their own

families in providing help to others. Jane MacCaw volunteers with The Silver Line, talking to lonely old people who have no family or friends, and Charles Hague works with homeless people and makes sure they get fed, particularly at Christmas when they are alone. April Stern volunteers with young students at the Wirral Design and Fine Arts Society, and restores antique books at The Athenaeum Library in Liverpool. Sally Foster volunteers as a companion with Ryedale Carers Support, assisting people with dementia.

Whether you are working or volunteering to help others, or are raising money to help those in need, you are doing something good. But I'd be relieved if you wouldn't travel on the outside of a plane in order to do it.

XXV

Back in the 1800's life was a constant round of births and deaths. Both were ever with you and taking place around you, and you could only hope and pray that the rule of natural order would be followed. When I say natural order, I mean that the old would go according to their age, and always before the young. Sadly, too often it was the little ones that left us first.

There are other rules to follow, though nature itself doesn't care about such things. One of these is the rule that says a wedding should take place at least nine months before a baby is born. Of course, the child will be born either way, although I agree it's better for all concerned if the mother and father get married first. But you don't have to get the timing exactly right. If a baby arrives eight months after a wedding, you can still put on a straight face and act surprised that the little bairn came so early.

I'm not bringing up the timing of weddings in order to point a finger at my daughter, Florence, although it might as well be mentioned here. Florrie and Arthur Holroyd were wed in April 1908, and in July of the same year Florrie gave birth to baby Arthur. None of us could explain how such a big, bouncing boy could have been produced in three months and we didn't try. My husband had passed away the previous summer and, fortunately, didn't have to go to the trouble of silencing those villagers who wouldn't have been able to resist pointing out that his "rabbiting" had been passed down to his children, or at least to his daughter, Florrie.

I didn't blame Florrie and Arthur for getting caught doing what countless other couples got away with, but I'd been upset with my daughter for not letting me know sooner about her condition. As you know, at Lizzie's wedding two years earlier, she'd been in tears because she wanted to marry Arthur so badly. So why did she take her time telling me she was in the family way when she would have been guaranteed a quick ceremony? I was never given a satisfactory answer or, in fact, any answer at all.

Florrie was bewildering at times, often behaving in contradictory ways. It's a shame to say this about my own child, but later in life she became a bit of an oddity, living in a shabby house and barely getting out.

Florrie was such a contrast to Lizzie and Effie, her two elegant sisters with their beautifully furnished houses and manicured lawns. Both those girls spent a great deal of time working in their gardens: Lizzie at "The Elms" on Sledgate Lane in Wickersley, and Effie at "Fairleigh" on Moorgate Lane in Rotherham. They each paid gardeners to help them, but nevertheless did a lot of the work themselves.

Lizzie loved to visit famous parks and gardens and would take cuttings from shrubs and plants, which probably wouldn't be allowed today. In particular, Lizzie loved roses, always pruning and dead-heading them to keep them in bloom. With her bonnie fair face, she was a true English rose. Upon Lizzie's death, her ashes were scattered, as she wished, in the rose garden of remembrance at the Rotherham Crematorium.

Florrie and Arthur had five children: Arthur, Effie, Neville, Peter and Ruth. Florrie's husband died almost twenty years before her so she was a widow for a long time. But she always had the companionship of her son, Neville, who, though he lived to be ninety, spent close to seventy of those years living at home.

Had Florrie and Arthur had an earlier wedding, it would have helped present baby Arthur's arrival in a more orderly manner. But Arthur was my first grandchild, and we soon forgot that he'd been growing in his mother's womb for a full six months before she'd married his father. Arthur grew up to be a successful man who liked to be in charge, becoming an Army major and later the boss of the local water works. He married Edith Riley when they were both over thirty and the couple had a good life together.

As you know, Florrie and Arthur's daughter, Effie, had a wonderful marriage with Reginald Wadsworth and, together with their daughter, Gay, they enjoyed an elegant life. Effie loved to shop which, fortunately, the family could afford and she was a keen golfer, serving as president of Thrybergh Golf Club. Florrie and Arthur's son, Peter, married Alice Colclough and had a son, Peter. And Ruth, the youngest child of Florrie and Arthur, married farmer, Guy Sampson, and has spent a lovely life in scenic North Yorkshire.

Of course, it was not unusual to learn that an unmarried girl was expecting, and the problem was almost always corrected with a speedy ceremony. Before too long, no-one would remember whether a baby had been born the same year as the wedding or the one after. But when death came to call in the wrong order, it could never be corrected.

What everyone wanted back in the 1800's is the same as you want and pray for now: that the old should die before the young, and that the members of one generation might pass before death stakes its claim on the next. What was so tragic back when I was alive was how often death took our babies and children, leaving parents, grandparents, brothers and sisters, aunts and uncles to suffer and mourn their loss.

Birth itself killed many newborns and their poor, suffering mothers. Then after struggling into the world, the first few years were a dangerous time. Babies died because they were premature and too small to thrive, they died of cot deaths or had breathing and heart problems. Older children would come down with pneumonia, measles and all manner of childhood illnesses.

Desperate parents fervently hoped and prayed, begged and pleaded to God, whether they believed in Him or not. They made faithful promises of the good they would do and the bad they would never do again, if He would spare their baby, their little girl or their little boy. But in spite of their pleas, death would swoop in as if no-one was watching or had bothered to lift a finger to stop it.

In my own family, my two brothers, John and Joseph, passed many years before our parents, leaving us all at a loss to understand why they should have gone first. Neither was the natural order of death followed in the Smith family.

On July 9, 1869 my husband's firstborn son, George E. Smith, died at the age of fifteen. He left behind his mother and father, his sisters, Annie, Jessie and Mary, and his brothers, Herbert and William. Margaret and Georgie would be born after he was gone, and Georgie would be given the name of the older brother he would never know. A few years later their mother, Mary Crawshaw, died, leaving the world before she could get to see her youngest children grow up. Much later, Herbert would pass away, a good five years before his father.

During the same year young George Smith was taken, a total of fifty four people died in Greasbrough. Nineteen of those who died were less than a year old, and another nine were under ten. Yet 1869 wasn't considered an unusually bad year. I know it's hard for you to imagine so many youngsters dying in one year.

If today, in a single year, almost thirty children died in your little town or village, the entire community would be devastated, medical experts would be desperate to uncover the reason, newspapers would report on it far and wide, and great steps would be taken to ensure it could never happen again. Fortunately, today you have vaccinations and medicines, and you are strict about hygiene and sanitation which was sadly lacking back then.

You won't associate a country like England with cholera, but Rotherham had two terrible epidemics in the 1800's. After that, more care was taken with water, drainage and sewers. By 1869, it had been twenty years since Rotherham had suffered its last cholera epidemic, although there were plenty of people alive who knew the fear and terror of the disease. Cholera could kill you within a few hours if you didn't get treatment.

The Rotherham Cholera Burial Ground is located on Park Road in East Dene. A monument lists the names of those who died in the outbreaks of 1832 and 1849. It's important to visit this special burial ground, not only to honor those who perished, but to understand what a better world you live in now and how vital it is that you preserve it for those who will follow.

Most of all you must ensure that your water belongs to everyone and does not fall into the hands of those whose only interest is to profit. As you know, Florrie's first baby, Arthur, worked at Rotherham Corporation water works and later became the boss of the whole plant. I'm proud my grandson played a big part in ensuring so many people got a good supply of water straight from their own town and reservoirs. Never, never take clean, running water for granted – your very lives depend upon it.

One can't help but think about those children who died in 1869, and the lives they might have led if they'd survived. Their names and ages are noted on Greasbrough's Burial Register and show what a brief, fleeting chance at life these little ones had: Arthur Hall and William Skelton were eighteen months, Thomas Dawes was one, Martha Watson and Elizabeth Teal were four.

William Race and William Hopkinson were eleven months, Erdley Bryan, eight months, Ernest Ibberson, twenty-one months. Thomas Carnelly was six weeks, Arthur Fulwood and Larrett Widdison, seventeen months. Elizabeth Rodgers and John Allen were five weeks, Joseph Ward, five months, and Joseph Chadwick, nine months. George Read was four months, dying in the same year as his fourteen year old brother, also named George. That's a sad example of a new baby being given the name of his deceased brother, only to follow him so swiftly in death.

The list goes on: Edward Cook was sixteen months, Samuel Blake, ten days, Sarah Ann Hizzard, two, Lilley Stansfield, three weeks. John Clark, seven weeks, Alfred Howard, four weeks,

Florence Glossop, six months, William Monks, two weeks. Arthur Bolton was three weeks, Emma Loy, ten months, and little Arthur Lee was just two weeks old.

Several older children also died in Greasbrough in 1869: Frank Mitchell, thirteen, Mary Emma Smith, seventeen. And our own George Smith, aged fifteen.

Every year on July 9, Mr. Smith and his children would visit George's grave and leave wildflowers they would pick on their way to the cemetery. What my husband didn't know as he mourned his son on that day each year was that he was also marking the day of his own death. My husband died on July 9, 1907, thirty eight years to the day since his eldest son had passed.

In Far Yonder I've grown fond of the poem "For the Anniversary of my Death" by the American poet, W. S. Merwin. It expresses so beautifully that the date which is so important to us and will be inscribed on our tombstones, and possibly on dozens of documents, is a date we will never know.

Except I know mine. I died on May 15, 1932. I was eighty six years old and it was time for me to go. I left long before my four children, but not before my little grandson, Tony. I wish, with my heart and soul, I could tell you that every other death in the family has occurred in the right order. It hasn't.

XXVI

Baby Jesus was fussing and whimpering and a nervous titter travelled around the audience. A boy called out with a loud, piercing cry that he didn't know the baby was real! A dozen voices piped up, telling him to shut up and, though I was sitting in the front row and couldn't see behind me, I could practically feel his mother sticking her elbow into the boy's ribs.

The audience grew quiet, waiting for the play to continue but baby Jesus was kicking and his swaddling clothes had started to unravel. Mr. Smith was sitting next to me and I didn't have to look at him to know that his eyes, along with every pair in the audience, were fixed on his daughter sitting center stage, a bright light shining down upon her.

Mary started to stroke the baby's head and lowered her face close to his. The baby's eyes were shut and his mouth started to twist and everyone in the audience knew that he was ready to let out a screeching wail. Mary shifted slightly in her chair, propped the baby up a bit, pulled him tight towards her and folded her blue wool shawl around him. A fine muslin scarf covered her head – Potter Hill Farm had been turned upside down before she'd finally settled on the right shawl and headdress – and the expression on her face had not been one of panic or confusion, but of serenity and peace.

Baby Jesus settled into his mother's bosom, such as it was, and as she stroked his little fair face it became as peaceful as her own. The audience started to murmur its relief and a woman sitting next to me clapped her hands together, and everyone joined in. The noise became deafening and I was fearful that baby Jesus would be frightened and start fussing again. Mary neither looked up nor smiled, but continued to hold the baby close to her and to stare at his face as if he was truly the Son of God. With poise and maturity, young Mary Smith, our Virgin Mary, had stolen the show.

I'd been in the Nativity Play every year at Billinghay School and had always played an angel. This meant standing at the back of the stage, draped in an old sheet with hooks fashioned on the edges for you to stick your thumbs in so you could pull out the cloth to spread your wings. I'd always been content to be in the background making my wings go up and down in time with everyone else's, and none of my brothers and sisters had cared a jot about what part they played. The only difficulty had been in the autumn when we were given our parts and went home to tell our parents that, once again, the girls would be angels and the boys would be shepherds.

Every year, as if on cue on a stage all of his own, our father would snort in disgust about the stupidity of making the sons of a shepherd play the shepherds. Without giving any of us chance to say that it didn't matter or that we didn't care about our roles, he would go on exclaiming in his loud, urgent way, that things never change, that's just the way it is! Why aren't the shepherd's boys made to play the Kings? He would pause for breath, as if waiting for a response, but none of us would say anything because we knew the silence only meant he was about to answer his own question. Raising his voice even louder, our father would shout that the shepherd's lads couldn't be Kings, not even pretend ones, because that might give them ideas that they could do better than follow in their father's tired, worn footsteps.

Our mother would try to hush him, saying that the children were happy with their parts and it was just a Nativity Play and there'd be another one next year and the year after. Our father would shake his head and then go outside to turn over the dirt in the vegetable garden to ensure it was done before the first frost arrived. Every year he refused to go to the play, but our mother would attend, not wanting to miss a rare chance to sit back and be entertained and not caring a jot that her children hadn't been given the chance to seize the limelight.

Years later at Greasbrough's Nativity Play, it would be me, a former angel, who'd enjoyed being in the audience, not caring a jot that a troublesome Smith child had, in fact, seized the limelight. I'd known from the day Miss Green had cast Mary as the Virgin Mary, that she was the best choice for the lead part. She'd practiced her lines every evening and laid books out on the parlor rug to mark where she would stand on stage. Mary's fine performance on the night had been a result not only of her inborn ability, but because she had practiced until the role came naturally to her.

There's nothing like being prepared to stop you from panicking when a carefully scripted plan changes. I'd known this from my years in Shireoaks and the constant changes to dates and guests and menus. Just be ready with a mountain of mashed potatoes, I would say to myself, and you'll be able to feed as many people as Mrs. Browne can invite. On the night Mary stood on stage, she'd been ready with her own version of my mashed potatoes, and was able to soothe a fretting baby before he screeched and squawked and ruined the performance.

The real reason, however, that I'd enjoyed myself that evening was because of the person I was with and where I was sitting. I'd been happy even before I'd learned that two seats on the front row – which on arriving I'd been surprised to find were empty considering the number of people who'd pushed to sit up front – had been reserved by special request of Mr. Smith. Had I known at that time that the request had been made to none other than Miss Green, I would have slithered off my seat and melted into a puddle on the floor right there in front of the whole audience. Now that would have stolen the show!

A few days before the performance, I'd overheard Mr. Smith ask Mary if she'd invited me to go to the play. He'd taken her aside in the parlor, believing to be out of earshot, but the door had been ajar and I'd stopped what I was doing so I could hear what was said. I hadn't caught every word, but had heard Mary say she didn't need to invite me because I knew about the play and could go if I pleased. Her father had reminded her, in no uncertain terms I'd noted with satisfaction, that I was their housekeeper, lived in their home and had helped her with her costume. That meant Mary must personally invite me to go to the play.

The following morning Mary had dropped her eyes as she'd been eating her porridge and mumbled that as the whole family was going to see her in the play there would be no need for me to stay at home and that I should go as well. I'd known not to take offense at such a back-handed invitation and, instead, had smiled and said I would like to go very much and would make sure not to miss a minute of her performance. She'd gobbled down the rest of her porridge and rushed off to school and I'd felt a broad grin spread across my face.

It wasn't that I'd been happy to be going to the play that made me smile so much, but that her father had insisted I should be invited. And be invited properly. This small, but simple, fact put me in a state of excitement which for the next few days made me fumble through my duties, including forgetting washing on the line and a pie in the oven. The washing got wet, and the pie got burned.

Most alarming of all, the day before the play I'd lost my to-do list and had turned the kitchen inside out in search of it, while Margaret and Georgie excitedly ran around trying, in vain, to help find it. I'd later found the torn and twisted sheet of paper tossed on my bed as if I'd discarded it right there, which I never did. I always threw my list on the range fire after I'd crossed everything off – and only after I'd propped up the next day's list on the kitchen dresser.

It's so important to keep regular habits and to establish a routine. You can keep your mind clear if it's not cluttered up with the little jobs and tasks you do all the time. It's why Mr. Smith likes to know that he'll find his pipe and tobacco in exactly the same place on the mantel when he goes into the parlor to smoke after his dinner. It's why I write my list and put it in exactly the same place on the dresser every evening. The fact that it ended up on my bed, with some items not even crossed out, was a sure sign that I was upset and discombobulated. As they say here in Yorkshire, I'd got myself in a right state.

That night I'd got into bed and, though exhausted, hadn't been able to sleep. You would think for all my physical work that I would collapse into bed every night and sleep a deep, dreamless sleep. Unfortunately, since being a youngster I'd slept poorly and had been easily disturbed by the noises and movements of my sisters in the bed we'd shared. The only time I recall sleeping well were those nights when I'd skipped until dark with the rope Joseph made. The rhythm and repetition of skipping lulled me to sleep before I climbed into bed.

But as a grown up, no matter how hard I worked, the slightest anxiety would keep me awake half the night, tossing and turning and wishing dawn would break. My sleeplessness would finally go away when I had a good man to hold me close in the bed we shared. But I hadn't known that on the night before the Nativity Play.

Immediately after tea on the evening of the play, Mary had rushed out of the door in order to get back to school in time. Margaret had begged to go with her and, having been told by her father that she could go, had then begged to take Georgie with her. Mr. Smith had agreed and had also reminded William and Herbert, as they too headed out of the kitchen, not to be late. Jessie had already been up at school making final changes to the costumes, and Annie had told her father she would be going to the play with her friends.

Peace and quiet had descended on the kitchen and I'd hurried to clean up, hoping for a few minutes to go upstairs to tidy myself up after the bustle of tea time. I hadn't forgotten the advice of

Hattie and the girls in Shireoaks, and at least once a day I would remember to look in the mirror and check my appearance. I'd also started the habit of going up to my room for five minutes to clean myself up before the men came home. Had Hattie and the girls known this, they would gleefully exclaim that, finally, I was doing things their way. But I'd told myself I was only making sure I was neat and tidy before I served the men their food.

I'd been heading towards the back stairs fully expecting Mr. Smith to remind me, as he had everyone else, of the time the play would start and to say that he hoped I would enjoy it. But, instead, he said he was going outside for some air and would wait for me at the back gate. I'd started to mumble but then remembered Mrs. Browne's lessons in manners, and I'd turned to Mr. Smith, smiled and said I'd be ready in less than five minutes.

Mr. Smith could not abide waiting. Not for anyone. The only way he could tolerate it at all was to do something that needed doing. Walking up and down the path kicking at the bricks to check if any were loose was preferable to standing around doing nothing. I'd started up the scullery stairs and, after reaching the landing on the first floor, had run as fast as I could up to my room in the attic. I'd looked in the mirror, tucked my hair back into its pins, draped myself in the thick red shawl I'd bought for my train journey to Greasbrough, brushed a few pieces of lint off my skirt, and flown back down the stairs.

As promised, Mr. Smith had waited for me at the back gate and opened it as soon as I stepped through the kitchen door. In the brief time I'd been upstairs, I'd been wondering if he'd already regretted offering to wait for me and that he would have hurried off to take care of some business on the way, leaving me to go to the play alone. But, like so many of my anxieties, I'd been wrong.

It is pitch dark early in December in Yorkshire. Cloudy skies block the stars and, if not for gas lamps, it would be impossible to see in front of your nose. Mr. Smith was used to walking around Greasbrough at night, but that evening he brought a lantern to help guide the way. He said he didn't need it for himself, but was aware that I didn't know the streets in the dark like he did.

We'd walked down Potter Hill, with Mr. Smith taking the side next to the road. The ground was wet from the rain which had poured down all day but now, blessedly, had stopped. I'd known I wouldn't look my best if I got soaking wet! A few times I had to step around puddles and once, in a hurry to keep up with his fast pace, had almost slipped. Mr. Smith immediately thrust his arms out to catch me and then, instead of releasing me when it was clear I wasn't going to fall to the ground, had taken my arm and crooked it in his own. We'd walked together, arm-in-arm, all the way to the school.

We passed a number of people on the way, overtaking them at the first chance, as Mr. Smith also had no patience for walking behind people who were moving at a slower pace than his own. From each person there were greetings of "Evening George", "Hello Mr. Smith", "Cold tonight", "Goin' to t' play?", and, "Is that your Annie on your arm, George?"

To the last question, Mr. Smith had turned and, with warmth in his voice that I'd scarcely dared register, had replied "No, it's not my Annie. It's my Miss Mary. Miss Mary Stennett".

XXVII

What a pleasure it is to walk arm-in-arm with your husband, whether strolling along enjoying the evening air or – more likely to be the case with George – striding ahead so we could get to where we were going as fast as possible. But whether we were rushing or dawdling, some of the happiest times of my life were spent with my arm thrust through the crook of my husband's, feeling the strength of his upper arm hugging me tightly against him.

Those times together arm-in-arm, two people moving as one, were always special treats for me, whether we were out in Greasbrough or Rotherham, or were on a real outing. With my arm through my husband's, I'd felt a keener sense of belonging than I'd felt when I first became Mrs. Smith, even more than the pleasure we shared when we lay in the rumpled sheets of our marriage bed. You may be shocked by this latter remark, but I'm happy to let you know that when it came to our love life, me and George were a far cry from the lonely, practical widower and the not-getting-any-younger housekeeper.

But I'm not talking about sex right now. I'm talking about walking along, happy to be out in the world together, be it only in our village or local town. And, always, that special thrill when we were strolling, arm-in-arm, when on holiday in Scarborough or on a day trip to a wonderful place such as Harrogate.

George wasn't fond of going on holiday. His idea of a perfect day was to have his breakfast, dinner and tea at home, go to work, drink beer in the local pubs, and sleep in his own bed. The only time we went on holiday was when the children were little and we would go to Scarborough for a week – holidays never lasted a fortnight in those days. But as we grew older, I could sometimes convince him that I needed a change of scenery, and he would be willing to enjoy a day trip to a nearby town or city.

Harrogate was my favorite place. It's a beautiful old medieval city in the West Riding of Yorkshire which has always been popular for its baths and sulfur water. I was never able to persuade George to go to the Royal Baths to take a dip. Bathing was one of the many things he believed should only take place at home, and certainly never in company. Or, at least, only in the company of his wife! I agreed with him on this matter, but on each visit I'd partake of a glass of sulfur water in the Pump Room and enjoy afternoon tea at Taylor's. I think the latter did me the most good.

If I could go to Harrogate today, I would have a fine time indeed as my great-great-granddaughter lives there. Harriet Foster, and her husband, Nicholas Heron, live in a lovely Victorian house in Duchy Grove, just a quick walk from the center. Harriet works in sales for a famous food company, which is the kind of job I would have liked if I'd been able to stay at school and hadn't had to go into service. However, I know I'd be better at making the sweets and chocolates than I would be at selling them. Nicholas is a solicitor, so between the pair they've got food on the table and the law on their side and you can't get much better than that. I like Harriet's name now that she is married. She is Harriet Heron of Harrogate!

Effie and Bert enjoyed taking their granddaughter, Jane MacCaw (née Hague), to Harrogate and she remembers those visits with great fondness. It's important to take your grandchildren on outings as they will remember those special days when countless others have been lost to memory. In Far Yonder we have a saying that we die when the last person who remembers us has gone. Though I am painfully aware it doesn't always work out the way you hoped, there is a good chance that your grandchildren will live for decades after you. Make sure you have some enjoyable times with them because they will be the ones who keep your memory alive. And, if you don't have grandchildren, find a young 'un or two to spend some special time with. Those lucky children will remember you for the rest of their lives.

My granddaughter, Ruth, and my grandson, Nigel, are the last people to remember me. They are both elderly now, but Nigel recalls, as clearly as if it was yesterday, walking with me to the bridge at Willow Garth, just down the road from Rossiter Villa. He was a little boy, but remembers my Victorian clothes. Between Nigel's memory, Far Yonder and this book, I'm still going strong!

My husband, George, has been gone a long time and there is no-one left to remember him. That wouldn't bother him in the least as he believed you have one go at life and it's up to you to make the most of it. When he was with us he was very much alive, always filled with energy and busy with his life. His mind was as active as his body and he enjoyed learning about new inventions and talking about new ideas. He read a lot and could discuss the state of the country, whether with a miner or a member of the gentry. People of his own ilk, as well as others, listened to him and trusted his judgment.

Though my husband would envy much of what you have seen and experienced on your world travels, he wouldn't have wanted to take those trips himself. George's life was a rich and varied journey from start to finish, and he was quite contented that it all took place in a small corner of Yorkshire.

Fortunately, though George was not a traveler, he believed it was important for youngsters to play on the sand and in the sea. Beginning when Clement was little, and lasting until Lizzie, Florrie and Effie were grown up, we went on holiday every year to Scarborough, an old, seaside town on the north coast of Yorkshire. Years earlier, George and Mary Crawshaw had taken their children to Scarborough, and three of them, Georgie, Margaret and Mary, were still young enough to come with us.

My husband was careful with his money, but once he

committed to making a purchase or going on holiday he wouldn't try to cut corners or do it on the cheap. If we were going to spend a week in Scarborough, we were going to stay at one of the best hotels. And the best at that time was the Grand Hotel overlooking the bay which, when it was built in 1867, was one of the largest hotels in the world.

To the everlasting delight of the children – not to mention the luxury for me of not having to cook and clean for a whole week – we always stayed at that beautiful hotel. When we sat together in the elegant dining room with its fine furnishings, draperies and spotless, starched table cloths, I felt as if I was in paradise.

I wasn't to know as I stood at the reception desk in the lobby of the Grand Hotel that so many years later my great-granddaughter, Jane, would work behind that very desk. Imagine if I could have seen her standing there! And it would have been even more remarkable if I could have told Effie – who loved picking up and dropping off the keys at the reception desk like the little lady she always was – that one day her granddaughter would be there to wait on her. The same little girl that she and Bert would enjoy taking to Harrogate!

So many of you know and love Scarborough and have spent many happy times there. My great-granddaughter, Gay Stephenson (née Wadsworth), grew up spending Christmas, Easter, Whitsun, and a week every summer at the luxurious Pavilion Hotel. Gay met her husband, Bruce Stephenson, at a wedding at that same hotel so she is particularly fond of Scarborough. Her parents, Reginald and Effie Wadsworth, later owned a flat on The Esplanade, opposite the Clock Tower and the Italian Gardens. Many of you rented beach chalets on the South Bay overlooking the swimming pool, and ran freely as children to the beach and up and down the endlessly winding paths to and from the Esplanade.

When my grandson, Nigel, married Stella, her family had moved from Manor Farm in Greasbrough to Scarborough, having purchased the Delverne Hotel on Granville Road. Her mother,

Hilda Jefferson, and sister, Mary Jefferson, ran the hotel for many years. Nigel and Stella took their holidays in Scarborough, and Jane, Veronica, Sally and William grew up swimming in the cold North Sea, paddling in the warm water which collected in the rock pools, and jumping into the South Bay salt-water pool. The paddle boats at Peasholm Park and a trip on the North Bay Railway to Scalby Mills were always a favorite.

The children enjoyed the helter skelter, dodgems and slot machines in the arcades on the Foreshore. They fished off the pier, played endless games of miniature golf, and fought over deck chairs. But, before the day ended they would have a '99 from one of the many ice cream shops, and eat cockles and winkles out of a bag on the pier. A lasting memory is of the donkey rides and of Nigel racing down the beach when a donkey Sally was riding suddenly took off at a gallop. Fortunately, Nigel was faster than the donkey!

And, always, there was the ever-present figure of Stella's sister, Aunty Mary, bronzing in the sun before she went back to Delverne to prepare the evening meal for the hotel's many guests. Other than the odd sea fret rolling in, it always seemed to be nice weather in Scarborough. Childhood's hazy memories are so precious, aren't they?

Sally's mother-in-law, Margaret Foster, also owns a flat on The Esplanade overlooking the South Bay. Sally and Robert's daughters, Rebecca and Harriet, have had many opportunities to enjoy Scarborough, and their American cousin, Edward Clinton, will never forget playing cricket on Scarborough's wide, expansive beach when the tide was out.

My daughter, Lizzie, and her husband, Albert, went to Scarborough every summer with their children, George and Joan, and later George Schonhut took his own family, along with his mother, to spend Christmas there each year. George and his wife, Ethel, often stayed at the Pavilion Hotel with Reginald and Effie Wadsworth. Joan and her husband, Arthur Hartley, made sure their children didn't miss out on Scarborough, and often stayed at Delverne with Nigel and Stella. Robin and Elizabeth have many happy memories of their time there.

Scarborough was founded by the Vikings a thousand years ago which makes the difference in time between my life and yours seem short. Time is a funny thing and we must remember how brief our lives are and make the most of the flash of time we are given. It's wonderful to know that such an ancient town still has a place in the heart of Yorkshire folk.

You will think with all these happy reminisces of the family in Scarborough, and my delight at being waited on in a luxurious hotel, that I must have loved being at the seaside. Unfortunately, I was afraid of the sea from the first time I stood on the beach and watched those dark, rolling waves heading towards me. I'd grown up inland in Lincolnshire and didn't see the sea until my first trip to Scarborough after I was married.

I would let the children enjoy the water but wouldn't step in the sea no matter how much they urged me to take off my shoes and stockings, lift up my skirts, and paddle at the edge. Instead, I would stand as close as I could get to the children without getting wet. Fortunately, I never had to go in and rescue any of them, as they all quickly became capable of looking after themselves in the water and loved jumping over the waves and ducking under the spray.

One of the most remarkable swimmers in the family was my grandson, Charles Hague, who in 1951, at the age of forty, swam the full length of Lake Windermere. Charlie and his wife, Mabel, were fond of the Lake District and visited every year. During a visit, Charlie learned that one of England's most famous swimmers, Captain Matthew Webb, had declared that, for swimmers, Lake Windermere was more difficult than the sea. Upon hearing this, Charlie vowed to return the following year and complete the difficult and dangerous swim.

Captain Matthew Webb was the first recorded person to swim

the English Channel, a feat he accomplished in August 1875. Though he declined to swim Lake Windermere because of the difficult conditions, he was destined to lose his life swimming in the Niagara River below Niagara Falls in 1883.

Lake Windermere is ten and a half miles long and famous for being very deep and cold. Charlie was an experienced swimmer and had previously swum across New Pond on the Wentworth Estate. On the day of his Windermere swim, Mabel daubed Charlie in grease which, though it might not help with the cold, could prevent chafing. His brother, Nigel, rowed in a boat alongside him. Charlie not only successfully traversed the full length of Lake Windermere, but did it swimming against the current.

Like his cousin, George Schonhut, Charlie owned a Rolls Royce which is a very posh car. Soon after completing his swim, he received a telegram from Rolls Royce which read, "As an owner of one of the world's finest cars, we are mystified as to why you should choose to tour the Lakes in this manner." They must have been so proud of him!

There is less to fear from the sea when you can swim like Charlie, and as all of you do now. You've been in oceans and waters far beyond the North Sea. I've watched you plough through the waves of the Atlantic, Pacific and Indian oceans, and seen you swim in the Mediterranean, the Adriatic, the Balearic, the Irish Sea, and the English Channel. I've watched you wade into the Persian Gulf, the Gulf of Mexico and the Gulf of Oman. I've seen you bobbing and floating in the warm, blue waters of the Caribbean Sea, the Arabian Sea, the Red Sea and the Dead Sea, and in such far off waters as the South China Sea, the Coral and Tasman seas, and the Great Barrier Reef.

As good as you are at swimming, you also snorkel, waterski and sail. Robin MacCaw is an experienced mariner and has sailed many of those seas, particularly during the ten years the family lived in Hong Kong. Jane and Robin's children, Mimi and Joseph, were both born in that far-off British territory. Robin was also privileged to travel as a passenger aboard a submarine, sailing from Gibraltar to Plymouth across the Bay of Biscay.

Jane and Robin's son, Joseph, is a skilled sailor and was a member of the crew on the top sail schooner, "Eye of the Wind" which was built in 1911. Rigged as a brigantine, the ship sailed from Antigua to England in 2006, taking two months to cross the Atlantic Ocean after running into very bad weather.

Two other sailors in the family are my great-great-granddaughter, Elizabeth Sayers, and her husband, Adrian, who is an experienced yachtsman. Years ago, they bought a boat in Portugal and sailed it to Lanzarote in the Canary Islands off the west coast of Africa. Over the years, they had many holidays sailing around those islands. Such adventurers! Elizabeth and Adrian still sail and now keep a boat moored in Scarborough.

All I ever knew of those oceans and seas was what I'd learned from looking at an Atlas. But there you all are, swimming in those great bodies of water as if you're down at the local swimming baths! But, looking back, I believe from the first moment I saw the sea I'd known it wouldn't be a friend to me. The North Sea claimed Wilfred when he was brave enough to be protecting his country. And it was just a hairsbreadth away, rolling and churning in its menacing way, when Tony and Stephanie were lost to us forever.

XXVIII

My granddaughter, Pauline, was extremely sociable and loved to go out, never refusing an invitation to a party, or a golf outing, or a gin and tonic at a friend's house. She wouldn't turn down an invitation to lunch, or a dinner dance at the golf club or rugby club. She would rush out to meet friends in the pub in the evening, always with her husband, Stan, who also knew how to enjoy himself. Pauline was a wonderful hostess and would throw parties in her home, serving mountains of food and drink, and inviting people from all around.

Pauline was quick and lively, and a gifted comedian. With her high spirits and outgoing nature, you would imagine her to be an adventurous woman who was willing to go anywhere at any time. It was true that she would never miss a social occasion, but only if it didn't involve going too far from home. Pauline's reluctance to travel even made her anxious about visiting her family in Rotherham, a distance from Redcar of only one hundred miles.

When you know the ending to a story, it's easy to look back and pinpoint why someone behaves a certain way, or to be convinced that if a particular incident hadn't occurred, everything would have been different. But, we often have trouble understanding our own behavior, let alone someone else's. And though it might be experience which has created a person's fears, it could also be a deep-seated sense of foreboding.

As you know, Pauline met Stan while on a cruise in the Mediterranean, a trip she voluntarily undertook with her cousin, Joan, and which had a lasting, happy outcome. But, I believe the reason that Pauline genuinely preferred not to travel was for two reasons. The first was the terrible tragedy which took place when she was a child on a family holiday. And the second – the great sorrow of her life – occurred near her home, but in circumstances so similar to the first it would be hard not to imagine that the two incidents shared some dreadful connection.

Just up the coast from Scarborough is the picturesque little fishing village of Sandsend. At low tide you can walk on its wide sandy beach down to Whitby. Sandsend has always been a popular place for families and, in September 1929, Bert and Effie took the children to Sandsend for their annual holiday.

I didn't say anything at the time, but from the moment Effie told me they were going on holiday, I had misgivings. For the rest of my life I wished they'd stayed at home or gone somewhere else. When you are grieving, your mind constantly churns, rearranging times and places. You keep asking why, why, why, wishing you could come up with a different answer and prevent what has already taken place.

I'd thought it was late in the year to be going to the seaside, even though the weather had stayed so warm that year. And, why did Effie and Bert choose Sandsend? Why not Scarborough? They could have gone to Bridlington or Filey, or stayed in Whitby. Bert and Effie liked Flamborough. Why didn't they go there? Whatever the reasons, and whether or not they made sense at the time, they would be questioned and dissected for the rest of everyone's lives.

Effie chose a hotel in Sandsend that had reception rooms and bedrooms with views of the North Sea. She had such fond memories of staying at the Grand Hotel overlooking the bay in Scarborough. Sandsend was a good choice for Bert because there were plenty of pubs where he could find some new friends and make several more attempts to satisfy his unquenchable thirst.

Bert's new Humber was filled to the gills when the family, or at least most of them, set off from Greasbrough on a fine September morning. Their eldest boy, Charlie, was eighteen years old and would stay at home to be at the business in Parkgate. He was a fine young man and a very good worker, and hadn't needed his parents to tell him he must stay behind. Charlie was happy to be at the factory, and even happier to be free for a week of his mother's ever-vigilant oversight.

Pauline, aged nine, was wedged in the back seat of the Humber with her little five-year old brother, Tony. Pauline spent most of the journey playing games with her brother, tickling him and stroking his legs which were golden brown from playing outside in the fine weather everyone had enjoyed that summer. Nigel was just over a year old, propped up happily on Effie's knees in the front.

How Bert managed to get himself, his wife, three children, and a mountain of luggage in that car, I don't know. But, somehow they all fit in and took off on what turned out to be an easy journey, arriving in Sandsend a few hours later. How they ever found the strength to drive home with an empty seat where a dear, precious child should have been, I have never been able to fathom.

Just as despair makes you want to rearrange time and the sequence of events, it can make you believe that you knew something bad was going to happen. Like I've said, I had misgivings from the beginning, but later I became convinced that I'd known for certain they shouldn't have gone. And that it had been up to me to stop them. After all, if I'd been found dead in bed on the morning they were leaving, Bert and Effie wouldn't have gone on holiday. If I'd died a day or two before the accident, they would have come home early and wouldn't have been in Sandsend on that dreadful day. I was eighty three and it was my time to die, not the time for my little five-year old grandson.

What I remember about that day is that I was at home working in the kitchen and suddenly realized that Lizzie was standing across the table from me. It was as if she'd been transported into the kitchen without making a sound, yet she was crying so hard she couldn't speak. Albert was holding on to her as she sobbed, her body shaking so much that I'd started to cry before I could even hear what they'd come to tell me. I remember thinking that if Lizzie and Albert were here to tell me some horrible news it must not be about their family. It must be about Clement or Florrie, or Effie. Within seconds Florrie had come bursting through the door crying out Tony's name.

Unimaginably, thirty six years later, Effie would be working in her own kitchen when her son, Charlie, and his wife, Mabel, would unexpectedly appear at the back door. Effie had smiled, saying what a lovely surprise it was to see them. She'd stopped speaking when she'd seen the tears streaming down Mabel's face. Just as I had learned in 1929, Effie would be told, in 1965, of the sudden, tragic death of a grandchild. And all she would know on that terrible day was that it was her time to die. It was not the time for her sixteen-year old granddaughter.

I'd listened to the details of the accident in Sandsend a dozen times in the first few hours, but didn't take it in until later. Pauline had gone with Tony to get an ice cream, just as thousands of sisters do with their little brothers when they're at the seaside. Effie had stayed in the hotel bedroom looking after Nigel, reminding Pauline to hold on to Tony's hand when crossing the road. The ice cream cart was parked over by the sand and the road was busy. Pauline had listened to her mother, but already knew not to let her five-year old brother cross the road by himself.

As they'd waited to cross The Parade, the main road in front of the hotel, Pauline had clasped Tony's sticky, sweaty little hand in her own. He was a lively, bonny boy with a calf-lick which made his bright blonde hair stick up straight off his brow. Effie was always wetting it and patting it down, but as soon as she was done Tony would flick it back up just as if a calf had come and taken a lick at his face.

The Parade was busy with vehicles on the afternoon of September 22, 1929. The weather had been unusually warm and dry for months, and in some parts of England it was the driest it had been for sixty years. Later that year it would start raining and it would seem as if it would never stop. By that time, our hearts were so heavy we didn't care whether it was wet or dry. But in Sandsend that Sunday afternoon, people were still happily enjoying the long summer season, all too aware that it could suddenly come to an end.

Like Bert, a growing number of people could afford the luxury of owning a car and were able to decide at the last minute to take a ride out for the day. The pretty village was bustling, and Pauline's head quickly darted back and forth from left to right as she watched the cars speed up and down the street. She held on to Tony's hand, clutching him more tightly as he struggled and wriggled to be free, impatient to get to his ice cream.

Suddenly, without warning, Tony snatched his hand out of his sister's and ran headlong across the road. Cars screeched and swerved and people cried out in alarm, but it was too late. My little grandson, Anthony Duncan Stennett Hague, who just as his cousin, Wilfred, bore my family name, was gone.

Tony would have been six on March 12th of the following year. Born on the same day as his father, Bert had been thrilled to share his birthday with his little boy. It was a date Bert and Effie could never celebrate again. Many years later, however, Effie would live to welcome the arrival of her great-grandson, Nigel James Hubert Goodswen, on March 12th 1972. Also on that day, Joe Sayers, a great-great-grandson of my Lizzie, would be born in 1988.

I've never rid my mind of the notion that the last word Tony heard was the sound of his sister crying out his name. Or that, amidst the noise and confusion of the horrific scene that lay before her, nine-year old Pauline had stared up at the hotel searching for her mother's face in the bedroom window. I've imagined that she watched as Effie looked out in horror before snatching Nigel up off the floor and taking the longest journey of her life down the hotel's staircase and out into the chaos of the street.

As Pauline had looked up at that hotel, had she had a dreadful premonition that one day she, too, would stare out of an upstairs window directly across from the North Sea at the scene of a fatal accident? And, had she known, that she would look down in horror upon the remnants of that accident and the pools of her daughter's blood on the road?

XXIX

More than fifty years after the death of her little brother – and sixteen years following a tragedy from which neither would ever recover – Pauline's husband, Stan, would pass away while traveling. Just as the couple had met on a cruise ship which had been forced to head swiftly back to port, their lives together would come to a sudden close after disembarking from a boat.

In 1981, Pauline and Stan were returning from a holiday in the Isle of Man and took the car ferry to the mainland. After leaving the ferry and driving a short distance, Stan had felt unwell and Pauline urged him to pull over to the side of the road. A police car drove by and, fortunately, returned to check if the travelers needed help. Pauline was sitting in the passenger seat with her husband already dead beside her. Stanley Goodswen was sixty six years of age, dying behind the wheel of one of his beloved cars.

Stan was fortunate in life to be a prosperous businessman, the owner of a number of butcher shops. But in a similar manner to Bert Hague, his father-in-law, Stan preferred to spend his time socializing and driving around town in his Bentley, rather than being at work on the business premises. For many years, Pauline herself managed the books and the staff.

Their son, Philip, joined the family business after leaving school early. He'd contracted the Asian Flu in the pandemic of 1957, aged 15, and developed pneumonia. He was seriously ill for a year and never returned to school. Philip hated the butchering business and didn't get along with his father, so Stan's regular absences from the shop were a mixed blessing. But when his father would arrive at the end of the day to check on the receipts and the condition of the shop, Philip would find it hard to contain his frustration.

One day, late in the afternoon after a long day behind the counter serving their many customers, Philip had finished the meticulous cleaning so essential to a place where meat is butchered. Stan had pulled up outside and stepped through the door. He'd walked around the shop, stopping to point out a speck of fat under a table. The argument that resulted brought to an end, at least temporarily, Philip's involvement in the family business.

A few weeks later, Philip sailed from Southampton on the Union Castle Line headed for Capetown in South Africa. He'd taken a job as a ship's steward and, for over a year, sailed between Southampton, Capetown and Durban. Philip was about as far away from his father as he could get.

Pauline had been extremely unhappy to see her son go, having doted on him from the second he'd been born. But she would have accepted Philip's desire to get away, and given every single day of the ninety one years she would live, if she could have prevented the tragedy that would bring her son home for good. And she would have given each of those days all over again if they would prevent Philip from dying before her, leaving Pauline, in her later years, with the grim distinction of outliving both her children.

The sense of adventure that had taken Philip Goodswen to South Africa was shared by a young woman he would soon meet. Dorothy Leigh had spent two years working as a secretary in Los Angeles and over a year in Vancouver in Canada. She had recently moved to San Francisco, but had been called back home to Redcar because her father was dying. Sadly, her father passed away soon after her return and she'd felt compelled to stay at home.

One evening, dispirited and missing North America, Dorothy went out with some friends to the Ship Inn at Marske By Sea. There she met Philip Goodswen. Married just a few months later, the couple would enjoy forty-one years of marriage prior to Philip's death in 2008. It is strange how often, in Far Yonder, we see good coming out of bad.

Years later, Philip and Dorothy's daughter, Charlotte, would relocate to Canada with her husband, Simon Schoch, and their children, Emily and Alexander. Simon is from Sissach in Switzerland, and he and Charlotte met during the time she worked as an au pair in Basel. After living in Switzerland, the couple moved to North Yorkshire and lived there for several years. In 2014, Simon and Charlotte and the children moved to Vancouver Island.

Dorothy recalls that in forty-one years of marriage, Philip mentioned his sister's name twice, though he told her he thought about Stephanie every day. She also noticed that in the home of her in-laws on the Coast Road, there was not a single photograph of their daughter, nor was Stephanie's name ever mentioned. It was as if her loss could be borne only if her parents and brother could pretend she had never existed.

Stephanie was a pretty, lively girl, as might be expected given her good-looking, sociable parents. At sixteen, she was popular and spent many evenings out with girls of her own age, along with several boys, many of whom were older. Some of the boys had driver's licenses and already owned sports cars. On a Saturday evening in May 1965, a young man picked Stephanie up to take her out and, as he earnestly assured her parents, would drive her home again.

Pauline and Stan went out to Redcar Rugby Club just around the corner from their home. A few hours later they left the Club with their friends, laughing and joking, calling out to each other that they would see each other soon. They got into their car and Stan drove down Green Lane, turning left onto Coast Road. After the glorious weather which everyone had enjoyed for many days all over the country, it rained heavily that weekend.

Suddenly Stan stopped the car, pulling up sharply when he saw the police had blocked the road just ahead of them. As Pauline surveyed the scene, she must have felt the first feeling of dread that the unimaginable was unfolding before her eyes. She recognized the figure of Stan's brother, Doug Goodswen, standing in the road. Doug's job brought him into regular contact with Redcar police and he knew many of the officers. Pauline turned to Stan and, with her usually strong voice low and hollow, asked why his brother was there. Why was Dougie standing in the road?

People often think that those of us in Far Yonder are angels. We are not. We can see what is happening down below, but we can't step in and change the course of a person's life, or even save it. Most of us here in Far Yonder have experienced a time, possibly more than once, when we have wished with all our hearts that we could have swooped in and rescued our loved ones. But I couldn't save Wilfred in 1941, nor Stephanie in 1965.

During her journey back home that evening, Stephanie had argued with her young man. As they'd approached her house overlooking the beach, she'd told him to pull up and drop her off on the side of the road. He'd said it would be best if he pulled into the drive, but she'd insisted he didn't have to go to the trouble. She just wanted to get out of the car. The young man pulled up on the side of the road opposite number sixty-one, and Stephanie opened the door.

The first drunk driving laws were introduced in England in 1872. It's strange to think that I was working in Shireoaks when it first became an offence to be drunk while in charge of a carriage, horse, cattle or steam engine. In the decades that followed, it became illegal to operate any vehicle while unfit due to drinking. But no legal limit on alcohol was set until 1967 and, prior to that, it was up to the police and witnesses to determine whether or not a driver was drunk. Drivers who were involved in accidents would always say that they had had a few drinks, but had been fit to drive.

In June 1965, the month following Stephanie's fateful night out, the British government announced it would introduce a maximum alcohol limit for drivers in an attempt to reduce the increasing number of deaths caused by drunk drivers. The new law went into effect in 1967 and, with it, came the first breathalyzers which made it possible to measure the amount of alcohol a person has consumed.

My great-granddaughter would have celebrated her seventeenth birthday on October 15 of that year. But in the early hours of Sunday, May 16, 1965, as a cold wind blew in off the North Sea, Stephanie jumped out of her friend's car and started across the road. A vehicle was heading towards her and she began to run. She didn't know the car was traveling far in excess of the speed limit or that the man behind the wheel had not just had a few drinks, but was drunk.

In court several months later, the driver was charged with speeding and levied a small fine. The man told the judge he was very sorry, but he hadn't seen the girl until she'd been right in front of him. He didn't know she was in the road until his vehicle hit her and he'd felt a thud as she tumbled under the wheels of his car.

The following morning, Pauline stood at her bedroom window and stared out at the sea. Friends and family were filling the house and the sound of their subdued voices drifted upstairs. Pauline's gaze fell on the road and on the policemen who were at work in front of her house. Hours had passed since the accident but the officers were still busy at the scene. Carefully and silently, they were cleaning Stephanie's blood from the surface of the road.

XXX

One morning Georgie and Margaret burst into the kitchen calling to me that the rag-and-bone man was outside. The poor fellow came once a month pulling his cart up Potter Hill, always ready for a rest by the time he got to our house. We threw very little out at Potter Hill Farm, but I was always happy to get rid of the bones we saved for him.

On that particular day, I was also giving him a pair of curtains that used to hang in the downstairs hall. They had collected so much dust and dirt by the time I'd had the chance to take them down, they'd fallen apart when I'd washed them. I'd told Mr. Smith that the curtains were damaged and couldn't be hung up again and I'd thought he'd be annoyed but, instead, he'd smiled and said he always thought they were dark, dreary things, and that I should tell Jessie to make another pair. He'd added that I should choose something I liked.

That had got me all of a flutter to a degree that had nothing to do with the simple – though in my case rare – pleasure of picking out something new. I'd spent the rest of the day forcing myself to get on with my jobs and not turn into a fanciful fool just because my employer had asked me to pick out the material for some new curtains.

Every time I saw the rag-and-bone man I would realize that he, too, suffered from letting his head fill with ideas which bore no relation to his circumstances. He always had an air about him and acted as if he was doing us a favor by stopping at our house. He made it clear that he expected more from Potter Hill Farm and had long been disappointed in our meagre offerings. The fellow makes a living scavenging people's unwanted items but, as with any job you do long enough, he had grown to criticize his customers, especially those he believed were holding on to stuff that should, by all rights, be passed on to him.

When I was first in Greasbrough, the rag-and-bone man would stare at me when I came out of the house with nothing but a cracked pot or two, looking as if he'd like to spit on the ground in front of me. Surely, he would say, there must be some metal for him or, with all those lasses in the house, some material going spare. One day Jessie had cleaned out her rag box and put together a fat wad of fabric. That had made him smile, for once.

But in the Smith home, everything got re-used or passed down or just plain worn out. I'm sorry to say that I smile when I see you making such a fuss about recycling nowadays. We re-used, re-purposed, re-cycled, or whatever you want to call it, as a matter of course. We did it either because we had to, or because we couldn't abide waste even when times were plentiful. We didn't know we could boast about it! Mr. Smith, in particular, was proud to head a thrifty household and had no tolerance for waste, which is why his calm reaction to the ruined curtains had taken me by surprise. Not to mention it got my head and my heart spinning.

Last year I'd started saving bones for the rag-and-bone man because, in spite of his manner, I'd felt sorry for him dragging his cart around in all weathers with no horse to aid him like those who, years later, followed in his line of work. But I would remind myself that at least he had a cart and wasn't carrying a bag on his shoulder like the poor fellows I used to see in Shireoaks. The bones would be of use to him and, given the appetites of Mr. Smith and the children, were practically picked clean at the table. The man will dry them out and sell them to be made into handles, hooks and toys.

On that particular morning, Margaret ran out to the street and handed over the bin full of bones. When the rag-and-bone man saw Georgie struggling towards him with the heavy curtains, he'd bent down to help him with his load. I'd been looking out of the kitchen window and the man caught my eye and nodded to me in acknowledgement of our greater contribution. I waved to him and went back into the scullery where I was peeling potatoes and burst out laughing. I was imagining Mr. Smith's outrage if he learned that the rag-and-bone man not only passed judgment on how little we give him, but had finally deigned to give us his approval.

Margaret and Georgie had come back inside and joined me in the scullery. It was the week after Easter and the girls were off school. Margaret asked me why I was laughing, and I'd told her that I was bemused by the high-and-mighty airs of the rag-and-bone man and that he should try to be more grateful, or at least appear to be so. I'd added that her father would be annoyed if he knew the man didn't appreciate what we gave him.

Margaret, who was sympathetic all her life to those with less, remarked that the man was very poor and needed whatever we could give him. I'd agreed, adding that when we are dependent on others we find a way to criticize them because it makes us feel less helpless if we take on a superior attitude.

Georgie, who was then four, had gone into the back yard and was using a muddy stick to beat the washing we'd hung out on the line together. He'd given the sheets such a beating that one of them had wrapped itself around his head. I sent Margaret out to stop his antics and she grabbed the stick and unraveled his head from the soggy sheet. Georgie started to wail and I went outside and told them to help me check for marks on the washing, and the three of us went down the line knocking bits of grass and dirt off the sheets.

Georgie loved being given a task and was happy running between the wet washing as it blew up and down on the line. Soon, he gleefully shouted that he'd cleaned off more dirty marks than me and his sister combined. I remarked to Margaret that Georgie was like the rag-and-bone man, wishing he wasn't so dependent on us. But, I added, Georgie is a child who will grow to be a man, sooner than he knows, and will be free, or at least as free as most of us ever get to be. But the rag-and-bone man was a grown-up who was still dependent upon the goodwill of others, and the only way to bear it was to behave as if he was better than the rest of us.

I told my little companion that I could understand how the man felt. I understood because I'd been in service for a long time. I'd lived in the homes of strangers and been dependent upon their goodwill for twenty years. I'd started when I was thirteen in Walcott and, at thirty three years old, I was still in service in Greasbrough.

As I said those words I felt more akin to the rag-and-bone man than I'd previously thought, and realized that the man's superior attitude was one I shared. If I thought Mr. Smith would be upset at the man's lack of humility, surely Mrs. Browne had been upset with me when I criticized the design of her butler's pantry and dining room? Where was my appreciation for being given the work, the roof over my head, the food in my belly and the fire blazing in the hearth? Instead, I'd found a way to criticize the large, elegant vicarage, though such a property could no more have been mine than the moon itself. Little had I known that by a miracle yet to come, I would get to the moon right here in Greasbrough.

I went inside and added a note to my list to write to Mrs. Browne to thank her for all she'd done for me. The following day, I posted the letter and she soon wrote back telling me that she should be the one thanking me for my loyalty and hard work. But the letter I'd written had been as much for me as for her. I hadn't wanted to feel that I'd been ungrateful, particularly for all the kindness she'd shown me. And I hadn't wanted to criticize the rag-and-bone man for a quality I shared myself. But neither did I want him to complain about the Smith household!

The rag-and-bone man hadn't been the only one who thought Mr. Smith was well off and should have plenty to spare. During my time in Greasbrough, a seemingly endless parade of widows and spinsters had come courting, though it could never be described that way back when only men could act as suitors. As you know, I had no experience when it came to courting, but I did know from Hattie and the girls in Shireoaks that, more often than not, they were in control of the young men, not the other way round. The girls just had to make it appear otherwise. And, as Hattie kept reminding me in her letters, it was only a matter of time before one of these ladies got Mr. Smith to follow her down the path she was busily strewing with roses or, more accurately, pies, crumbles and tarts.

In fact, the lady visitors had stopped coming to the house right after Mrs. Bowman had been sent away when she'd come bearing that one last pie. Word soon got out that the unfriendly housekeeper said she couldn't accept baked goods or any kind of food, and she was so rushed off her feet she couldn't even stop to make a visitor a cup of tea.

I'd heard remarks along those lines when I'd been out doing the shopping. Not surprisingly, I'd always been in a hurry to get back to my jobs and I'd never been inclined to waste time with idle gossip. Most importantly, I had never forgotten Martha's warning to me to never, ever talk about your employer. And, thus, it had soon become known to everyone in Greasbrough that a warm welcome could not be expected in the kitchen of Potter Hill Farm.

XXXI

I'd always thought of myself as being quite intelligent and wished with all my heart that I'd been able to stay in school longer. I know I've said this before, but it's wonderful that you can be a pupil until you're eighteen and then have the chance to spend a few years at university. I could have done well with my studies if I'd been given the opportunity. But I must admit that though I always thought I was sharp, I was sometimes disappointed with myself for not noticing what was right under my nose.

I'd been in Greasbrough for two years by this time and I'd spent a lot of time thinking about the ladies who were looking for a husband and hoped to find that man in Mr. Smith. I'd hardly dared admit to myself that I too was hoping for the very same thing. I'd been afraid to let such a thought fill my head in case I let it slip one day when I was talking to Margaret. Or, even worse, when sitting with Mr. Smith in the parlor on the days he wanted to talk after his dinner. I'd pushed any fancy ideas about marrying my employer as far back in my head as I'd been able.

In the front of my mind, however, I'd been genuinely puzzled by how many ladies had set their sights on Mr. Smith, though I'd understood he was a good prospect. After all, he had a business, he was intelligent and good company, and he was handsome and trim for his age. But Mr. Smith still had children at home, and keeping house at Potter Hill Farm was hard work, day in and day out. There was no help, other than me. We didn't even have a young lad like Fred who'd been such a help to me in Shireoaks.

Why, I wondered so often to myself as I scrubbed and cooked

and cleaned, were so many women interested in my employer? Some of them were widows with means of their own. Why would they want to take on the Smith household? True, there were some spinsters still hoping for a husband and for whom Mr. Smith, and his ready-made family, would be quite a catch. But didn't they, too, realize that once the courting was over they would have to work extremely hard for many years to come?

Like all things that are stuck under your nose but you're too preoccupied – or too stupid – to notice, the answer had suddenly come to me like a bolt of lightning. Early one morning, as a grey dawn started to peep through the curtains of my attic window, I'd woken with such a start that I'd sat bolt upright and banged my head on the eaves above my bed. Later, I'd thought how much I'd needed that thump on the head. I'd hoped it had finally lodged in my brain what I'd needed to see all along. I couldn't believe how stupid I'd been and for how long I'd ignored what must have been as plain as day to everyone else.

The reason so many ladies were after Mr. Smith, in spite of knowing about the children and the Yeoman's work of Potter Hill Farm was because they'd be marrying a man of means. And they believed that a man of means wouldn't make them solely responsible for the children and all the house work. They believed they would have help. In fact, they believed they would have excellent help. They would have a full-time housekeeper. And that housekeeper would be me. These ladies believed they would marry Mr. Smith and get me into the bargain!

I'd got up as fast as I could though I hadn't known what to do at five o'clock on a cold spring morning except check that my vails were still safely stored away. I hadn't spent any money in the two years I'd been in Greasbrough, other than buying material for two house dresses and new undergarments. Admittedly, I'd chosen better quality material and a prettier pattern than I would have done in the past, even though I hadn't been sure why I'd decided to spend more than had been necessary. But my wages had covered that little extravagance, which meant my vails were still intact in the exact spot I'd left them in the dresser drawer. I'd reminded myself that I'd saved that money so I'd be able to leave a place where I was no longer contented. That thought had calmed me down a little.

But I hadn't been able to get back into bed, no matter how warm it might be, with such terrible thoughts flooding my mind. I couldn't believe it had taken me the better part of two years to see what had suddenly become crystal clear. If Mr. Smith got married again, it would be me who would care for the children, clean the house and cook the meals. Meanwhile, the new Mrs. Smith would not only walk around giving me instructions, but would be the one to sit with Mr. Smith in the parlor after dinner and by the range in the evening.

I'd been so proud of myself for putting a stop to the visits from Mrs. Brown and Mrs. Bowman, and it was true that nice Miss Green had only come to the house because she'd needed a Virgin Mary. Thankfully, our little Madonna had returned to her normal self after the Nativity Play, although she'd put in another fine performance the year after. Mary would get the role again, but one day she would leave school and her years of playing the Virgin Mary would be over.

I'd known that morning that it was time for my years of playing a virgin to be over. It was time to bring to a close the twenty years I'd spent as a single girl in service. It was time to change my life and become a married woman. And it was time to accept that the man in whose home I was employed was the man I wanted. The only thing I didn't know was how to make him mine.

By that time, I'd lost control of Mr. Smith's admirers. As challenging as gatekeeping duty can be, you at least know what's going on when the visitors come to the gate. You can stop them dead in their tracks or as close to that as you can get. But because word had got round about the unfriendly housekeeper and the fact that Mr. Smith wouldn't eat anyone else's food, the ladies were no longer coming to Potter Hill Farm.

Instead, and much worse, they were finding ways to talk to Mr. Smith when he was out in the village. Some of them would send notes to him at his building sites asking him to fix their roof or repoint their bricks. Why would they think that a man who builds houses from the foundation up would have time for every widow's and spinster's little repairs?

If you wonder how I'd known about these women's overtures to Mr. Smith, it was because he'd told me himself. As I've said before, Mr. Smith enjoyed talking to a woman and I'd soon begun to look forward to our time together in the parlor. Unfortunately, that didn't mean I would always be happy with what I would learn.

One day, Mr. Smith told me that a lady from Sheffield had invited him for tea. I know I hadn't managed to hide my alarm at hearing this news but, with his eyes twinkling, he'd said he'd politely declined the invitation. He'd added that he had no reason to go as far as Sheffield when a perfectly good tea was always ready for him at home. I'd been so relieved that I'd blushed and giggled like a young girl, and then grown even more flustered when I'd recalled that not only had Mr. Harrison and Reverend Browne never made me blush, they had certainly never caused me to giggle like a fool.

Now that it had finally dawned on me that the ladies believed I would be their housekeeper, I'd known I had to be honest with myself. I could no longer pretend that I wasn't in love with my employer. Not only could I not fool myself, I hadn't been sure I could hide it from him, or the children, much longer. A few days earlier, I'd caught Mary giving me sly looks when her father and I talked together and, on those same occasions, I'd catch a little smile spreading across Margaret's face.

But, after a few days passed since banging my head on the attic eaves, I'd begun to feel more optimistic. It was the same day the rag-and-bone man had shown appreciation for the pair of curtains we'd given him. I'd felt proud of myself for not only being able to acknowledge the difficulty of the man's position, but seeing that my own circumstances were quite similar. I'd accepted that it was time for my life to change and felt confident that, with that acceptance, I would find a way to get what I wanted.

I'd known, however, that nothing could be done on that particular day, of all days. My newfound confidence would be needed simply to get to the end of it. As soon as dinner was done, I would be busy preparing a special tea of boiled eggs, pork pies, boiled ham, and Mr. Smith's favorite Cheshire cheese. I would be setting the dining room table with Rockingham cups, saucers and plates, the family's best china.

On that particular day, Mary and Margaret had been instructed by their father to help Miss Mary serve their guests. Jessie would be home on time instead of out pinning fabric on her customers, and Annie would come round and stay longer than the time it took her to tear through the house looking for Georgie and Herbert. Only William had been excused on the grounds that he was too far away.

I'd been shocked when first I'd learned that on the days these particular occasions took place, Mr. Smith and Herbert came home from the public house at half past five instead of six o'clock. This fact, more than any other, always threw me into a tizzy as everything had to be brought forward half-an-hour.

Fortunately, this kind of entertaining took place no more than twice a year. It would always be for the same reason. Mr. Smith's sisters were coming for tea. There were three of them: Mary, Jane and Eliza.

XXXII

Two of the Hague sisters are in the photograph. Veronica and Sally are on holiday in Arizona, with Steven and Robert, and the two couples are spending a day visiting Monument Valley. That great valley spreads from Arizona into Utah and contains numerous sandstone formations which provide fabulous scenery. Like all tourists, the visitors drove around the flat desert valley in awe of the magnificent buttes, mesas and spires.

Discovering that one of the monuments is named The Three Sisters, Veronica hurriedly asks Steven to stop the car. He quickly pulls over and Sally jumps out of the vehicle, calling to Robert to grab the camera and to take a photograph of the two of them. She reminds him to make sure to get The Three Sisters in the distance behind them.

Throughout the bustle of activity, Steven and Robert exchange glances, each wondering what the rush is all about considering the monuments have been there for over a hundred million years and aren't about to be packed up like when the traveling fair left Shireoaks. It seems they share my sentiments that, when it comes to travel, everything could be done at a slower pace. But some things are better left unremarked upon, and the photograph was dutifully taken with the two sisters in the foreground and The Three Sisters behind them, standing for all time in the dust of the desert.

The Hague girls are dressed for the warm weather, with Sally in a short skirt and Veronica in Capri pants. This makes me envious because they are the kind of clothes I would have liked to wear.

The photograph would be sent to their sister, Jane, at her home in Whitchurch-on-Thames in Oxfordshire.

Monument Valley is part of the Navajo Nation Reservation which was established in 1868, during my own lifetime. The Reservation covers twenty seven thousand acres and is the largest in the United States of America. The Indians were treated terribly by the Europeans who settled America, so it's nice to know that some of the tribes now own their native lands.

Monument Valley is one of the most majestic sights in all of North America and every visitor must pay an entrance fee to the Navajo Nation which is at least a little bit of compensation for their dreadful history. The monuments were named by a mixture of white settlers and the Navajo, and The Three Sisters is said to represent a Catholic nun facing her two pupils. You could just as well imagine, however, that the monument was named by a man who had three sisters and had weathered their formidable, immovable presence in his life.

There are several sets of three sisters in our family, beginning with my own three daughters, Elizabeth, Florence and Effie. In the next generation, Nigel and Stella Hague had Jane, Veronica and Sally. In the generation to follow, Clement's grandson, Anthony Smith, and his wife, Elizabeth, had Sarah, Joanne and Lesley, the latter two being a lovely set of twins. Also in that generation, Robin and Judith Hartley had Elizabeth, Clare and Fleur. More recently, Clare produced three girls, Mia, Amber and Mabelle.

But the key difference between these sets of sisters is that, in the first two instances, there was also a boy: my oldest child, Clement, came before his three sisters, and in Nigel and Stella's family, William came after the three girls.

Navajo women are known to be strong and in charge. In families and marriages, it is the women who own the livestock and the land, and inheritances pass to daughters or to other women in the family. This seems like a very sensible arrangement and I wish more societies had had the sense to set things up this way. A lot of trouble could be avoided if the ladies were in charge. Nevertheless, it must be said that women have a way of taking control even when being treated like second class citizens.

Needless to say, neither Clement nor I ever got as far as Monument Valley. But there were times when my three girls could have passed for Indian princesses, and Clement knew only too well that their strength could rival that of the Navajo. My son was fortunate, however, to be the firstborn. As in all families, this placed him in a superior position and there were times when the three girls, even when ganging up on him, would be forced to back down.

My great-grandson, William Hague, was not so fortunate. Coming seven years after Sally, the youngest girl, there were times when the poor lad would have willingly traded his birthplace, the tranquil Yorkshire village of Greasbrough, for the harsh terrain of the Navajo Nation's tribal lands. Just imagine if he had! William might have become a Chief, although given his fair coloring he would never have been able to pass for a native Indian.

The three sisters of Mr. Smith who came for tea that day weren't born one after the other, but alternated between himself and his two brothers, James and Herbert. First there was Mary who was seven years older than George. Mary had moved to London as a young woman and, in 1840, married William Rossiter, a railway laborer from Woolwich in Kent. They couple settled in Bermondsey and had five children: Mary, William, Albert, George and Herbert. Once again, you find the same names!

Mr. Smith's second sister was Jane, who'd been followed by James. His third sister was Elizabeth, known as Eliza. Eliza had been followed by the Smiths' youngest child, Herbert.

Mr. Smith was fond of his sisters and often spoke well of them in their absence, though he could become irritated rather quickly when they were present. The oldest two were quite vocal when it came to complaining about their brother, most especially because he refused to consider them an exception to his rules about uninvited visitors. Eliza never complained. She was just excited to be taken out for the evening.

Several years ago, Mary and Jane had protested that, as family, they should be free to call round whenever they were in Greasbrough, or wanted to see their nieces and nephews. Their brother had not budged from his practice of not welcoming uninvited guests, and so they had turned his rule to their advantage by insisting that they be invited properly for tea. These occasions would take place when Mary was making her visits up North which were more frequent since she'd been widowed several years earlier. And so, a tradition had been established that, twice a year, Mary, Jane and Eliza would be guests for tea at Potter Hill Farm.

Similar to this tradition is the lovely invitation which William and his wife, Ffion, send out twice a year, not only to William's three sisters, but to all the Hague family, to stay for a weekend at Plas Cyfronydd, William and Ffion's home in Powys. Welsh names can be hard to pronounce, but even if you can't spell it or say it properly, dates are set and the whole family is made very welcome. The Hagues' are joined by Ffion's family and everyone is treated generously and has a wonderful time.

George's sisters would be gratified to know that, not only did they start a tradition with their twice yearly visits, but that some members of the family have become fine enough to live in a Plas, or Hall. They might be surprised that this particular branch of the family tree sprang not from their brother and his first Mary, but from me. Not surprisingly, there had been some comments when their brother married his plain little housekeeper.

Mary and Jane had had the nerve to tell George that they were bewildered by his choice of bride as he, more than anyone else in the family, had grown into a man of good position and could have married a woman of some standing. Only Eliza had shown genuine pleasure at gaining a new sister-in-law. People like Eliza don't pass judgment on others. It takes the rest of us a lifetime to get to that special place.

211

My new husband would tell his sisters that they had no need to be bewildered by his marriage. He was of sound mind and free will and had chosen to marry Miss Mary Stennett and that was the end of the discussion. He'd told me to ignore their comments and not let them spoil my happiness. As we all know, that's easier said than done, but I'd appreciated the fact that my new husband had stood up for me in the face of criticism.

But, back at Potter Hill Farm in the spring of 1879, there'd been no time to do anything on the day of the tea party but to get ready for the visitors. Mr. Smith's brothers, James and Herbert, weren't invited because they were too far away. As you know, James and his wife, Christiana, lived in Nottinghamshire.

Herbert, too, would have had too far to travel as he lived in Sheffield. After starting out as a gardener for Wentworth Estate, Herbert had married Alice Cartwright, a girl from Sheffield. Herbert and Alice lived in Nether Hallam where Herbert worked as a gas meter inspector. They had recently lost their little nine-year old daughter, Martha. In a year or two, they would have a boy, William, who would grow up to stay in the Sheffield area and work as a gas meter fitter.

I could only be grateful that we didn't have more members of the Smith family to seat at the dining room table. I'd walked around that table dozens of times that afternoon, making sure there were places set for the ten members of the family. That included the children, who would be free to go after they'd finished eating as long as they were polite and asked for permission to leave the table. Their aunties would smile at their good manners, and Mr. Smith would nod his assent and remind them to help Miss Mary wash the pots.

I'd known from their visits over the last two years that, as soon as the children left, Mary and Jane would turn the conversation from general chatter about food, school, farming and building, to more personal topics. Mary owned a piece of property on Willow Garth in Greasbrough, and she and Mr. Smith generally spent a few minutes talking about its value and whether or not she should sell it. I'd noticed that he always urged his sister to hold on to the property. This recommendation would turn out to be quite beneficial to Mr. Smith as well as – though I could not in my wildest dreams have imagined it at the time – to me.

Most of all, Mary liked to talk of her life in Bermondsey and her daughter, four sons and grandchildren. Mr. Smith took a genuine interest, always keen to hear about the brass finishing business which his niece, Mary, and her husband, William Wellman, ran in Croydon, Surrey. On their last visit, Mary had proudly related that the Wellmans' employed over a dozen men, and that her daughter was still finishing brass even though she had the four boys, William, Arthur, Herbert and Alfred. Mary Wellman was thirty years old when she married, but gave birth to six babies, with five sons living to adulthood. She would die in 1932 at the age of ninety one, far outliving her four younger brothers.

It would turn out, however, that the talk at this particular visit would not be of George's niece, but of his nephew, William, his sister's second child. Seventeen years ago, at the age of nineteen, William Rossiter had left for America and settled in Utah Territory. He'd joined The Church of Jesus Christ of Latter-day Saints while still in England, and had traveled with hundreds of new Mormons to the Salt Lake Valley where a new Mormon development had been established.

You will learn that William became a prominent member of the Mormon community and created, with his two wives, a large family. William Rossiter's descendants live in the Salt Lake City area of Utah to this day. If you are descended from "Rabbit George", you are related to William Rossiter's descendants. You are all descended from William and Elizabeth Smith, the parents of George Smith, and of Mary Smith Rossiter.

Salt Lake City is just four hundred miles north of the Three Sisters in Monument Valley and would have been an easy journey for the Hague sisters to take to look up their Rossiter relatives. But at that time, no-one knew that the descendants of William and Elizabeth Smith included the Rossiter men and women in Utah.

Nor did anyone know that back in 1879 at the table in Potter Hill Farm, Mary's news from Utah would keep everyone enthralled until the night had drawn in and it was well past time for the three sisters to wend their way home.

Mary Smith Rossiter (1820-1884) and William Rossiter (1816-1870)

MARY (1841-1932) *m. William Wellman (1845-1917)*
William *m. Ada Murden:* Doris, Arthur, Douglas, Cyril
Arthur, Herbert *m. Alice Appleyard,* **Alfred, Percy**

WILLIAM (1843-1913) *m. Eliza Crabtree (1848-1915)*
Phoebe *m. Henry Baddley,* **William** *m. Maria Baddley* (Edith, Bryan, Eliza, William, Frank)**, Elizabeth** *m. David Campbell,* **Frederick** *m. Sarah Shannon* (Ruth, Frederick, William, Afton Eliza, Lawrence, Alfred, Shannon, Belva)**, Edith** *m. William Lovesey,* **George** *m. Nettie Boyle,* **Lucy** *m. William Evans,* **Ernest** *m. Venus Robinson* (Ernest, Babette), **Elmer** *m. Luella ____* (Robert)
m. Shamira Young (1853-1915)
Clifford, Lillian, Russell *m. Leah Farr*

ALBERT (1848-1907)

GEORGE (1851-1905) *m. Emma Ashton*
Beatrice, Herbert, Maud, Alfred, Arthur, Jay, Gilbert, Frank

HERBERT (1859-1897)

XXXIII

At half past five on the dot, there'd been a loud rap on the front door. I'd been startled the first time I'd heard the sharp sound of the brass knocker, but realized that as the sisters believed they were not being treated like family who could call round whenever they liked, they would behave like visitors and stand at the front door until someone let them in. That imposing, heavy door was rarely opened, although earlier in the afternoon Margaret, busily helping with the preparations, had drawn open the heavy curtain which blocked cold draughts from blowing through the front door in anything but a warm summer.

Mr. Smith and Herbert had arrived home from The Ship in the nick of time, practically jumping through the scullery door with their faces flushed from supping an hour's worth of ale in half that time. As you know, Mr. Smith came home for tea at half past five instead of six o'clock only twice a year, a necessary change in his treasured habits if he was to meet the demands of his sisters.

In the past, Jane had complained about the lateness of starting tea at six o'clock, always stating her concern about getting Eliza back to Barrow. Eliza was over forty years old but was backward, as we called it then, and was a resident of Barrow Hospital in Wentworth. Barrow Hospital was, in fact, a group of alms houses and cottages with space for only twelve patients, most of them poor and elderly.

The fact that Eliza had been given a place at Barrow was a testament to the strength of the relationship between her father, the blacksmith, and Earl Fitzwilliam. Residents of Barrow helped

216

care for themselves and were allowed to go out, at which time they wore a red cloak adorned with a solid silver badge. I'd noticed that Eliza was always reluctant to take her cloak off when she came to Potter Hill Farm. She was very proud of the cloak and badge as they were proof that she was a resident of Barrow and gave her security when out in the village. With the red cloak and the badge, no-one could question who she was or what she was doing in Wentworth.

The cost of Eliza's care at Barrow was covered, in part, by an annuity which, as Mr. Smith explained to me much later, had been set up by his parents to ensure that their daughter would get the care she needed after they were gone. I'd known from first looking at Elizabeth Smith's photograph that she was a wonderful woman. I'd wondered what sacrifices a blacksmith and his wife had made to be able to set aside money for their daughter's care. Eliza was fortunate to come from such a family.

Mary had joined Jane in complaining about the timing of tea and the difficulty of getting home in the dark. This particular complaint seemed strange considering one of their visits took place in the early summer when it is almost ten o'clock before the last light leaves the sky in the north of England. But Mary had insisted that if the visits got off to a late start – not because the men were at work, but at the public house – she might have to come up North more often so they could visit Potter Hill Farm more than twice a year. Two visits were as much as their brother could manage, and he had readily agreed that tea would begin at half past five sharp.

That time had arrived and, on the dot, there'd been the rap on the front door. Mr. Smith told Herbert to stop dawdling in the scullery, as if he'd had chance to do so, and to open the door for his aunties. Georgie chased behind his brother and, after diving through Herbert's long lean legs, was the first to greet the visitors. The sisters each bent down to stroke his bonnie little head, exclaiming, loudly and in unison, just how much Georgie had grown!

Mary, Jane and Eliza gathered at the table with Mr. Smith and the older children, and I rushed in and out, with Mary and Margaret scuttling behind me, carrying plates of ham, boiled eggs, pork pies, pickled onions, bread buns, scones and lemon curd tarts. As expected, the talk wended its way through the weather, Wentworth, Greasbrough, Mr. Smith's building work, the high price of food, and how hard it was for the young ones to get work. Though the visit had barely begun, I'd mashed not one, but two, pots of tea.

After consuming a veritable mountain of food, Herbert had asked to be excused from the table and, upon receiving a nod of assent from his father, swiftly left the room. Annie and Jessie had looked across at Mr. Smith and then they, too, had jumped up, mumbling apologies to their aunties about fittings and jobs to be done.

Mary had smiled at her departing nieces and then turned to her brother to ask about William. Mr. Smith reported that he was doing well and working hard. Mary and Jane nodded their heads approvingly and Eliza let out a sharp burst of laughter. This made Georgie jump off his stool and he ran from the room calling after his older brother and sisters, while Mary and Margaret started clearing the table.

As soon as the children left, I'd gone back into the dining room to ask Mr. Smith if he wanted another pot of tea. Before he could answer, Mary had turned to him and said she'd prefer a drop of sherry. As you know, it was highly unusual for Mr. Smith to drink at home, but he'd swiftly reached into the sideboard behind him and brought out a bottle of Harvey's Bristol Cream. He'd raised the bottle in the air and looked inquiringly at Mary who had responded in a low soft voice, unlike her usual confident tone, that she would need it as she had something troubling to tell them, and a little sherry would help her get the story out.

As soon as I'd seen Mr. Smith pull out the bottle, I'd gone to the scullery for four sherry glasses and placed one in front of each of them. Mr. Smith filled their glasses, giving Eliza just a tiny drop, and then asked me if I too would like a glass of sherry. Mary and Jane had looked at each other, each raising their eyebrows. The glances they'd exchanged had been so fleeting that their brother hadn't noticed. But, I had.

I'd declined Mr. Smith's surprising offer of a glass of sherry and gone back into the kitchen to start washing the pots. But I'd been curious to hear what Mary had to say and so, instead of closing the dining room door, I'd left it ajar. And, instead of going to the sink, I'd decided it was a perfect time to give the crockery on the dresser a quick dusting. So, I'd stood behind the half-open door and taken down a plate and started to dust, following the circles of blue and white stripes.

From out of the folds of her dress, Mary had taken out a thick wad of paper which turned out to be a letter from her son, William, written at the end of 1877, a year and a half ago. Mary explained that she hadn't brought the letter to read to them on earlier visits because she hadn't known what to think, let alone say, about its contents. Everyone in the family was aware that William was a Mormon and was doing extremely well in Utah, but his latest news was something quite different.

I'd been standing, completely still, with my duster in one hand and a plate in the other, when Mr. Smith interrupted his sister and called my name. Mary, he'd shouted across the dining room, put down your rag and come in here! You must learn about my nephew! I'd been amazed that he'd known I was listening, but I hadn't needed to be asked twice and I'd pushed the duster into my pocket and approached the table. This time Mary and Jane made no effort to hide their surprise at their brother's invitation for me to join the family group, and they'd stared at him in astonishment. Eliza had burst out laughing, which I'd already learned was her way of joining in a discussion.

Jane had started to say that their talk was a private matter, while Mary slowly nodded her head in agreement. Mr. Smith cut them off and said that considering he trusted Miss Mary to bring up his children, prepare his food and keep his house running like clockwork, he could trust her to hear about his family, no matter how private such news might be considered to be.

He'd then instructed Mary to start at the beginning with the story of her son because he wanted his housekeeper to know that the Smith family included such an adventurous man. This latter comment cleverly touched his sister's proud, maternal heart, and she'd nodded her head in agreement that I should join them at the table.

As I'd sat down, Mary had started to fumble with the letter and Mr. Smith reminded her to start her story at the beginning. He'd said it was no trouble to him or to Jane to hear, once more, the tale of their nephew's travels and life in Utah Territory. And, he'd added, Eliza would enjoy learning about her nephew in America, not to mention her great-nieces and nephews, as he doubted she recalled any of the facts.

Mary needed no more encouragement as she was always happy, as I would learn over the years, to be the center of attention. Mary expected recognition when she believed it was due and felt that the Potter Hill Farm tea parties were held as an acknowledgement of the countless trips she'd made up North in order to stay close to her family.

Mary would be flattered beyond her wildest expectations to know that, several years after she passed away, recognition of her commitment to her family in Yorkshire would extend to a road in Greasbrough being named after her. Though it was never proclaimed officially, I have always been of the belief that Rossiter Road was named in honor of Mary and her husband, William Rossiter. You will learn more on that subject later in this book.

Once again, Mr. Smith had picked up the bottle of sherry and filled Mary's and Jane's glasses, both of which I'd noticed had been polished off in a jiffy. He'd motioned over to me with the bottle in his hand and a question on his face, but I'd shaken my head and smiled. If being invited to sit at the table had been an achievement, partaking of the sherry would have been taking it too far. Though I would have very much enjoyed a drop of the sweet, dark liquid, my mind had been whirling with excitement at Mr. Smith's treatment of me as a trusted confidante. I'd known that when I went up to my attic later that night, I would be beaming with joy. But, before I could indulge my own fanciful ideas, it had been time to listen to Mary and to pay respectful attention to the story of her remarkable son.

XXXIV

Born in 1842, William Alfred Rossiter was the second son of Mary and William Rossiter. At the age of nineteen, he'd informed his parents that he'd joined The Church of Jesus Christ of Latter-day Saints and become a Mormon. He'd added that by saving money from his earnings as a gas fitter in Bermondsey, he had enough to pay for his passage on a Mormon ship set to sail from Liverpool to New York.

Mary had paused in her story to say she didn't know what had drawn a young man to join the Mormons who, as far as she understood, didn't consume alcohol, coffee, tea or tobacco, and whose primary commitment was to spread their faith. It didn't seem like much of a life for a lively, young Londoner.

Mr. Smith's face had grown long and he'd nodded his head in agreement at the mystery of a young man giving up the simple pleasures of beer and tobacco, and replacing them with proselytizing. But he'd nodded at his sister to encourage her to continue with her tale. I'd looked at him across the table wanting to say that now I understood why he'd said I would have to go to Utah to find a true man of faith in the family.

On May 14, 1862, William had embarked on the "William Tapscott" ship, sailing from Liverpool with over eight hundred Mormons. The ship docked in New York on June 25, 1862, ending a journey which had lasted six weeks in severely cramped conditions with many of the passengers suffering from sea sickness. William had then traveled by rail over fifteen hundred miles to Nebraska, again suffering overcrowded dangerous conditions.

Florence, Nebraska, was the outfitting post for Mormon wagon trains leaving for the Salt Lake Valley, a thousand miles west. William joined the company of Captain William H. Dame, along with one hundred and fifty men, women and children. The wagon train consisted of fifty wagons, hauled by oxen and laden with supplies. Leaving Florence on August 14, they traveled the vast distances across Nebraska and Wyoming, arriving in Salt Lake City on October 29, 1862. Due to winter's onset, it was the last wagon train to arrive that year. William's journey from London to Salt Lake City had taken almost six months.

I'd thought of my own anxiety when I'd moved from Billinghay to Walcott, from Walcott to Shireoaks and, finally, from Shireoaks to Greasbrough. I'd moved a total of only seventy-five miles yet had felt the weight of those journeys and struggled with the strangeness of my new surroundings. I'd barely been able to imagine taking William's journey of over five thousand miles in such harsh conditions.

Mary had again stopped her story to say that during that time she'd feared for her son's life, and had even prayed for him never to return if he could just get safely to his destination. Later, she'd known from receiving her son's first letter from Utah that he would not be coming home, at least not to stay. These kinds of moves alter you forever, she said, because of all the changes you have to make. She'd known that because she'd left Wentworth for London when she was a young woman and, after all the time and trouble she'd taken to settle in, she could never have moved back home.

It turned out that William Rossiter had borne his arduous journey well. After arriving in Salt Lake City, he'd been hired by its founder, Brigham Young, to serve as his coachman. Brigham Young had served as the first governor of Utah Territory, having been appointed by President Millard Fillmore in 1850, and governing until 1858. Most significantly, Brigham Young was the president of The Church of Jesus Christ of Latter-day Saints, and had spent time in England promoting Mormonism and recruiting new members. Mary didn't know for sure, but it was possible her son joined the Mormons after meeting Mr. Young himself.

William had quickly settled into Mormon life and, in December 1863, a year after his arrival, married Eliza Crabtree. Fifteen years old at the time of the marriage, Eliza had arrived in Utah in 1853 with her parents, Charles and Elizabeth Crabtree. Mr. Smith had interrupted Mary and urged her to talk about his nephew's in-laws.

Charles Crabtree was born in the Yorkshire town of Kingston Upon Hull. His wife, Elizabeth Aston was Welsh, having being born in Flintshire. The couple had several children and, with the exception of Eliza who'd been five years old when she arrived in Utah, all had been born in the new territory. Like their future son-in-law, Charles and Elizabeth Crabtree were true pioneers. What a journey they made with their little Eliza!

After working as a coachman for five years, William had been appointed General Superintendent of President Young's business affairs. Like his Uncle George, William obviously knew the importance of being positioned where the money is changing hands. He served in a trusted position within his community and, together with his father-in-law, Charles Crabtree, is listed in "Pioneers and Prominent Men of Utah" by Frank Esshom. Copies of the book are available today, providing a wonderful testament for members of the Rossiter family of the courage and faith of their forebears.

After once again hearing the tale of his fellow Yorkshireman, Charles Crabtree, Mr. Smith had nodded to Mary to continue her tale. She'd proudly reeled off the names and birth years of her Mormon grandchildren: Phoebe born in 1865, William in 1867, Elizabeth in 1872, Frederick in 1874, Edith in 1876, and baby George, born just last January, in 1878. Suddenly she'd stopped and picked up the letter from the table in front of her.

Jane had glanced at Mary, then at her brother, and then at me. After a brief pause Mary had continued saying that she knows it sounds selfish but she can't help but think that she has all these grandchildren who she will never see, let alone get to know. Thankfully, she has her daughter's brood because Albert, a younger son, is over thirty and shows no signs of leaving home, let alone marrying. Another son, George, is younger, but he too prefers to live at home. Herbert, the youngest, is twenty and lives at home. She didn't know how she and her husband produced William who, though happy to get married and have a family, took off so far away.

It would turn out that Mary's fears that her son, Albert, would never leave home would be well-founded. He spent his life in the family home at 8 Guilford Place, Bermondsey, working as a plumber's laborer and dying at fifty nine years of age. Herbert too, a leather finisher by trade, never married and lived at home until his death at the age of thirty eight.

By contrast, though well into his thirties at the time, Mary's son, George, married Emma Ashton and had eight children, the last one being born only a year before George died at the age of fifty four. Mary Rossiter passed away before any of George's children were born. It seemed she'd been right to place such stock in the grandchildren produced by her daughter, Mary. They were the only ones she would get to know.

Once again, Mary had fumbled with the letter. Jane had remained silent and even Eliza had sat quietly staring at her sister. Mr. Smith had begun to get impatient and moved to snatch the pages out of his sister's hand, causing Mary and Jane to lean across the table and swat at him in unison. Eliza, thinking this a wonderful game, flung her arms out towards her brother and then slammed her hands down on the table, by some miracle missing the sherry glasses.

Mr. Smith had quickly backed away from the table and put his hands up in the air, saying his sisters would have done well on a wagon train because they would have been the first to shoo away attacking Indians. Everyone had laughed and as Mary tossed the pages back on the table and wiped a tear from her eye – I hadn't known if it was from smiles or sorrow – murmured that William had taken another wife.

The table had fallen silent which had given me time to consider what Mary had said. William Rossiter, husband and father, had got married again, yet no mention had been made of the death of his first wife. Jane's pointed silence was proof that she had heard this news earlier, if not some time ago.

Mr. Smith, who somehow always managed to maintain a calm demeanor when hearing news that got everyone else in a tizzy, had looked carefully at Mary and gently asked about William's wife, Eliza. Had something happened to Eliza? Why had no-one been told of her passing? Mr. Smith had become so solemn I'd wondered if he'd been thinking about his own first wife, Eliza, and her early, sad death. Mary had quickly interjected that Eliza was very much alive, and reportedly strong and healthy since the birth of her youngest. Mr. Smith's solemn face turned into one of relief, and then puzzlement.

But now, Mary continued before her brother could ask the question which was undoubtedly hovering on his lips, there was a second wife. A silence had fallen, once again, as Mary spoke the name of William's new wife. Her name was Shamira Young, and she was the daughter of Brigham Young and his wife, Lucy Ann.

Mary added that she understood Mr. Young had many wives, and that Lucy Ann was his third. In fact, we would learn that Brigham Young had a total of fifty-five wives, although many were widows and divorcees he'd promised to take care of. He had children with sixteen of the wives, one of whom was Shamira's mother, Lucy Ann Decker.

William Rossiter married Shamira Young on October 9, 1877. His father-in-law-to-be had passed away a few weeks earlier in August. Upon his death, William had been appointed agent of his estate. Twenty three of Brigham Young's wives were living, but his Will included only the sixteen he had lived with and the estate was split between them. It's hard to imagine how an estate could be divided between sixteen wives! William Rossiter must have had a strong head for business and fairness.

Mary had gone on to say that the Mormons were polygamous and allowed what they called 'plural' marriages, which meant a man could have more than one wife at the same time. Mr. Smith had started to smirk, but quickly straightened his face when Mary and Jane had glared at him. I'd had to stop myself from giggling although in the years to come we would joke that, though George had had three wives, he hadn't had them all at the same time! We'd always enjoyed that joke, but been careful to add that we didn't mean to be disrespectful to his nephew and his brethren. Now in Far Yonder I have finally learned not to pass judgement on others, but sometimes it's hard to understand the ways of others.

We apparently weren't the only ones who found some humor in the situation. Mary had reported that when she told her daughter, Mary, that her brother now had two wives, her harried daughter had remarked that she too could use another wife in the house. Her mother had replied that she doubted her daughter would want to share her husband with another woman, but Mary had saucily raised her eyebrows and said he'd be welcome to another one if it took the pressure off her.

Mr. Smith had guffawed at hearing his niece's remark and, once again, I'd had to look down at the table to hide my reddening face and to stop myself from laughing. Mary had sniffed, but then acknowledged that her daughter had her hands full with her boys, William, Arthur, Herbert and baby Alfred. Mary and her husband work hard, her mother added, so she supposed it was understandable that Mary might want some relief. At that, Jane had smiled, Eliza had guffawed loudly and Mr. Smith had been free to join in the laughter.

But the laughter had immediately been followed by tears as Mary had added that a later letter from William reported that Shamira had given birth last December to a boy, but he was ailing and not expected to make it to spring. William would later confirm that Clifford Young Rossiter died on May 10, 1879, having lived but a few months.

In the years that followed, Mary would learn that Shamira again gave birth in May 1880 but the baby girl, Lilian, would live only a year. The following year, in August 1881, Shamira gave birth to Russell Young Rossiter, the only one of her children to live to adulthood.

During the years William was having children with Shamira, he was still very much married to Eliza. She gave birth to Lucy in 1880, Ernest in 1882 and Elmer in 1886. In total, William Rossiter sired nine children with Eliza and three with Shamira. Though Mary and William Rossiter wouldn't get to know their Mormon grandchildren, they each live on in the Salt Lake Valley. To the present day, many of their descendants remain in Salt Lake City.

Mary Rossiter would also be comforted to know that Mormons believe that families are eternally sealed to each other in heaven, including those of the past and the future. Because of this belief, Mormons research their ancestors in great detail and learn as much as they possibly can about the men and women from whom they are descended. They believe that knowing ones ancestors helps build connections between past and future generations. I think this is a wonderful belief, and I hope everything you are learning in this book helps connect all of us together.

It would be over a hundred years before another member of the family would move to America, and in much easier circumstances. On March 14, 1981, my great-granddaughter, Veronica Hague, flew from London to New York to start work in the New York office of a London-based publishing company. Landing at John F. Kennedy Airport some eight hours later, she was greeted by Rick Clinton, a young American she'd met in London a few months earlier. Rick had grown up in Clark, New Jersey, with his mother and step-father, Gladys and Claude Krasse.

Rick had driven to Kennedy Airport from his apartment in Belmar, a popular beach town on New Jersey's long shoreline, and, together, they made the one hour journey from Queens to the apartment of Veronica's friend, Eileen Crittle. Eileen lived on the corner of Second Avenue and East 40th Street in Manhattan, and was employed by the same publishing company. The girls had become friends while working together in the London office. Eileen, too, had been transferred to New York City, making her own journey to America several years earlier in 1977.

The friends ate dinner in Eileen's apartment, drinking beer from Colorado and wine from California as the lights glittered in the high rise buildings surrounding them. Two days later, Veronica reported for work in The Chanin Building on East 42nd Street. As the position was a company transfer, she started her job that Monday morning in New York City exactly where she left off the previous Friday afternoon in London. Later that same week, Veronica would be out buying furniture for her studio apartment on East 22nd Street, and would settle into life in America with little trouble or inconvenience.

Neither William nor Veronica would ever look back from their new homes across the Atlantic Ocean, each settling in as though they'd arrived at the place they were meant to be. America calls many to its shores. It is likely William returned to England to fulfil the Mormon obligation to serve as a missionary, though his travels would have been long and arduous. Over a hundred years later, Veronica would be able to take advantage of inexpensive air travel to make regular trips home, bringing her son, Edward Clinton, to visit the Hague family two dozen times during his childhood.

Edward has since brought his wife, Carla, and their son, Theo, to meet their English relatives, and it won't be long before their youngest son, Wesley, will land on English soil. The world is much smaller since the time William Rossiter pledged his heart and soul to the Mormon faith, and left his comfortable home in Bermondsey for the rigors of the Salt Lake Valley.

XXXV

I couldn't have told you how many cups of tea were brought to my little attic bedroom as I lay there, feverish and chilled, first barely able to take a sip of the hot liquid and then desperately trying to quench a raging thirst. I couldn't recall when I'd last been so poorly, if ever. I slept in fits and starts, tossing and turning, my body cold and then hot, and I ached and coughed until I'd thought death would surely take me. Sometimes when I was half awake but too weak to lift my head or speak, I'd seen a shadow dance across the wall as a little figure had peered in, tiptoed towards the bed and left a cup or a plate on the bedside table.

It was the beginning of May, but I hadn't known whether it was Monday or Sunday, or some day in between. The doctor had been sent for – the sound of his heavy boots thumping up the stairs making me fearful of who'd been about to open my door – and declared that I had a bad bout of influenza. He'd added that I would live to make a full recovery but, if I was to regain my strength, I must stay in bed, get plenty of rest, drink lots of fluids, and eat lightly. I'd learned later that these instructions had been relayed to Mr. Smith and the result had been a continuous delivery to my room of cups of tea and little slices of bread and butter.

It was unusual for me to be ill. Though I'd always lived in houses full of children and had dealt with all manner of illnesses, I'd rarely become poorly myself. Other than the childhood diseases we were all stricken with, I'd barely caught so much as a cold.

I've always credited my long healthy years to a strong constitution which had come from growing up, though poor, with decent food and plenty of work, both inside and out. Being outside in all weathers doesn't kill you if you are properly dressed and well fed. From being a youngster, I'd always been in motion and I believe that is the reason why I lived to be eighty six, staying in fine fettle until the end.

If you want to live a long life free of illness, you must keep moving! When you stand still or sit for too long, illness can stake its hold on you. I've seen from Far Yonder that even though you know idleness is bad for you, you all sit so much now. In my day, we were always on our feet, upright and moving. I don't know how you can tolerate lounging in front of televisions and computers and sitting in cars for hours on end. Needless to say, I never sat in front of a television or computer and the only carriage I ever owned was nature's transport – my own two legs!

But the influenza I caught in May 1879 hit me hard, and not just physically. The fever and sleeplessness and the long hours I spent with only myself for company had my mind whirling and left me fretting and fearful for my future. Much of the time I'd been convinced that my life was over and no future, good or ill, would be mine. At times that prospect had seemed like a blessed relief because I'd known that if my life wasn't at stake, which the nice doctor had declared it was not, my future and position in the Smith household must come to an end. I'd known that my recovery must be followed, with all due haste, by my departure from Potter Hill Farm.

Though I'd been very ill and not thinking clearly, I'd been of sufficiently sound mind to know that leaving would be the only way to avoid becoming housekeeper to a new Mrs. Smith. I'd known also, without a shadow of a doubt, that there would soon be a new Mrs. Smith. I'd known because I'd heard it from Mr. Smith himself.

On the night before I became poorly, I was sitting in front of the range darning socks and sipping my ale when Mr. Smith returned home. It was a Wednesday and he'd burst into the kitchen after walking the short distance up Potter Hill from The Crown Inn. Mr. Smith always enjoyed the evenings he spent at The Crown because he thought highly of Mr. Booth, the landlord. A few years later, Luke Booth would take over The Prince of Wales and would be gratified to find that Mr. Smith and Herbert were amongst his regulars.

The weather had stayed cold and felt more like March than May so I'd put a hot water bottle in Mr. Smith's bed, just as I did during the winter months. I'd thought he'd be pleased to find a warm bed waiting for him. I don't mind saying that whenever I went up to his room and turned down the covers to put the hot water bottle in place, I would imagine climbing into that bed myself. Though I'd barely admit it to myself at the time, I'd picture Mr. Smith coming home to find me laying, attractive and seductive, in his big, comfy bed. In my fantasy, I'd skip over how I would make myself attractive and seductive as I had no idea how to accomplish such a daunting feat.

A fantasy is meant to be just that, however, and so I'd place the hot water bottle in the middle of the bed and go back downstairs to my darning. I know that some women would have the courage, not to mention the feminine wiles, to climb into their employer's bed and his arms, but I wasn't one of them. We have to be true to ourselves, and it would have been a mistake for me to act in a manner which was not in my nature.

That evening when Mr. Smith had returned home he'd talked to me for a little while, as was his usual habit, before saying goodnight and starting up the stairs. I'd called out to him that the hot water bottle was in his bed and that the sheets would be nice and warm. All at once the sound of his footsteps had ceased and, as I'd pushed my needle through the thick wool of his sock, I'd lifted my head listening for either his voice or the sound of his steps on the stairs. But there had been only silence.

I'd started to say once again, only louder, that the hot water bottle was in his bed, when all of a sudden he'd come back into the kitchen. I hadn't heard a single footstep and it was as if he'd flown down the hall. Mr. Smith had stared at me with an expression on his face that I hadn't seen before. He'd looked so serious that I'd worried I'd done something wrong, and I'd instantly felt a yearning to see the handsome face and the dancing eyes which had become so familiar to me. From the beginning, my husband's face was most appealing to me when he was feeling lighthearted.

Not wanting to stare back at his serious expression, I'd lowered my head and busied myself, suddenly needing to change the wool in my needle. After what seemed like an endless silence, Mr. Smith had started to speak, his voice sounding as if he was making an effort to stay calm. He'd thanked me for being thoughtful and said he'd enjoy getting into a warm bed. I'd looked up at him and smiled.

He'd continued to speak, staring at me so intently I'd put my head back down, as if my only concern was threading the needle and stitching up the hole in his sock. He'd said that he hoped it wouldn't be too long before he would have no need of a bloody hot water bottle. His voice had risen when he'd said bloody. As I've mentioned before, Mr. Smith rarely swore at home so I'd known he was upset. This had made me nervous and I'd giggled, starting to say that it wasn't fair to call the hot water bottle names when its only purpose in life was to keep us warm. But I'd stopped when I'd heard what he said next.

I don't intend to sleep alone for the rest of my life, Mary.

Mr. Smith had said that he didn't intend to sleep alone for the rest of his life. I'd known in an instant what that meant. It could mean only one thing. Mr. Smith was going to take another wife.

It had been clear that Mr. Smith didn't expect a response to his comment because as quickly as he'd reappeared in the kitchen, he'd left again and I'd sat staring at his sock as he'd thudded up the stairs. I'd told myself that it was a cold night and Mr. Smith must be fed up of depending for warmth upon a hot water bottle that grew cold before dawn. Though I had no experience of sleeping with a husband, I'd spent every night of my childhood sharing a bed with two or three brothers and sisters. You don't have to be married to know that a human body keeps you warm all night, whereas a hot water bottle turns into a cold mass well before dawn and has to be tossed onto the floor. It wouldn't be surprising that Mr. Smith wanted a wife in his bed, not a bottle.

I'd also had to accept, right there and then, that Mr. Smith's announcement had been a warning that the friendliness and easy chatter that took place between us would be coming to an end. After all, a new wife wouldn't tolerate her husband talking so cozily with his housekeeper! A new wife would be sitting by the range every evening waiting for her husband to come home so he could share his stories with her.

In my sick bed, my mind had swirled with images of the widow Bowman and pretty Miss Green. Yet, I would also remind myself that Mr. Smith had spoken my name at the same time he'd stated that he wasn't going to sleep alone. But, as soon as that thought entered my head, I'd dismissed the fact that he'd used my name. Though in public Mr. Smith referred to me as Miss Mary, he always called me Mary when we were alone. That was just his friendly, easy-going manner.

Mr. Smith hadn't meant that I, Mary, would be the one he would be sleeping with. And even if that was his meaning, he hadn't said anything about a wife. It was me who'd put the idea of a new Mrs. Smith into my head, along with my own tortured imaginings of the bride-to-be and her superior position in the household.

I'd also known that Mr. Smith would have no reason to make Miss Mary Stennett his wife. After all, every evening when he came home, there she was sitting by his range darning his socks, his youngsters sleeping soundly up above. He knew there'd be food on the table for his whole family the next day, and the day after, and the day after that. Mr. Smith had no need to go to the trouble of making Miss Stennett his wife just so he could get rid of the bloody hot water bottle.

I'd listened to his feet thud up the stairs and made a few final stitches to his sock. I'd cut the wool, set my needle aside and wiped my hands on my dress. Somehow, though the weather was chilly, the kitchen had grown hot and I'd become clammy and damp. I'd started to worry that my face had been sweating when Mr. Smith had arrived home. Then I'd decided that I was tired of worrying about my appearance. So I screwed the sock up into a ball and flung it across the kitchen.

My great-granddaughter, Elizabeth Brain (née Hartley), is married to Brian Brain, a professional cricketer who played for Worcestershire and Gloucestershire in the 1960's and 1970's. He was an opening bowler and I believe would be impressed with the strength of my arm.

The sock landed on the dresser and, though no more than a bundle of wool, the force of the throw – from a skinny arm that had spent years lifting, scrubbing, kneading, carrying and mashing – brought one of Mary Crawshaw's dishes clattering to the ground. In the silence of the house, it sounded as if the whole dresser had come crashing down. It was like when a cricket ball hits the wicket with a swift, resounding thud, and the spectators jump up to clap and cheer.

I'd known, however, not to anticipate the sound of applause and, instead, had heard rapid footsteps thundering down the stairs. Mr. Smith, with his shirt pulled out from his trousers and his hair disheveled as if he'd been pulling his hands through it, had once again appeared in the kitchen. I'd already been down on my knees picking up the pieces and had started to mumble that I was sorry for making such a noise and breaking his wife's pretty pottery. He'd laughed and bent down beside me, saying he didn't care about the broken plate, but wondered what had possessed it to suddenly fly off the dresser and crash onto the floor?

I'd turned to look at him and seen that his face was relaxed and handsome again, his eyes twinkling in the dim light. I'd smiled with relief and, together, we'd picked up the pieces of the shattered plate and thrown it in the rubbish bin.

Mr. Smith said goodnight once again and I'd listened as he'd stepped swiftly up the stairs. I'd waited until his bedroom door closed, then taken a candle, walked through the scullery and up the back stairs. I'd stopped on the landing and stared at the closed bedroom door for a moment and then continued, slowly and silently, up the stairs to my room in the attic.

XXXVI

The following day the influenza had me in its grips. I'd been right as rain all day, working in the kitchen, cooking and cleaning, but by tea time my head had been spinning and my body ached. As soon as tea had been cleared, Margaret had helped me up the stairs and from then on I'd spent days in my room with nothing but my imagination for company.

You're never more hopeless than when you are poorly. Instead of wanting to get up and fight, you can only lay and weep. Instead of looking for the bright side of a problem, you see only blackness. For several days and nights I'd tossed and turned. Other than delivering the little morsels of food and drink, the children had been told, quite sensibly, to stay out of my room. So, I'd lain there, alone and bereft, with nothing but Mr. Smith's words for company.

I don't intend to sleep alone for the rest of my life, Mary.

In a never-ending cycle, I'd replayed his words, desperately trying to find their meaning. Did Mr. Smith want another wife? Did he want me in his bed? I'd been wretched over either possibility. I hadn't dared imagine the happiest of alternatives. That Miss Mary Stennett, spinster of the parish of Billinghay, then Walcott, then Shireoaks and, now, Greasbrough, plain, thin and thirty three years of age, would be the new Mrs. Smith.

I hadn't seen how such an outcome could be possible, no matter how much I longed for it. In the Smith house, I already performed all the wifely duties – except the obvious one. How could I flatter myself that Mr. Smith would make me his wife for the sole purpose of getting me in his bed? Couldn't he find that, and a great deal more, with the other ladies? All those ladies whom, now that I was confined to my room, could stake their claim on him without my even knowing about it?

In my feverish state, I'd seen the gate left unguarded, the gatekeeper gone. I'd imagined Mr. Smith deciding it was worth his while, after all, to go all the way to Sheffield for tea. I'd pictured him taking a brisk walk up The Whins to see his friend, Mr. Yeardley, and then conveniently dropping in – this man who hated anyone dropping in on him – on Mrs. Bowman at her cozy cottage in Nether Haugh. I'd tortured myself with the picture of Miss Green stepping daintily out of school, all pretty and pert, at the exact moment her favorite pupil's father was passing by on his way to the building site.

After a few days, I'd begun to feel a bit better, but I'd been so confused about how long I'd been confined to my room, that I didn't know what was real and what was no more than my jealous imagination. For the rest of my life I would look back in amazement at what I truly hadn't known at the time: that just one year later I would have taken to my bed once again. This time it wouldn't be a result of contracting a terrible influenza, but for my first confinement.

I delivered my first child in May 1880 at thirty four years of age. At that time, I was no longer sleeping in my attic room, but in the bed I'd shared for the previous nine months with my husband. Just one year earlier, such an idea seemed as much a feverish dream as the flu-driven nightmares which plagued my addled brain.

Clement was born on May 11, 1880, a bouncing healthy full-term baby boy! A number of people had earnestly awaited his arrival for the previous two or three months, because they believed the only reason Mr. Smith suddenly wed his housekeeper was because she was in the family way. Those gossiping nosy parkers had been disappointed when Clement was born just shy of nine months after our wedding day.

I know now you can find out if you are expecting within days, but back then we didn't know for certain until two full months had passed. As disappointing as it was to those who wondered why on earth Mr. George Smith had married Miss Mary Stennett, everyone had to admit that there was no possibility that an August wedding had been arranged for a baby who wasn't born until the following May.

But, as recently as the previous year, a great deal had yet to happen before I would be sitting up in bed with Clement in my arms while a parade of half-brothers and half-sisters came to see him: Annie and Jessie, thankfully accepting that they must help downstairs, Herbert stepping awkwardly into his father's bedroom to see the new baby, our very own Virgin Mary asking to hold him while Margaret all but elbowed her out of the way. Georgie, the only one allowed to climb on the bed because I was afraid he would think the new baby would take me away from him. And William, summoned home by his father to meet his little half-brother, patting the baby's head before rushing downstairs to ask Jessie if there were any forcemeat balls in the pantry.

Looking back, I'm sure this happy ending would have come about no matter what. But I'm not sure it would have taken place during the spring and summer of 1879. Like I've said before, I'd often been disappointed with myself for not seeing what was right under my nose. Just as I'd needed to bash my head on the attic ceiling to realize that the ladies thought they'd be getting me as a housekeeper, it had taken another knock for me to come to understand that there had been at least one person at Potter Hill Farm who, from the day of my arrival, had not viewed me solely as the paid help.

The knock that I'd needed would not come in the form of another knock on the head, but as a tap on my door. A little rat-a-tat-tat from Georgie who'd come to my room – just as I'd been starting to feel better – to tell me that there was a lady in the kitchen. This was the very last thing I'd wanted to hear, but because it was Georgie giving me this long-feared but not unexpected news, I'd managed to stop myself from bursting into tears. I'd held myself together so as not to upset him as I'd known that during my illness he'd been afraid I might go the same way as his mother.

Fortunately, Georgie's arrival in my room had swiftly been followed by Margaret's. She'd exclaimed that it wasn't just any lady in the kitchen. It was Miss Mary's friend. It was the same lady who'd sent the letter which was still propped on the dresser because Miss Mary hadn't been well enough to open it!

With Margaret's words, I'd started to recover from the image of a new Mrs. Smith standing in the kitchen. But who'd written the letter which was still on the dresser? My first guess had been that it was from Mrs. Browne as she continued to write to me weekly. But, confused as I might have been, I'd thought it unlikely that busy, overextended Mrs. Browne could have made a trip to Greasbrough and now be in the kitchen. If she'd heard of my illness, she would have been more likely to enquire as to my care and, having been assured I was being looked after, would have felt blessedly free to continue with her responsibilities.

So who was this friend who'd arrived at Potter Hill Farm? I hadn't had to wonder much longer before I'd heard the sound of a familiar voice coming up the stairs. A voice which – with its thick Yorkshire accent – seemed so much more in place in Greasbrough than in Shireoaks. As Georgie and Margaret stood aside grinning, Hattie bounded into my room.

My friend rushed towards me and placed her hand on my forehead. She'd announced that I was warm, but not hot, and had turned to shoo the children out of the room. They'd immediately obeyed her and I'd got the distinct impression Hattie had been down in the kitchen for some time. She'd closed the door behind them and turned to look at me. The tears which I'd managed to hold back so as not to upset Georgie had burst from me, and I'd buried my head in my pillow and wept like a baby.

XXXVII

Yorkshire folk have long been famous for their no-nonsense, matter-of-fact attitude. Emotional outbursts are accepted as a necessary release, but are expected to be brief and to the point. You're crying. There, there. Why are you crying? Well, I never. Crying won't change anything. Dry your tears.

Hattie let me sob for a couple of minutes which, for her, had been a genuine show of patience. She then got down to business. The unopened letter had been sent to tell me that Hattie would be visiting her mother in Leeds, and she would get off the train at Rotherham and come to visit me. She'd asked if I could arrange for someone to pick her up at the station and take her back again a few hours later. Not having received a response to my letter, she'd become concerned and had left Shireoaks a day early. She said she didn't have to tell me what all manner of arrangements she'd had to make in order to do that.

Hattie reported that it hadn't been difficult for her to arrive at the station without having a lift in place. She'd asked the station master how to get to Greasbrough and he'd said a tradesman was about to leave for the village and she'd got a lift with him. I'd laughed and said that was exactly how I'd arrived at Potter Hill Farm.

As I'd laughed, Hattie had ceased her frenetic tidying up and stared at me. Good, I'm glad you're laughing, she'd said, surveying me with an eagle eye, because we don't have time for tears. With that, she'd pulled back the covers and grabbed me by the shoulders and started to ease me out of bed.

I'd protested that I was cold and didn't have the strength to stand up, that I'd been in bed for days and my legs had turned to jelly. Hattie had listened to me and ignored me, all at the same time. Nodding her head that she understood, she'd nevertheless got me out of bed and upright and I'd managed to take a few steps. She then let me sit down on the bottom of the bed.

We have a lot of work to do, Hattie said. We don't have much time because it's eight o'clock and Mr. Smith has just left for The Ship. It was still light outside and I hadn't realized evening had arrived. I asked my friend how she was going to get to Leeds if it was already late. You must leave right away, I told her. But she'd shaken her head and said she couldn't leave until the job was done and, anyway, Mr. Smith had told her she must spend the night. She said she would sleep on my floor, even though Margaret had already offered her bed.

This had been startling news to me. Mr. Smith had not only accepted Hattie showing up unexpectedly, but had insisted she spend the night? This was unusual in the extreme. But I'd felt so grateful that my friend would be staying until the following day that I'd questioned it no further.

But then I'd remembered Hattie's other words. She said a job had to be done. What job had to be done? I was soon to learn.

As I sat on the end of the bed feeling a little stronger, Hattie bustled around pulling a clean nightdress from the chest of drawers, grinning broadly upon finding a pair of blue velvet slippers in the bottom drawer. The slippers had been a cast-off from a guest at the vicarage, but I'd never worn them as they were too delicate for the stone floors in the kitchen at Potter Hill Farm. I'd been saving them for best, should such an imaginary day ever come. It would seem that, as far as Hattie was concerned, that day had arrived.

Margaret had come back upstairs to say that the bath had been filled and everyone had gone out. Right, said Hattie, help me get Miss Mary downstairs. The two of them each grabbed an arm and a shoulder and guided me down the stairs to the landing, and then down the main stairs to the front hall. I'd said that I always go down the back stairs, but Hattie said it was high time for that to change. I'd been concentrating so much on getting my legs to work properly that I hadn't paid proper attention to her comment.

The tub had been placed in front of the range and filled with hot water. Two steaming pans of water were on the range, ready to be added to the tub as the water cooled. Hattie sent Margaret for soap and towels and, in spite of my clutching protests, yanked my nightdress over my head and lowered me into the hot water. After telling me to soak for at least ten minutes, she'd disappeared and I'd heard her run back up the stairs.

Silence had descended upon the kitchen and I'd wondered again what job Hattie had been referring to. She must mean the job she'd already done. She'd got me out of bed and downstairs and into a much needed bath. She'd found me a clean nightdress and a pair of ladies slippers. She was probably changing the sheets on my bed, and the rush would be to get me out of the bath and back upstairs before Mr. Smith came back from The Ship.

I'd started looking around the kitchen to examine the state of things since I'd been ill for almost a week. I'd been pleasantly surprised to find that, at least on the surface, everything looked neat and clean. Jessie had obviously done a good job and I'd hoped she'd had plenty of help from Mary and Margaret.

The hall door had suddenly opened again and Hattie had come in carrying a beautiful blue velvet robe. As you know, I have never been particularly interested in clothes or my appearance, but the sight of that shining, sapphire material made me gasp.

Hattie had been delighted that the robe received such an approving reception, and proudly related that it had been given to her by the lady of a big, fancy house her husband had worked on. She hadn't wanted it for herself as she'd known she would never wear it, but she was taking it to her mother. However, upon discovering the job she had to do here, she'd decided that her poor mother would just have to do without the robe because it was desperately needed here in Greasbrough. She'd said her mother hadn't known of the robe's existence so wouldn't know she'd lost anything.

Again, Hattie referenced the job she had to do here and, as she'd stood by the tub and held a towel out for me, I'd asked her what job was of such importance she'd had to stay for a night in Greasbrough. Unusually for Hattie, she'd fallen silent. I'd stood up and quickly wrapped the towel around me. She'd then held up the robe to check the length and declared that the lady of the big, fancy house was also a scrawny, little thing and the robe was exactly the right length. It was neither too long, nor too short. She'd added that when she'd found the velvet slippers upstairs, she'd known it was meant to be and that the robe must be mine.

Of course, I'd soon interrupted her praising of the robe and its measurements to point out that it could hardly be worn at Potter Hill Farm, at least not by me, as it was totally unsuitable for anyone who worked. And, I'd added, that when I sat in the kitchen in the evening darning and reading the newspaper, I always stayed properly dressed and wasn't about to start lounging around in a velvet robe when Mr. Smith came home from the public house. I'd told her I appreciated her thoughtfulness, but a better use of the robe would be to brighten her mother's evenings as she sat in her little house in Leeds.

That's where you're wrong, Mary, Hattie had said. That's where you've always been wrong. You don't see yourself as worthy, not even of a free garment. The robe was gorgeous, she'd added, getting worked up as she often did, adding that the robe was nothing more than a bit of cloth. Why, she'd asked, don't you deserve this bit of cloth as much as my mother does? And why don't you deserve it more than the woman in the big, fancy house who has so much to spare?

With that, she'd motioned for me to open up my arms and I'd let the towel drop as she'd helped me into the robe. The robe was lined with silk which made me gasp as its coldness hit my skin, but within seconds the fine fabric had grown warm. I'd stood in front of her like a child as Hattie buttoned up the robe from my neck all the way down to the last button at the bottom. She'd stood back and appraised me, and then stepped forward, unfastened the top button and fussed with the collar.

That's why, she continued, you've been in Greasbrough for two years and haven't seen what I've seen in three hours. That last remark had at least confirmed my suspicion that Hattie had arrived some time before her appearance in my room an hour earlier. Knowing the speed at which Hattie moved, I'd wondered what on earth she could have been doing at Potter Hill Farm for two hours.

I would later learn that Margaret and Georgie were both in the kitchen when Hattie suddenly stepped through the back door. She was a Yorkshire lass in Yorkshire, after all, so there was no need to knock and wait to be invited into the Smith home. And, as she'd pointed out to the children as they'd stared at her, her old friend was their housekeeper and they must have been expecting her to show up some day. Like I've said before, Hattie was never a stranger.

Jessie had been getting tea ready, and Hattie had torn off her coat and helped her slice up the leftover beef, get the jars of pickles out of the pantry, set the dishes on the table and had then announced that tea was ready. Without questioning Hattie's sudden appearance, Jessie had apparently gratefully taken a mouthful to eat and rushed out of the door muttering about Whitsun and fittings. It seemed my friend's arrival at Potter Hill Farm had been an exact copy of my own.

The children obediently sat down at the table, and the back door had opened and Herbert and Mr. Smith stepped into the kitchen. Both had smiled, assuming the female figure bustling around the kitchen was Miss Mary up from her sick bed, but then must have realized that it wasn't me, but an unknown woman. Herbert, never one to question something unless it concerned building, sat down and started to eat, but Mr. Smith had stopped stock still and stared at her.

Hattie said at that moment she'd known my employer was not only fond of me, but in love with me. And that's when she'd known that she not only had a lot of work to do, but that the robe would come in handy because it was highly unlikely her friend had a single decent thing to wear for the splendid occasion which was about to take place. She'd been relieved to find, upon going up to the attic, that I was feeling better and she'd have time to get me cleaned up when Mr. Smith went out to the public house. Hattie was familiar with my employer's habits from the weekly letters I wrote to her about life in the Smith family.

I'd pretended to listen to Hattie's torrent of words but had got stuck at the beginning. Hattie had said Mr. Smith was in love with me. I'd interrupted her and asked her to repeat the first bit. She'd said there was no time for talk and that there'd already been too much time for that. It was time for deeds, not words, and those deeds must happen that night.

I'd slowly asked her what exactly she meant when she said deeds. Did she mean getting me out of bed, bathed, my hair washed, clean sheets on my bed and a cup of tea in my hands. Did she mean dressing me in the beautiful robe and the dainty velvet slippers?

Hattie had laughed and shaken her head. The little deeds that have been done so far are to get you ready for the big one, she'd said. The proposal, Mary, the proposal!

I'd stared at her in silence as, with a mixture of exasperation and delight, Hattie had raised both her voice and her arms up in the air: Mr. Smith, Mary! Mr. Smith wants to marry you!

XXXVIII

The following afternoon I'd been peeling potatoes in the scullery when Mr. Smith, I mean George, came through the door. I'd looked up at him and smiled, feeling suddenly shy in his presence. He'd walked up behind me, kissed the back of my head and run his hand down my back. He'd said he liked the way I stood up straight as it showed I was a proud and determined person. I'd thought of Mrs. Browne remarking that when she'd seen me standing so straight at the sink, she'd known I would one day leave Shireoaks. It's funny how much we reveal about ourselves without ever saying a word.

I'd felt a bit embarrassed that my employer had touched me out in the open and I'd quickly looked around afraid one of the children might be in the kitchen watching us. George had laughed and said that though it might take some getting used to, it was quite acceptable for a man to kiss his bride-to-be, even in front of his children.

I'd laughed and put down the potato peeler. There were already enough spuds in the pan and there'd be plenty more to peel the following day. I had no illusions that getting married would bring my potato cathedral to an end. In fact, it could well result in it growing even taller. I'd planned to leave the potatoes soaking overnight and the only reason I'd peeled them that afternoon was to get started on my jobs for the following day.

My bout with influenza was over, but I'd been left feeling weak and tired and would have to go slowly for a few days. The events of the previous night had filled me with happiness and given me a jolt of energy which, unfortunately, had left my body as soon I'd risen that morning and started working at my usual brisk pace.

Hattie had left that morning on a train to Leeds. Mr. Smith had taken her to the station, interrupting his work day in order to do so. His willingness to drive my friend to the station made me feel confident that what I'd heard last night were not simply words. Of course, it could well have been that Mr. Smith wanted to make sure Hattie actually left! The events of the previous evening must have left him feeling that a whirlwind had come into his house and, before it was through, he was betrothed to his housekeeper.

After dressing me in the gleaming sapphire robe, Hattie had helped me into the parlor. I'd told her it wasn't appropriate for me to sit in that room when Mr. Smith wasn't there and that I would prefer to sit by the range like I always did. She'd placed a hand – strong like mine from years of fetching, carrying, lifting and scrubbing – on my shoulder and pressed me down into a chair. It would have been futile to protest. At least it was the chair I always sat in when I talked to Mr. Smith. She'd combed my wet hair and moved my chair closer to the fire so I would keep warm and my hair would dry.

Hattie had left me in the parlor for some time before returning with a hot toddy. She'd put the kettle on the hob and found whisky and honey. The heady mixture felt warm in my hands and even warmer in my belly. I told her that she'd been a bit heavy handed with the whisky and she'd said I would need it, and not to complain when being waited on like the lady of the house. Which is what you're about to be, she'd said, once again throwing her arms up in the air.

Before I'd been able to argue with her, the back door had opened and Mr. Smith had stepped into the kitchen. Hattie must have silently indicated to him that I was in the parlor because, within a flash, he was sitting in the chair opposite me. He was smiling, his blue eyes twinkling and I realized that he was enjoying Hattie's visit and whatever they'd cooked up together.

I would learn later that Hattie had known from my letters that I was totally smitten with my employer. She'd explained, a little unnecessarily, that not only could she read my words, she could read between the lines. She'd said she'd had more than an inkling that Mr. Smith was just as keen on me. She'd noticed all those confidences he'd shared with me in the parlor after dinner and the cozy chats by the range at night. She'd taken notice of our walking arm-in-arm to the Nativity play and my seat at the dining room table with Mr. Smith's sisters. My friend was painfully aware that I knew nothing about men and was as stubborn as a mule to boot and wouldn't have gleaned what my employer was trying, in vain, to tell me.

Hattie said she'd known she would have to step in the minute she'd seen the consternation on Mr. Smith's face when he'd come home and found her in the kitchen instead of me. She'd served everyone their tea and quietly asked to speak with him in private. Following him into the parlor, she'd closed the door behind them. Without giving him chance to open his mouth, she'd told him that she knew he did not want Miss Mary to leave and to have to go to the trouble of finding a new housekeeper. She knew that he wouldn't want to come home and find someone like herself, as nice as she was, standing in the kitchen.

He'd agreed that he did not want me to leave, but added that he hadn't known that was a possibility. Hattie said he'd asked, in such a pretend casual manner it was obvious he'd known the answer, if there was anything he could do to make me stay. You can stop beating about the bush, she'd told him. Mr. Smith had adopted a puzzled expression which she could tell was a complete put on. He's not a good actor, she'd said, his face is honest and tells you everything you need to know.

She'd then added, with genuine exasperation, that if I wasn't a complete idiot I could have seen in two years what she'd seen in two minutes. It seemed an angel had been holding me in his wings, after all. The only problem was that I hadn't been able to see him. Hattie had then looked him dead in the eye and said: "Mr. Smith, you must marry Mary."

I'd asked her if it could really have been that simple. Mr. Smith isn't the kind of man you can push around. He does things his own way and in his own time. Yet you march into his house and say you must marry her and he says alright. How can I believe that?

All men need a push, Hattie had exclaimed, giving me the same look as in Shireoaks all those years earlier when I'd asked why she'd wanted to push the trumpet player into inviting her to the colliery dance. Mr. Smith hesitated, she'd added, because if it all went wrong he would have been guilty of turning over his own apple cart, wouldn't he? You run his house and take care of his children. He wouldn't want to risk losing you. What if he'd courted you and you'd turned him down? He would have lost a good housekeeper, and they are much harder to find than a good wife!

When people are honest and straightforward with each other, it's simple, Hattie had continued, adding that men and women play too many games. Again, I'd thought of the trumpet player. Hadn't she been playing a game with him? She must have read my mind because she'd immediately said she'd played plenty of games when she was young, but there was no time for that nonsense when it came to me and Mr. Smith. He'll find himself a bride, Mary, and you will leave and you will both be unhappy. All it takes is some plain speaking.

So, earlier that evening Hattie and Mr. Smith had laid out a plan together. He would go to the pub as usual and she would try to get me up and about. As long as I was able to get out of bed, they could get the job, as she called it, done. Fortunately, I'd not only been able to get out of bed, but had been sufficiently recovered to be sitting in the parlor in a beautiful velvet robe and with a hot toddy in my hand when Mr. Smith came home.

After some enquiries as to how I was feeling, and kindly saying how relieved he was that I was much better, the room had fallen silent. How I'd wished to be sitting at the range with my darning so I could look down and occupy myself with my stitches. It would have been so much easier to avoid the look on his face which, just as on the night I'd broken his wife's plate, had become so serious. How much I preferred the lighthearted look on his handsome face.

Mary, he'd said, breaking the silence. Or should I say, Miss Stennett, he'd added, his face starting to brighten. Mary, will you marry me?

During all the times I'd dared to imagine this scene, the reality hadn't been what I'd expected. I'd pictured bells starting to ring and gongs proclaiming such astounding news. Yet, as my future husband has risen out of his chair and knelt down before me, I'd felt merely a comfortable familiarity. It was as if I'd been welcoming home a husband of many years, one who had been away at sea or far away to a long war. It seemed the only person who'd been at sea was me.

Marry me, Mary, he said. I looked down at the thick, blue robe and at his hands resting upon mine on its folds. Yes, I said. Yes, Mr. Smith, I will marry you.

A crashing of pots had suddenly sounded as Hattie and Margaret, who'd pretended to be busy in the kitchen, dropped an earthenware bowl on the stone floor. They'd shouted out in alarm at being caught eavesdropping, but then dissolved into laughter. Mr. Smith had taken my hand and helped me out of the chair, and we'd stood in the parlor doorway watching Hattie and Margaret dry the tears from their eyes.

Fortunately, the pair had immediately gone upstairs to bed and, hours later when I'd finally gone to my room, I'd found Hattie curled up in a ball of blankets at the foot of my bed. The next day she'd declared that she'd slept in my room to make sure I was chaperoned. You were a dirty stop out, nevertheless, she'd added gleefully.

I'd jumped in to defend my honor, saying that we'd sat up in the parlor talking for hours. I am still a maiden, I'd let her know. Not for too much longer, Hattie had said, adding that she'd thought the day would never come.

It was true that George and I had sat up for hours that night. It was the most magical night of my life. For all the happy times we had after that, it was that night that I'd heard for the first time the reasons Mr. Smith wanted me to be not just his housekeeper, but his wife.

He'd said he loved my Lincolnshire accent which I'd been amazed to learn as some people made fun of the way I spoke and, on more than one occasion, I'd had to remind Mary and William not to mimic my accent. No, Mr. Smith had said, your accent makes you different and that's why I like it. I'd wondered out loud if I should have moved further away, saying that maybe the further you go from where you were born, the more interesting you become. But I'd added that Greasbrough was as far as I would ever want to go.

Mr. Smith said he'd had ideas about making me his bride ever since he'd come home that first night and seen my bum sticking out of the oven. I'd blushed at this comment because no matter how familiar he now seemed to me, I'd been embarrassed to know he'd been thinking about my behind. I'm not going to talk about our lovemaking but, as you know, Mr. Smith was a man of experience. I'd had none, as Hattie had reminded me before she'd left for the station that morning. Just go along, she'd said, in her wise, matter-of-fact manner. Just go along, and you won't go wrong. But don't forget to enjoy it, either.

I'd been most flattered to hear that Mr. Smith enjoyed our chats together and felt he could talk to me. He liked that I read the newspapers and discussed the news with him. He liked that I was good with his children, and that I loved Margaret and Georgie.

For a brief silly moment, I'd felt sorry for the ladies who'd called at Potter Hill Farm. I'd felt sorry that they hadn't realized the many advantages I had over them. That I cared for Mr. Smith's children and was patient with the ones I hadn't grown to love. That

I sometimes sat in the parlor with him after he'd eaten his dinner. That he'd liked my bum when he'd seen it sticking out of the oven. That in every way, except the bedroom, I was already his wife. All the cakes and pies in the world couldn't compete with that.

XXXIX

The church bells rang on a bright Monday morning in August. Even the sun came out to celebrate, shining down on us in what was otherwise one of England's wettest, coldest summers. Monday had always been my day off and George had joked for weeks that we couldn't waste time getting wed on a work day. I would have got married anytime from Monday to Sunday, but I'd been happy to be a bride on the day of the week that had been mine since going into service twenty years earlier.

George had also said, with his eyes shining at his own joke, he would no longer have to pay for my housekeeping services because a wife doesn't collect wages from her husband. And as if that wasn't enough to make me nervous, he'd wondered out loud as we'd snuggled in his chair in the parlor late one evening, if the money he'd already paid me, and the vails I'd scrupulously saved, would become his property. I'd bitten hook, line and sinker on his teasing and had immediately jumped off his lap and reminded him about the Married Women's Property Act. The Act had passed almost ten years earlier in 1870, and had made it the law that the wages a woman had earned would remain hers upon marrying.

As I'd gleefully told him that the vails would be mine to keep, George had looked at me curiously. He'd then nodded his head saying what a good thing it was that not only had that law come into effect, but every woman in England was aware of it. At least, he'd added, those who read the newspaper from front to back every day. Had I read about it in the daily papers? Or, maybe I'd seen it in the Rotherham *Advertiser*?

This last question had been asked with another predictable gleam in his eye because soon after I'd arrived in Greasbrough I'd learned that a weekly newspaper had been started a few years earlier by a woman. In fact, I'd learned about it from a woman standing in the queue at Willey's shop, which shows that you need to get out if you want to keep up-to-date. But you don't have to fly to the other side of the world. A walk down to the butcher's shop might be all that you need.

Ann Hinchcliffe ran a printing company in Rotherham, and had started the weekly *Advertiser* herself. I'd been so impressed that a woman had started her own newspaper that I'd asked Mr. Smith if he would order a copy. He'd already noticed me pouring over his crumpled copies of the *Sheffield Daily Telegraph* and the *Sheffield and Rotherham Independent* and had gleaned that I liked to read. He'd said that being informed could never be considered a frivolous expense, so it would be alright to get another paper. But, he'd added, it couldn't replace the weekly *Barnsley Chronicle* which he enjoyed reading every Saturday, as did I.

In fact, I'd read about the Married Women's Property Act in all those newspapers as it had been given a lot of coverage and there had been many opinions about it, good and bad. There were many aspects to the law regarding property and inheritances, but the only money I had was from the wages and tips I'd earned in twenty years of service.

You might think it odd that I'd been concerned about my meager savings when I was about to become the wife of a man of means, though just saying that makes me sound like one of the ladies who were after Mr. Smith! But some habits are hard to drop even when your circumstances are much improved, and having a little money of your own is a habit no woman, or man, should ever give up.

The wedding was held at St. George's Church in Doncaster, about fifteen miles north of Greasbrough, and the ceremony was conducted by Reverend Charles Sisum Wright. The church had burned to the ground years earlier and been rebuilt and consecrated in 1858. That beautiful church is now known as Doncaster Minster, and if you visit it today you will be able to picture us there, me feeling giddy and George smiling from ear-to-ear.

We got married in Doncaster, not because of the grandeur of the church but because George didn't want to be wed in Greasbrough. Or at least that's the reason he gave to me and everyone else. He said that getting married was a private matter and had never understood why hordes of people stood outside church whenever there was a wedding. I'd thought his notion of hordes of people was a bit exaggerated, although in the case of George Smith, farmer, builder, father, widower, there had been the distinct possibility that crowds of people might show up to see the groom, though certainly not the bride.

But I'd known all along that the real reason George had insisted on getting married at St. George's Church was because there was efficient train service between Lincolnshire and Doncaster. It would be a great deal easier for my parents to attend the wedding than if they had to come to Greasbrough. The ease of the journey also made it possible for Mrs. Browne to be at the ceremony, bringing two of her daughters with her, which was a wonderful surprise for me. All in all, I'd been touched at George's reasons for insisting we marry in Doncaster, as they had all contributed to making it a very special day for the bride.

The most important people for me at the wedding, other than the two of us, were my mother and father, John and Elizabeth Stennett. My father had proudly walked me down the aisle and other than a few loud remarks that "it was about time" and "Mary's caught a good 'un", he'd been quiet and contained, at least for him. But I'd known he'd been genuinely happy to meet George, and be with us on the big day.

To my delight, another Elizabeth Stennett was at the wedding. Following us down the aisle was my baby sister, Elizabeth. For a number of years, Elizabeth had worked in Peterborough as a nurse for Henry Townsend, an architect, and his wife, Helen. She looked after their four children and had been fortunate that the family also had a cook, a housemaid and two other servants. I never had the chance of such help!

If I'd thought I was getting old to be married at the age of thirty three, it turned out I was a spring chicken compared to my baby sister. Elizabeth married Henry Harris, a police constable, in 1901 at the age of forty one. They lived for a time in New Windsor, Berkshire and later in Dartford, Kent. Elizabeth had one child, Harry Harris, when she was forty four. No matter what Hattie might say, it's never too late to find love and happiness.

Hattie, of course, was at the wedding, having said when she'd left that May morning that wild dogs and horses wouldn't keep her away. She'd sat in the front pew between Margaret and Georgie, like an aunt or old family friend. As far as I'd been concerned, she was both.

Sitting alongside them were Annie, Jessie, Herbert and Mary. William was at the far end of the pew, sitting away from the group, but with a surprisingly happy smile on his face. That had, undoubtedly, been in anticipation of the forcemeat balls and dinner that awaited us all at Potter Hill Farm. I'd been flattered that George had insisted that all seven of his children be at church. Whatever they thought of their father getting married they kept it to themselves, knowing he wouldn't tolerate any questions or criticism of his decision. Back then, parents didn't seek the approval of their own children.

There were many things I'd liked about being a bride, but most of all I'd loved feeling younger and prettier than on any other day in my life. As much as I'd always resisted spending money, I'd decided to treat myself and, one Monday, I'd gone to the market in Rotherham to buy material. The outing, in itself, had been an unusual treat and I'd enjoyed examining the bolts of fine fabric as if I went out to buy material very week like some of the Rotherham ladies.

I'd bought three yards of beautiful pearl-colored cotton which Jessie had expertly fashioned into a gorgeous dress. I'd asked her to make something suitable for a bride, but not so fussy that I couldn't wear it on another special occasion, should the opportunity arise. But the truth was that I'd been so excited to be getting married, I'd been willing to spend my money on a dress I might wear only once.

Jessie's design for my bridal dress was simple, but it flattered me so much I'd barely recognized myself when I'd studied my reflection in her dressmaker's mirror. The slender shape cinched my waist, and the soft cotton dropped down to the ground in elegant folds. She'd designed a low square neckline which emphasized my bosom. By some miracle, which so many women in the family who came after me knew instinctively, the choice of material and the pearl color suited me perfectly. I'd looked feminine and pretty without appearing fussy or overblown.

Jessie did my hair, raising it high on my head at the back. In the front, she'd placed a small wreath of white and pink roses, which put a shine on my usually drab brown hair. I'd felt like a princess.

I'd arrived at St. George's Church and my groom had turned to watch me walk down the long aisle. He'd been visibly surprised at my appearance, staring at me so intently I'd been afraid his serious face was going to appear. More than anything I'd wanted to see his light, friendly face. Fortunately, I'd got my wish as George had been happy and relaxed the rest of the day.

There had been many changes and interruptions to our regular daily lives that Monday. Most surprisingly, George had announced that he wouldn't be going to The Prince of Wales later that night. And, so, as the long evening had finally drawn in and the children were either out or in bed, we'd walked together up the front stairs to the main bedroom. George closed the door behind us and, for the first time, we were alone in his room together. By the time that bedroom door opened again, the virgin Mary was well and truly gone from Potter Hill Farm.

When Tuesday dawned, the household routines returned to normal. I'd risen early to make breakfast and to clean up what hadn't been put away the night before. George had gone to work on time and come home for dinner at noon and for tea at six o'clock. That night he'd gone to The Yellow Lion as he did every Tuesday. In the evenings that followed, I'd do my usual darning jobs and read the paper in the quiet of the kitchen. But sometimes I'd get into bed before he came home and wait until I heard him step quickly up the stairs, eager to get into the nice warm sheets. Mr. Smith had no more need of a hot water bottle.

On the Friday after the wedding, I'd been reading the *Advertiser* while George was at The Ship. I'd turned to the page which listed the week's births, deaths and marriages, and had immediately found what I was looking for. Printed in black and white, nicely positioned in the middle of the page for everyone to see, it was reported that on August 18, 1879, at St. George's Church, Doncaster, Mr. George Smith, widower, and Miss Mary Stennett, spinster, were joined together in matrimony, and were now man and wife.

XL

For many years into our marriage, we continued to live at Potter Hill Farm. Much later, the front rooms of the house were converted into a shop, with a big window and an entrance facing down Potter Hill. Nora Hartley, sister-in-law of my granddaughter, Joan Hartley (née Schonhut) owned the shop and sold general provisions. Nora was a real beauty in her day and she married a wonderful Polish man named Frank Sobkowiak. Frank was a bomber pilot in the Second World War who, tragically, was killed in action in 1942. For his exceptional bravery, Frank Sobkowiak was awarded Poland's highest medal, the equivalent of the Victoria Cross. Nora and Frank's daughter, Carole, was only a few months old when he was killed. Sadly, Nora did not know where her young husband had been killed or where he was buried, and never got over losing him.

After we'd been married almost twelve years, we moved into the house my husband built for us down Willow Garth. It was finished in 1892 and, like many of my husband's properties, the house still stands today, tall and proud on Rossiter Road. The four distinctive bay windows were my design. When I'd shown George my ideas for the house, he'd asked where the door was supposed to go if the entire front was taken up with windows. I'd said that the front door would be at the side of the house, adding that it would suit him perfectly. Why put an entrance on the front of the house if you don't want uninvited visitors to call round?

With that, he'd told me I could design the whole house and, as long as he had a chair by a fireside and a place to put his pipe and tobacco and read the newspaper, he didn't care about the rest of it. At the time, I'd been thrilled to be put in charge of the design, but looking back I'd realized it was the first sign that my husband was getting tired. As we get older, we don't care as much about the layout of a house and every detail of it inside and out, because we are beginning to realize that the day will dawn when neither the house, nor our opinion, will matter.

Nevertheless, as many of you would agree, designing your own house is an exciting task and I'd enjoyed every minute of it, no matter how much work it turned out to be. I'd made sure that the living room and dining room each had a fireplace, and that there was enough space for a man to spread his legs and enjoy some peace and quiet. I'd separated those rooms from the noise and clamor of the kitchen with a large hall with high stained glass windows to let in the northern light. Going up from the hall was a solid staircase, also with a stained glass window, which led to three large bedrooms and an upstairs bathroom, which was a complete luxury.

After a few years of living in our new house, the lane became formally known as Rossiter Road, and we named our house Rossiter Villa. The name, Rossiter, is familiar to you as you know that George's sister, Mary, married William Rossiter, a railway laborer from Bermondsey. You will also recall that Mary Rossiter owned a piece of land down Willow Garth.

It turned out that as far back as 1856, Mary's husband, William Rossiter, had purchased the land from a Mr. Benjamin Sellers. When William Rossiter died in 1870, he left the land to his widow, Mary. Years later, on September 25, 1883, Mary Rossiter sold the property to her brother, George. I believe my husband had his eye on that land for a long time, which is why – shrewdly and with more than a bit of self-interest – he always advised his sister to hold on to it.

William and Mary Rossiter owned the property on Willow Garth for twenty seven years, beginning with William's purchase in 1856, and Mary's eventual sale of it to her brother in 1883. Mary died in 1884, the year following the sale.

I have always been convinced that George named our road after his sister and brother-in-law. My husband and I talked about many things together including his business dealings, yet he never told me whether or not he'd personally chosen the name. Whenever I asked him, he would smile and his eyes would twinkle, but he would say that some things in life are just a coincidence.

I didn't believe for a minute that a somewhat unusual name had been chosen for our road, and that it was just a coincidence that it was the name of my husband's relations, the very same couple who originally owned our property. Given that my husband was a prominent builder in Greasbrough, it stands to reason that Mr. George Smith had a say in naming the road on which he built his family home. Throughout his life, however, George took great pains to ensure that he wasn't viewed as having an unfair advantage over other men. He believed you should get the contract on a building job because you do the best work, not because you have the best connections. He would often remind the children to make sure their work spoke for itself and didn't depend upon the words, or favors, of others.

So, it is quite likely that my husband didn't want to put himself in a position where it might be suggested that George Smith used his influence to put his relative's name on the road. There were other, earlier, owners on that same lane who might complain. However, it's clear that George may never have owned the Willow Garth land were it not for the initial purchase by his brother-in-law, his sister's inheritance of it from her husband, and her eventual sale of the property to him.

The road was named Rossiter Road by the time of the 1901 census, and I remain certain that George wished to honor William and Mary Rossiter's long investment in Greasbrough by naming the road after them. I just wish it had been documented so I could prove it!

Our youngest child, Effie, had been three years old when we'd moved to Rossiter Villa which, it would turn out, would play a big part in her life. First, she would spend her childhood there, and later would live at Rossiter Villa with Bert and their children. Their youngest, Nigel, was born in the back bedroom in 1928. During that time, Effie was fortunate to have a wonderful housekeeper named Mary Bielby. You see how the next generation lived so differently. I spent much of my life as a housekeeper, but my daughter employed one!

In a similar example of how future generations can do so much better than the last, Mary Bielby would have a nephew, Andrew Bailey, who, with his wife, Jean, would own Rossiter Villa in the 1970's and 1980's. It's nice to know that my daughter and Mary Bielby's nephew did so well.

In 1941, Bert and Effie moved to Moorgate Lane in Rotherham and rented Rossiter Villa to Mr. Rhodes, the manager of the Yorkshire Penny Bank, who lived there for many years.

In 1955, Effie's youngest child, Nigel Hague, moved to Rossiter Villa with Stella and their three daughters, Jane, Veronica and Sally. William was born during the time the family lived there, and his older sisters remember standing excitedly on the stairs as their father announced they had a new baby brother. Nigel and Stella stayed at Rossiter Villa until 1971 when they moved to Wentworth and, for the first time, the house was sold outside the family.

Rossiter Villa is now owned by Stephen and Amanda Pilgrim. Amanda works for an organization which promotes the work of small and medium-sized building companies. My husband would be happy to know that his house is in the hands of a woman who supports builders!

During his later years, George had been very concerned about what would happen to Rossiter Villa after he was gone. He often mentioned that he didn't want the house to be sold right away, and he assured me it would remain my home for as long as I would need it. As I mentioned earlier in this book, when my husband passed away in 1907, he left me a Life Estate in Rossiter Villa, which was to be followed by a Life Estate to his son, Georgie. My Life Estate lasted until my death on May 15, 1932 but, sadly, Georgie would be gone before his could even begin.

Georgie and his wife, Annie Edwards, lived at 39 Westgate in Rotherham, where he made a living as a fruiterer. Georgie's passing in 1930 meant that, upon my death, Rossiter Villa was to go to his son, George Albert Smith. George Albert was a school teacher who lived on Wharncliffe Street in Rotherham.

The property was left to George Albert with full ownership, and he was, therefore, free to keep it or dispose of it as he wished. There's only so much you can control from the grave, and I believe my husband accepted that his wishes should come to an end with a grandchild. However, he'd be happy to know that our daughter, Effie, acquired the property from George Albert, and that Rossiter Villa stayed in the Hague family until 1971.

During the time I was at Rossiter Villa as a widow, Florrie and Arthur lived at home with me. Their second child, Effie Wadsworth (née Holroyd), was born in the house in 1910. I, too, am happy that the house my husband built for us in 1892 stayed in the family for almost eighty years. As I've said before, try to leave something you've made behind when you are gone. You will live longer that way.

By the time we moved into our new house, much had happened since the day we'd got married. Clement had been born the year following our wedding, making me the mother of my own precious boy. George was fifty three when Clement was born and, as there'd been no opportunity to suggest we'd got married because there was a bun in the oven, there had, instead, been some gossip about Mr. Smith adding another child to the eight he'd had with Mary Crawshaw. But everyone knows that a new wife, particularly one bringing up the previous wife's children, will want a baby of her own. And so it had been expected that another Smith baby would come along.

It was almost five years later when, on February 21, 1885, our daughter, Elizabeth, was born. Back then, no-one was in the least bit surprised when a baby arrived, even if the mother wasn't getting any younger and a few years had gone by since the last. There were often big gaps between babies, and there's nothing new about older mothers. But George had just turned fifty eight years of age when Elizabeth was born, and the first comments about "Rabbit George" started to be made. Fortunately, George was always popular and self-confident and, not only knew how to take a bit of good-natured ribbing, but how to silence anyone he thought was taking it too far.

Two years later, not long after my husband turned sixty, Florence was born on March 31, 1887, and "Rabbit George" came into popular use throughout Greasbrough. This nickname was further cemented when, on February 12, 1889, Effie came forth into the world. Just the week before, George had turned sixty-two. My dear husband would be known evermore as "Rabbit George".

I've enjoyed getting to know you all from Far Yonder. I hope you've learned a lot about your forebears and that you will pass this knowledge on to the generations to come. We all leave this earth hoping our family members will stay in touch and that the connections will be strong. It's an unrealistic wish because, though you are part of my family, you also belong to others. But, I'm sure you now know more about each other than when you first opened this book.

Happy years are made up of hundreds of different days and "Rabbit George" and me had many of them. But looking back from Far Yonder, I know that the happiest day of my life was the one which followed our wedding day. It was the Tuesday when everything had returned to normal.

Tea was ready on the table and, as I was waiting for George and Herbert to come home at six o'clock, I'd gone up to my attic room to tidy up from the whirlwind of the day before. I'd sat down on the bed and a great relief had washed over me at being able to gather myself in the familiar surroundings of my room. Though truly happy to be a bride, I hadn't forgotten who I was overnight. You don't lose yourself in the space of a day, not when you've been so long in the making.

My sampler was still hanging on the wall and I'd got up from the bed to take it off its hook in order to move it down to the main bedroom. I'd studied my work for a moment, thinking of all that had happened since the day I'd put in the last stitch.

On my sampler was everything I'd known I would need in life: the alphabet, so I could read the newspapers and discuss the state of the world with my husband; numbers, so I could count my wages and save my vails; my family name, Mary Stennett, which, though I hadn't yet known it, would live on through my grandsons' Clement, Wilfred and Tony; the year, 1858, so it would always be known when the sampler was completed – and that it was done on time! The words "feed my lambs" to remind me to care for the young ones: the Harrison children, the Browne children, Mary Crawshaw's children, and, as yet unknown to me, my own four precious lambs. And, at the bottom, a shepherd, so I would always remember my parents.

I'd gone over to the window and, still clutching my sampler, looked down Potter Hill. George was coming up the road with his usual fast stride and, though busily talking to Herbert, must have sensed he was being watched. He'd glanced up at the house and, not finding anyone peering out of the ground or first floor windows, had bent his head backwards to look up at the attic. Seeing me, he'd stopped so quickly that Herbert had taken several more steps before realizing his father was no longer at his side.

George had smiled up at me with the light, friendly face I loved best. I'd waved and smiled and turned back into the room. As I lay the sampler down on the bed, I'd been surprised to see it was splashed with tears. I'd wiped my eyes and rushed down the stairs to welcome my husband home.

THE DESCENDANTS

APPENDIX I

MARY STENNETT'S FAMILY:
DESCENDANTS OF JOHN STENNETT (1813-1882) AND
ELIZABETH STENNETT (1814-1898)

Children

Martha Stennett Beaumont

Joseph Stennett

Mary Stennett Smith

John Stennett

Ann Stennett Loweth

Thomas Stennett

William Stennett

Elizabeth Stennett Harris

Grandchildren (known)

Mary Ann Beaumont

Charles Beaumont

Fanny Beaumont

Henry Beaumont

Elizabeth Beaumont

Clement Smith

Elizabeth Smith Schonhut

Florence Smith Holroyd

Effie Smith Hague

Henry Loweth

Elizabeth Loweth

Annie Loweth

Lucy Loweth

Thomas Loweth

Joseph Loweth

Annie Stennett Ashworth

Thomas Stennett

William Stennett

Arthur Stennett

Cyril Stennett

Elizabeth Stennett

Harry Harris

Great-Grandchildren (known)

Robert Beaumont

Martha King

Charles King

Albert King

Nellie King

Cyril Ashworth

Wilfred Smith

Clement Smith

George Schonhut

Joan Schonhut Hartley

Arthur Holroyd

Effie Holroyd Wadsworth

Neville Holroyd

Hubert Peter Holroyd

Ruth Holroyd Sampson

Charles Hague

Pauline Hague Goodswen

Anthony Hague

Timothy Nigel Hague

Thomas Stennett

Winifred Loweth

Jack Loweth

Robert Loweth

Val Loweth

Great-great-grandchildren (known)

Eric Smith

Anthony Smith

Pauline Schonhut Tear

Hilary Schonhut Hoskins

Charles Robin Hartley

Elizabeth Hartley Ogley Brain

Gabrielle Wadsworth Stephenson

Peter Holroyd

Leonard Mark Sampson

April Sampson Stern

Julia Hague Ross

Charles Hague

Philip Goodswen

Stephanie Goodswen

Jane Hague MacCaw

Veronica Hague Clinton

Sally Hague Foster

William J. Hague

Great-great-great-grandchildren (known)

Julie Smith Ford
Wendy Smith
Neil Smith
Sarah Smith
Joanne Smith
Lesley Smith
Jacqueline Tear Houghton
James Tear
Rupert Hoskins
Elizabeth Hartley Sayers
Clare Hartley Kitt Erskine
Fleur Hartley Shaw
Richard Ogley
Jonathan Ogley
Mark Stephenson
Deborah Stephenson Gill

Henry Sampson
Cordelia Sampson
George Stern
Edward Stern
James Ross
Mark Hague
Robert Hague
Lucy Hague
Emily Hague
James Goodswen
Charlotte Goodswen Schoch
Marina MacCaw Lewis
Joseph MacCaw
Edward Clinton
Rebecca Foster Carruthers
Harriet Foster Heron

Great-great-great-great-grandchildren (known)

Jack Ford
Sam Ford
Isobel Smith
Libby Smith
Robert Shaw
Sophie Bird
Emily Houghton
Suzanna Houghton
Charles Tear
Alexander Tear
Henry Tear
Adele Elizabeth Sayers
Joe Sayers

Joshua Sayers
Mia Kitt
Amber Kitt
Mabelle Erskine
Kara Shaw
Quillen Shaw
Isla Ogley
Lucie Ogley
Charles Ogley
Lucas Stephenson
Chloe Stephenson
Adam Gill
Alex Gill

Aaron Ross
Harry Hague
Evi Hague
Thomas Goodswen
Hannah Goodswen

Alexander Schoch
Emily Schoch
Theo Castaneda Clinton
Wesley Castaneda Clinton
Mina Lewis

Great-great-great-great-great-grandchildren (known)

Logan Sayers

APPENDIX II

GEORGE SMITH'S FAMILY:
DESCENDANTS OF WILLIAM SMITH (1796-1864)
AND ELIZABETH FOULSTON SMITH (1801-1872)

Children

Mary Smith Rossiter

George Smith

Jane Smith

James L. Smith

Elizabeth Smith

Herbert Smith

Grandchildren (known)

Mary Rossiter Wellman

William A. Rossiter

Albert E. Rossiter

George S. Rossiter

Herbert H. Rossiter

George E. Smith

Annie Smith

Jessie Smith Chambers

Herbert Smith

William J. Smith

Mary Smith

Margaret Smith Laver

George Smith

Clement Smith

Elizabeth Smith Schonhut

Florence Smith Holroyd

Effie Smith Hague

Walter T. Smith

Alfred Smith

William Smith

Guildford Smith

Marshall Smith

Annie Smith Stanley

Martha Smith

William P. Smith

Great-Grandchildren (known)

William J. Wellman

Arthur E. Wellman

Herbert H. Wellman

Alfred E. Wellman

Percy W. Wellman

Beatrice Rossiter

Herbert Rossiter

Maud Rossiter

Alfred Rossiter

Arthur Rossiter

Jay Rossiter

Gilbert Rossiter

Frank Rossiter

Phoebe Rossiter Baddley

William H. Rossiter

Elizabeth Rossiter Campbell

Frederick C. Rossiter

Edith Rossiter Lovesy

George A. Rossiter

Lucy Rossiter Evans

Clifford Young Rossiter

Lillian Young Rossiter

Russell Young Rossiter

Ernest Crabtree Rossiter

Elmer D. Rossiter

Jane Stanley

James L. Stanley

Elizabeth Laver Maxfield

Joseph Laver

Jessie Laver Dowden

Lucie 'Cissie' Laver Johnson

Margaret 'Ruda' Laver Jones

James Laver

Edward Laver

Frances 'Nora' Laver Senior

Herbert Smith

Hilda Smith

Henry Smith

Constance Smith

George Smith

Cyril Smith

William E. Smith

Harold Chambers

William C. Smith

Frank Smith

Reginald Chambers Smith

Oswald Smith

Lilian Smith

Edgar Rands Smith

George Smith

Walter Smith

Gertrude Smith

Harold Smith

Ada Smith

Ethel Smith

George Smith

Guildford Smith

Lewis Smith

Emma Smith Graham

Harold Smith

William Smith
Ernest Smith
Annie Smith
Ada Smith
Albert Smith
Annie Smith Wall
Sarah Smith Bowling
Elsie Smith Healey
Guildford Smith
Wilfred S. Smith
Clement S. Smith

George Schonhut
Joan Schonhut Hartley
Arthur Holroyd
Effie Holroyd Wadsworth
Neville Holroyd
Hubert Peter Holroyd
Ruth Holroyd Sampson
Charles Hague
Pauline Hague Goodswen
Anthony Hague
Timothy Nigel Hague

Great-great-grandchildren (known)

Doris Wellman
Arthur Wellman
Douglass Wellman
Cyril Wellman
Edith Rossiter
Bryan Rossiter
Eliza Rossiter
William Rossiter
Frank B. Rossiter
Ruth Rossiter Peck
Frederick S. Rossiter
William A. Rossiter
Afton Eliza Rossiter Heninger
Lawrence C. Rossiter
Alfred H. Rossiter
Sadie Rossiter
Shannon L. Rossiter
Belva Rossiter Bird

Ernest T. Rossiter
Babette Homolya
Robert D. Rossiter, Sr.
Phyllis Maxfield Thickett
Margaret Maxfield Charlton
Mary Laver
Jessie Dowden
Frank Laver
Margaret Laver
Patricia Laver
Albert Healey
Joan Skelton Smith
Irene A. Smith
Constance Smith
Alfred Wall
Edna Wall
Cecil Wall
Shirley Graham Atherton

John Smith
Guildford Bowling
Eric Smith
Anthony Smith
Pauline Schonhut Tear
Hilary Schonhut Hoskins
Charles Robin Hartley
Elizabeth Hartley Ogley Brain
Gabrielle Wadsworth Stephenson
Peter Holroyd

Leonard Mark Sampson
April Sampson Stern
Julia Hague Ross
Charles R. Hague
Philip Goodswen
Stephanie Goodswen
Jane Hague MacCaw
Veronica Hague Clinton
Sally Hague Foster
William J. Hague

Great-great-great-grandchildren (known)

Sandra Oakland Pounder
David W. Oakland
Allan G. Oakland
Linda Oakland
Susan Bowling Lane
Jane Bowling
Pamela Thickett
Peter Thickett
Diana Charlton
Monica Charlton
Clare Charlton Pattinson
David Skelton Johnston
Lindsay Skelton Johnston
Julie Smith Ford
Wendy Smith
Neil Smith
Sarah Smith
Joanne Smith

Lesley Smith
Jacqueline Tear Houghton
James Tear
Rupert Hoskins
Elizabeth Hartley Sayers
Clare Hartley Kitt Erskine
Fleur Hartley Shaw
Richard Ogley
Jonathan Ogley
Mark Stephenson
Deborah Stephenson Gill
Henry Sampson
Cordelia Sampson
George Stern
Edward Stern
James Ross
Mark C. Hague
Robert Hague

Lucy Hague
Emily Hague
James Goodswen
Charlotte Goodswen Schoch

Marina MacCaw Lewis
Joseph MacCaw
Edward Clinton
Rebecca Foster Carruthers
Harriet Foster Heron

Great-great-great-great-grandchildren (known)

Victoria Pattinson
Elizabeth Pattinson
Robert Pattinson
Rachel Thickett Holden
Natalie Thickett Swift
Jack Ford
Sam Ford
Isobel Smith
Libby Smith
Robert Shaw
Sophie Bird
Emily Houghton
Suzanna Houghton
Charles Tear
Alexander Tear
Henry Tear
Adele Elizabeth Sayers
Joseph Sayers
Joshua Sayers
Mia Kitt
Amber Kitt
Mabelle Erskine
Kara Shaw
Morgyn Johnston

Quillen Shaw
Isla Ogley
Lucie Ogley
Charles Ogley
Lucas Stephenson
Chloe Stephenson
Adam Gill
Alex Gill
Aaron Ross
Harry Hague
Evi Hague
Thomas Goodswen
Hannah Goodswen
Alexander Schoch
Emily Schoch
Theo Castaneda Clinton
Wesley Castaneda Clinton
Mina Lewis

Great-great-great-great-great-grandchildren (known)

Bailey Holden

Nyah Holden

Thea Holden

Finley Holden

Riley Whyte

Logan Sayers

APPENDIX III

GEORGE SMITH (1827-1907) AND MARY CRAWSHAW (1831-1877): DESCENDANTS OF "RABBIT GEORGE" AND MARY CRAWSHAW SMITH

Children

George E. Smith

Annie M. Smith

Jessie Smith Chambers

Herbert Smith

William J. Smith

Mary J. Smith

Margaret Smith Laver

George Smith

Grandchildren (known)

Elizabeth Laver Maxfield

Lucie 'Cissie' Laver Johnson

Margaret 'Ruda' Laver Jones

James Laver

Joseph Laver

Jessie Laver Dowden

Edward Laver

Frances 'Nora' Laver Senior

Herbert Smith

Hilda Smith

Henry Smith

Constance Smith

George Smith

Cyril Smith

William E. Smith

Harold Chambers

Edgar Rands Smith

Lilian Smith

Oswald Smith

Reginald Chambers Smith

Albert Smith

William C. Smith

Frank Smith

Great-Grandchildren (known)

Phyllis Maxfield Thickett
Margaret Maxfield Charlton
Mary Laver
Jessie Dowden

Frank Laver
Joan Skelton Smith
Margaret Laver
Patricia Laver
Albert Healey

Great-great-grandchildren (known)

Pamela Thickett
Peter Thickett
Diana Charlton

Monica Charlton
Clare Charlton Pattinson
David Skelton Johnston
Lindsay Skelton Johnston

Great-great-great-grandchildren (known)

Victoria Pattinson
Elizabeth Pattinson
Robert Pattinson

Rachel Thickett Holden
Natalie Thickett Swift
Morgyn Johnston

Great-great-great-great-grandchildren (known)

Bailey Holden
Nyah Holden

Thea Holden
Finley Holden
Riley Whyte

APPENDIX IV

GEORGE SMITH (1827-1907) AND MARY STENNETT (1846-1932): DESCENDANTS OF "RABBIT GEORGE" AND MARY STENNETT SMITH

Children

Clement Smith

Elizabeth Smith Schonhut

Florence Smith Holroyd

Effie Smith Hague

Grandchildren

Wilfred Smith

Clement Smith

George Schonhut

Joan Schonhut Hartley

Arthur Holroyd

Effie Holroyd Wadsworth

Neville Holroyd

Hubert Peter Holroyd

Ruth Holroyd Sampson

Charles Hague

Pauline Hague Goodswen

Anthony Hague

Timothy Nigel Hague

Great-Grandchildren

Eric Smith

Anthony Smith

Pauline Schonhut Tear

Hilary Schonhut Hoskins

Charles Robin Hartley

Elizabeth Hartley Ogley Brain

Gabrielle Wadsworth Stephenson

April Sampson Stern

Julia Hague Ross

Charles R. Hague

Philip Goodswen

Stephanie Goodswen

Jane Hague MacCaw

Veronica Hague Clinton

Peter Holroyd

Leonard Mark Sampson

Sally Hague Foster

William J. Hague

Great-great-grandchildren

Julie Smith Ford

Wendy Smith

Neil Smith

Sarah Smith

Joanne Smith

Lesley Smith

Jacqueline Tear Houghton

James Tear

Rupert Hoskins

Elizabeth Hartley Sayers

Clare Hartley Kitt Erskine

Fleur Hartley Shaw

Richard Ogley

Jonathan Ogley

Mark Stephenson

Deborah Stephenson Gill

Henry Sampson

Cordelia Sampson

George Stern

Edward Stern

James Ross

Mark C. Hague

Robert Hague

Lucy Hague

Emily Hague

James Goodswen

Charlotte Goodswen Schoch

Marina MacCaw Lewis

Joseph MacCaw

Edward Clinton

Rebecca Foster Carruthers

Harriet Foster Heron

Great-great-great-grandchildren

Jack Ford

Sam Ford

Isobel Smith

Libby Smith

Robert Shaw

Sophie Bird

Emily Houghton

Suzanna Houghton

Lucie Ogley

Adele Elizabeth Sayers

Joe Sayers

Joshua Sayers

Mia Kitt

Amber Kitt

Mabelle Erskine

Kara Shaw

Quillen Shaw

Isla Ogley

Charles Ogley
Lucas Stephenson
Chloe Stephenson
Charles Tear
Alexander Tear
Henry Tear
Adam Gill
Alex Gill

Aaron Ross
Harry Hague
Evi Hague
Thomas Goodswen
Hannah Goodswen
Alexander Schoch
Emily Schoch
Theo Castaneda Clinton
Wesley Castaneda Clinton
Mina Lewis

Great-great-great-great-grandchildren

Logan Sayers

APPENDIX V

HUSBANDS, WIVES AND PARTNERS
GROUPED BY GENERATION OF SMITH OR STENNETT
FAMILY MEMBER:

Hannah Parton Smith *(George's paternal great-grandmother)*

Charlotte Turner Smith *(George's paternal grandmother)*
Martha Batley Foulston *(George's maternal grandmother)*
Elizabeth Stennett *(Mary's paternal grandmother)*

Elizabeth Foulston Smith *(George's mother)*
Elizabeth Stennett *(Mary's mother)*

Of George, Mary and their siblings:
William Rossiter
John Beaumont
Hannah Ainge Stennett
Henry Loweth
Henry Harris
Eliza Jackson Smith
Mary Crawshaw Smith
Esther Stow Stennett
Sarah Staples Smith
Christiana Heppenstall Smith
Alice Cartwright Smith

Of George's and Mary's children, nephews, nieces:
Albert Holroyd
Albert Schonhut
Hubert Henry Hague
Dora Woodward Smith

Mary Townsend Smith
Annie Edwards Smith
Joseph Laver
William J. Wellman
Eliza Crabtree Rossiter
Shamira Young Rossiter
Walter Ashworth
Emma Ashton Rossiter
William Stanley
Mary Kine Smith

Of George's and Mary's grandchildren, great-nephews and nieces:
Stella Jefferson Hague
Charles Arthur Hartley
Stanley Goodswen
Reginald Wadsworth
Guy Sampson
Alice Colclough Holroyd
Mabel Issott Hague
Ethel Spittlehouse Schonhut
Edith Riley Holroyd
Ada Murden Wellman
Alice Appleyard Wellman
Henry Baddley
David Campbell
William Lovesy
Maria Baddley Rossiter
William Evans
Venus Robinson Rossiter
Luella Rossiter
Sarah Shannon Rossiter
Annie Hyde Smith
Jane Vessey Smith
Ada Elnor Smith

Mary Cook Smith
Annie Woods Smith
Mildred Hartley Laver
Ellis Dowden
Effie Dickinson Laver
Clifford Senior
Nettie Boyle Rossiter
Leah Farr Rossiter
Thomas Johnson
Hayden Jones
William Maxfield
Francis Graham
Millicent Fisher Smith
Fred Vertigan
Alfred Wall
Tom Bowling
Albert Healey
Beryl Price Brown

Of George's and Mary's great-grandchildren, etc.:
Charles Thickett
Joyce Daft Bowling
George Oakland
Gordon Atherton
John Charlton
Paul Tear
Paul Hoskins
Valerie Guy Holroyd
Judith Hewitt Hartley
Elizabeth Huttall Smith
James Ogley
Verity Smith Morcom
Dean Ford
Brian Brain

Dorothy Leigh Goodswen
Robin MacCaw
Rick Clinton
Robert Foster
Ffion Jenkins Hague
Steven McAuliff
Davina Smith Hague
Nicholas Ross
Bruce Stephenson
Angela Turner Hague
Philip Stern
Louise England Sampson
Rachel McAteer Hague

Of George's and Mary's great-great-grandchildren, etc.:
Jane Wright Thickett
Jacqueline Cowin Stephenson
Russell Gill
James Houghton
Johanna Rae Tear
Kay Garbutt-Leonard Goodswen
Simon Schoch
Richard Pattinson
Ben Lewis
Carla Castaneda Clinton
Scott Carruthers
Nicholas Heron
Audrey Falkner
Marietta Brown Hague
Sarah Heller Ogley
Karalyn Niven Ogley
Philip Shaw
Nigel Bird
Edwin Holden

Adrian Sayers
Steven Kitt
John Erskine
Matthew Shaw

Of George's and Mary's great-great-great-grandchildren, etc.:
Karen Buckley
Adam Croft

FACT OR FICTION?

The villages and towns noted in this book are actual places in which Mary Stennett, George Smith or another character lived. The names of family members and the dates of their births and deaths are factual. Where a first and last name is used it serves as confirmation that a person existed, for example, George and Mary Browne, and their servant, Frederick Elliott.

The employment history for George and Mary is factual: Mary worked in Walcott, Shireoaks and Greasbrough, just as George was employed at Wentworth Woodhouse, ran Potter Hill Farm and founded his own building company.

The story's named fictional characters are limited to Mary's friend, Hattie, and the ladies who pursued Mr. Smith: Mrs. Jones, Miss Green, Mrs. Bowman, and so on. Everyone needs a friend and it was necessary to create Hattie to serve as Mary's trusted companion. The friendship which developed between Mary and her step-daughter, Margaret, is imaginary, as is their trip to London.

If we all need friends in life, we all need a little romance. While it is possible that George and Mary's marriage was little more than convenience, it would be a shame to deny a loyal, hardworking woman a chance at love. Mary did eventually find her own true love – at least in the pages of *Rabbit George and Me*.

Great liberty has been taken with the personalities of some of the characters, most notably Mary's father, John Stennett, and George and Mary. The author employed reverse engineering in building their characters, borrowing from family members of the present and recent past. As it is generally understood that we take after our ancestors, we can confidently speculate that the women and men who came before us bore the characteristics, habits, talents and strengths found in ourselves.

The story includes numerous names and dates, all of which document the extensive research conducted by family members. The author acknowledges that these frequent references may interrupt the flow of the story, but affirms that the primary purpose of writing *Rabbit George and Me* was to produce a Smith family history. An attempt has been made, however, to tell a story which is of interest to readers beyond the family. The judgment as to whether or not such a lofty goal has been achieved may only be made by such readers.

The information provided on George and Mary's descendants is, to the best of the author's knowledge, factual. The names of many descendants, as well as those of George and Mary Crawshaw, and of George and Mary's extended families, are included in the story. Maiden and married names of female descendants are indicated and used according to the point of reference in the narrative. The author takes responsibility for any confusion which may result.

The old practice of using the same first name across generations creates challenges for researchers and writers. Multiple generations of the Smith family named their offspring George, Elizabeth, William, Mary and Herbert. The challenges created by this repetition of names is, in turn, passed on to the reader, who may have difficulty identifying a particular subject. It is hoped that the family trees distributed throughout the book will serve as a useful guide. These trees were produced by the author using information available at the time the book went into production.

The reader may also find it helpful to refer to the appendices, which include a list of the descendants of George and Mary, together with a list of those, where known, of George and Mary Crawshaw. Also included are the known descendants of Mary's parents, John and Elizabeth Stennett, and – most extensive of all – those of George's parents, William and Elizabeth Smith. These four separate lists will be helpful in clarifying the names of family members and the generation to which they belong.

A fifth list provides the names, where known, of the husbands, wives and partners who have enriched the lives of so many members of the Smith and Stennett families. The list begins with Hannah Parton Smith, born in 1734, wife of George Smith, great-grandmother of "Rabbit George". It is hoped that present and future generations will find such fine men and women with whom to share their journeys and that they, too, will be added to this list.

In all of the above, whether in the text, the family trees or the appendices, the author trusts that those readers who are surprised to find their name in print understand the importance of providing a comprehensive list. The author regrets any inaccuracies, misrepresentations or omissions and is interested in learning of new, or corrected, information: **rabbitgeorgeandme@gmail.com.**

The history of Rossiter Villa is based on factual information regarding occupancy and ownership, and has been verified by historic documents. The author's proposal that Rossiter Road was named in honor of Mary and William Rossiter, George Smith's sister and brother-in-law, is based on information as described in the text, but has not been confirmed.

PRINT AND DIGITAL RESOURCES

Images of England: Greasbrough by Anthony and Jane Dodsworth (Tempus Publishing Limited, 2005)

Black Diamonds: The Rise and Fall of an English Dynasty by Catherine Bailey (Penguin Books Ltd, 2007)

Pioneers and Prominent Men of Utah by Frank Esshom (Utah Pioneers Book Publishing Co., 1913)

The Big House and The Little Village by Roy Young (Wentworth Garden Centre, 2000)

"For the Anniversary of My Death" from The Second Four Books of Poems by W.S. Merwin (Copper Canyon Press, 1993)

St. Mary's Church, Greasbrough – Its History and Background 1828-1978 by Beatrice Light (1979)

A Brief History of St. Mary's Church in the Parish of Greasbrough by Graham Hobson (2013)

What's in a Name by Tom Cassell (2013)

Greasbrough Community History Society Newsletter

Deed of Conveyance between Mary Rossiter and George Smith, September 25, 1883 *(courtesy of Stephen and Amanda Pilgrim)*

Abstract of Title of Mr. George Albert Smith *(courtesy of Stephen and Amanda Pilgrim)*

Memorandum of Agreement between William Collinson, Charles Hague and Ellis Law, November 25, 1870 *(courtesy of Dr. Charles Collinson)*

Commonwealth War Graves Commission (www.cwgc.org)

The Church of Jesus Christ of Latter-day Saints (www.lds.org)

Websites:

www.ancestry.com
www.findagrave.com
www.myheritage.com
www.genuki.org.uk
www.Findmypast.com
www.Billiongraves.com
www.metoffice.gov.uk
www.Forebears.co.uk
www.chillswim.com